CREATING & KNITTING YOUR OWN DESIGNS FOR A PERFECT FIT

MONTSE STANLEY

1817

HARPER & ROW, PUBLISHERS, New York
Cambridge, Philadelphia, San Francisco,
London, Mexico City, São Paulo, Sydney

Acknowledgements

Many people have helped me while writing this book. It would be impossible to mention them all, but there are some to whom I am particularly indebted:

Bill Pollard, FBKS, for putting so much time and effort into the black and white photographs and Barbara Pollard for my photograph on the jacket.

Mercè Sopena, William Sharples, Mira Rathmell, Lorne Hepher, Isabel Shoolbred, and especially Trinitat Sopena, my mother, for their help in knitting the garments.

My husband Tom and my parents-in-law, Louis and Jean Stanley, for giving me the initial push, helping me with their advice and encouragement, and straightening up my English grammar.

To everyone, mentioned here or not, my most sincere thanks.

To Tom and *tothom*

CREATING AND KNITTING YOUR
OWN DESIGNS FOR A PERFECT FIT

Copyright © 1982 Montse Stanley

82 83 84 85 10 9 8 7 6 5 4 3 2 1

Library of Congress Cataloging in Publication
Data

Stanley, Montse.
    Creating and knitting your own designs for
    a perfect fit.
    Includes index.
    1. Knitting. 2. Clothing and dress. I. Title.
TT820. S796 1982   746.9′2   82–47549
    ISBN 0–06–015054–8   AACR2

Contents

APPENDIX

Introduction

WHY DESIGN?

Hand knitters are very rarely encouraged to consider design as an essential part of their craft. They are generally expected to content themselves with a passive role as copiers, obediently following a confusing mass of abbreviated instructions, in order that they may feel proud, not to mention privileged in some cases, to have reproduced exactly what somebody-that-must-obviously-be-terribly-clever has designed for their benefit.

This is reflected in the fact that some knitting patterns do not include a diagram showing the shape of every piece to be knitted, fully dimensioned so that adjustments can be introduced easily. How would dressmakers react, one wonders, if they were given written instructions for cutting the cloth? Should knitters accept what dressmakers would not? After all, they both have the same need for accurately shaped sections if they are to put together a garment successfully.

Always supposing they were free from errors, knitting patterns based exclusively on obtaining a specified tension would possibly be satisfactory for use with highly accurate machines. But, unlike machines, hand knitters do not possess adjusting mechanisms. In fact, they find it difficult to work for any length of time to a tension other than that which comes naturally to them. For a hand knitter a measuring tape is a far more convenient and accurate way of checking the work progress than counting rows and stitches.

Another big problem with ordinary knitting patterns is that they are intended for standard sizes. Even when you manage to find a pattern you really like, is it really worthwhile to spend days or weeks working with needles and yarn, deciphering instructions and trying to keep the correct tension, to obtain a garment that at best will look off the peg?

When you design, all these problems disappear. You knit to your own tension, your garments are made-to-measure and their style is exactly as you wish. But there are other reasons why you should want to design.

Apart from the satisfaction of having created something from start to finish, designing makes you improve your skills as a knitter because it gently forces you to widen your technical knowledge. In this way, designing gives you an understanding of the craft far deeper than a whole lifetime of pattern copying can achieve.

THE BOOK

Design is closely linked to technique, so a book on design cannot overlook the physical aspects of knitting, which is why this book is in two parts. The first part gives all the technical background likely to be needed. The second part deals entirely with design.

For the sake of clarity, design is presented as a series of clear-cut steps, but in real life the steps will not necessarily follow the same order. Indeed, they will probably amalgamate into a single process.

APPROACHING DESIGN

When you are about to start a design, especially if it is one of your first, it is highly probable that your mind will go blank and you will feel hopelessly inadequate. Do not worry if this happens. In fact, you should expect it and be prepared for it.

It occurs, with rare exceptions that come as pleasant surprises, every time anybody tries to design something. The frustration when faced with a blank sheet of paper is a well-known feeling amongst designers of all kinds, even amongst the very experienced.

The problem is that ideas do not come at command. On the contrary, they seem to have a great ability to appear and disappear at will (their will, not yours!).

Knowing this can happen, do not try to force the process. Give yourself a few days, even weeks, to mull over your ideas and to let them take shape. Chapter 3 might help you at this stage.

See what other people are wearing, what yarns are available, what is the coming fashion. Look at the shapes explained in Chapter 6 and the suggestions given in Chapter 7. Look up the stitch patterns in Chapter 5, and the techniques in Chapters 1 and 2. See what Chapter 4 says about the yarns you have found, or whether it mentions any others you might prefer; if this is the case, search for them. If you would like something colourful, look up art books, postcards, prints, fabrics, paintings, patchwork and cross-stitch samplers, or anything else that might be helpful.

Magazines are also useful when you are searching for inspiration. And that includes foreign magazines. The Italians and the French are renowned for their skills both as fashion designers in general and as knitting designers in particular.

The key word which will tell you whether a foreign magazine has any knitting inside is *maglia* in Italian, *tricot* in French and *punto* in Spanish. Since you are not going to copy the patterns, you do not need to understand the instructions. But you will find that most European magazines have pattern diagrams similar to the ones used in this book. That, plus the photographs, might be just what you need to trigger your imagination, and those elusive ideas might at last come.

Once you have a clearer notion of what you want to knit (clear*er* because it will keep changing and maturing as you go along), start to put pen to paper as indicated in Chapter 8. Things might not fit as easily on paper as they did in your head; they hardly ever do. But drawing will give you a new awareness, and this is what will help your ideas to mature. Again, do not rush. If you cannot see instantly how to solve a problem, sleep on it. The solution will come to you eventually.

Many designs can be finalized while knitting is already in progress. In fact, knitting might even help you to see ways of solving difficulties. Therefore, if you can start the garment and knit part of it before reaching a critical point, do so.

Once the garment is finished, make a note of its final dimensions, the amount of yarn used and the way it fits. Keep one of the yarn labels, any stitch samples you have knitted, and all the notes, sketches and diagrams you have drawn or written. They are invaluable for future reference.

You will then be ready to start the design process all over again. Unless, of course, you already know what you want to knit next.

Part One: Technique

Technique and design are two inseparable aspects in the making of a knitted garment, and they should both be considered of equal importance. Concentrating only on technique leads to uninspired results, while a design that turns to technique only at the last minute will rarely be a complete success.

Consider technique as a tool in your hands; it is there not to make life difficult but to help you translate your ideas into reality. Take it into account at every stage of the design process, but do not feel obliged to learn every existing technique before designing your first garment.

If your technical knowledge is limited and does not extend further than casting on and off, knitting and purling, aim at simple designs that make full use of what you know. When you can use a few basic techniques with confidence, then it is time to incorporate one or two new ones into your next garment.

When more than one technique can be applied (as is the case with increasing and decreasing) you will have to experiment to find out which technique best suits your particular needs.

Always make sure you have needles and yarn with you when you look at techniques. Knitting is learnt by doing, not by thinking, and it is far better understood with the fingers than with the head.

CHAPTER 1

Working Techniques

EQUIPMENT
The following list includes everything a knitter *might* need. Compared with other crafts, the equipment necessary for knitting is quite inexpensive and can be built up slowly. The most expensive items are not essential; use an obliging friend or the back of a chair instead of a swift, your own hands instead of a ball winder, and paper and pen instead of a pocket calculator.

EQUIPMENT FOR WORKING AND FINISHING
Knitting needles (also called **pins**) (**1**) Nowadays they are made out of lightweight metal, plastic or wood. They come in pairs, in several standard lengths and a wide range of diameters. It is worth having a good stock of needle sizes—old and foreign ones with different lengths or diameters may come in handy. Keep them well protected and carefully file away any roughness. (See Appendix for standard sizes.)

Double-pointed needles (**2**) For working in rounds. These come in sets of four (sometimes five). The selection of lengths and diameters is usually poorer than for ordinary needles.

Knitting belt or **stick** (**3**) To be tied round the waist in order to hold the free end of double-pointed right-hand needles.

Circular needles (**4**) For working flat or in rounds. They consist of a pair of very short metal needles connected by a strong, flexible, nylon cord. The length of this cord is variable and should be checked before purchasing the needles. The total length of the set must be shorter than the circle being knitted, when working in rounds, but must be long enough to hold the stitches comfortably. For this reason, more than one set of needles might be needed to complete a garment.

Needle gauge (**5**) For checking diameters of needles. The needle must fit exactly the perforation corresponding to its size.

Cable needles (**6**) Very short double-pointed needles used when crossing groups of stitches. Their diameter should be smaller than that of the main set of needles.

Stitch holders (**7**) These come in various shapes but all are designed to secure the stitches when it is necessary to remove the needle.

Safety pins (**8**) To be used as small stitch holders, as markers, and for pinning two pieces of knitting together.

Ordinary pins (**9**) For pinning, marking and blocking. Long pins with glass heads are best, but any dressmaking pins will do providing they are completely free from rust.

Sewing needles (**10**) These are special 'tapestry' needles with a blunt point. Keep two or three sizes so that yarns of different thickness can be threaded through with ease.

Crochet hooks (**11**) A few crochet hooks are useful for picking-up dropped stitches and crocheting edges. In the first case the diameter of the hook is not critical, provided it is not larger than the knitting needles being used. (See Appendix for standard sizes.)

Row counters (**12**) To be threaded on the needles to keep a tally of the rows (for instance, when working a long stitch pattern). No matter how light the material they are made of, they represent an additional weight on the needles and for this reason table counters have been developed. However, some people find it preferable to keep a tally with paper and pen.

Stitch stops (**13**) These can be fixed at the points of needles to stop the stitches from coming off when not working. They are useful when there are many stitches on a needle.

Swift (**14**) Expanding frame that turns on an axis. Used to hold the skeins when winding balls of yarn.

Ball winder (**15**) For winding balls of yarn by hand the fast way. Very useful, coupled with a swift, when many skeins have to be turned into balls.

Bobbins (**16**) Small pieces of card for wrapping small amounts of yarn when working colour patterns. They can have many shapes, the

simplest being a square or rectangle. The yarn is unwound in short lengths, as required, and is then passed through a slit in one of the sides of the card to stop it from unwinding further. You may need to make your own, or use old-fashioned mending-yarn cards.

Teasel (also spelled **teazle**) **(17)** Small wire brush used for fluffing up mohair and other brushed yarns.

Scissors (18) These do not need to be large, but they must be sharp.

Measuring tape (19) Use an accurate dressmaker's tape, or a rigid ruler if you prefer. Take all your measurements consistently in either centimetres or inches.

White cloth To place on your lap to protect both your clothing from yarns that shed fibres and delicate yarns from contact with clothing. It can also be used to improve your vision of the work when knitting dark colours. Make sure it is spotlessly clean.

Large bag For storing the work in hand. Bags with a flat base are best.

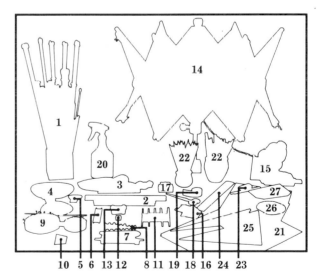

Large padded surface For blocking or pressing. Ironing boards are too small for most jobs.

Sprayer (20) For cold blocking. Use a fine garden or barbecue sprayer.

Iron and pressing cloths For blocking and pressing those yarns that do not respond to cold blocking.

EQUIPMENT FOR DESIGNING

Paper (21) You will use white paper and graph paper mainly, but tracing or other translucent paper comes in useful occasionally. Buy blocks or sheets of ordinary graph paper, not too small: 2·5–3cm per 10 divisions (8–10 divisions to the inch) are convenient for most people. Take photocopies of the special graph papers in the Appendix as required. Also keep a small notebook in your work bag, either to keep tallies or to make notes of anything you come across whilst knitting that might be relevant later on.

Pens and pencils (22) Both ordinary and coloured. Use a medium to slightly soft pencil for designing (if you need to buy one, get an F, HB or B, in order of increasing softness), bright felt-tip pens for any marks or writing you want to stand out from the rest, and subtly-coloured crayons or felt-tip pens for designing multicoloured garments or motifs.

Eraser (23)

Ruler (24) Should be stiff and accurate. A transparent one that will allow you to see what is underneath is best.

Set square(s) (25) Not strictly necessary but useful if you know how to use them.

Protractor (26) For measuring angles. Again not strictly necessary.

Pocket calculator (27) To help you with those simple mathematical operations that cannot be avoided; fewer than you might think, thanks to the special graph paper and tables in this book. Not strictly necessary.

File Use whatever system suits you best, but find a way of keeping a permanent record of all your ideas and designs. Do not throw away any sketches, colour studies or knitting notes. Also keep a yarn label for each yarn used, and a note of the amount used.

Sample box For keeping stitch samples and tension swatches. It is invaluable when trying to think of new ideas.

HOLDING NEEDLES AND YARN

There are several ways of holding the work, and every knitter has a favourite one. If you already knit, are used to one way *and have no problems with it*, do not change. Otherwise, try one of the two methods explained, which are probably the best both for speed and control over the work.

Whichever way you choose to hold needles and yarn, it is important that you adopt the correct posture. Unless you have been accustomed from childhood to knitting for several hours a day, you could easily strain the muscles of your neck, back and shoulders. Find a chair, not too hard and not too soft, that gives good support to your back and in which you feel comfortable. If necessary, add cushions until it feels right. Keep your arms and shoulders as relaxed as you can while you knit; there is no need to clutch the needles as if your life depended on it. Your movements should be as supple as possible. Bend your head down only as far as necessary to see the work, but *do not bend your back*. From time to time, take a break: have a good stretch, go for a walk, or engage in some physical activity, even if it is only for a few minutes, in order to loosen up your muscles and get your blood circulating.

It is equally important that you work near a good source of light. Even if you do not normally need to look much at what you are doing (some people can actually read books while they knit!), you must be able to see without straining your eyes whenever you need to look closely at your work, or read any instructions.

YARN ON RIGHT HAND

From the last stitch made, the yarn is wound over the first (index) finger, down between this and the middle finger, across the palm and up between the fourth and little fingers. This is done to maintain an even flow of yarn when the work is in progress; if you prefer to give the yarn a tighter tension, wrap it around the little finger once. From the little finger the yarn goes to the ball, which is kept in the work bag. The bag is generally left on the floor.

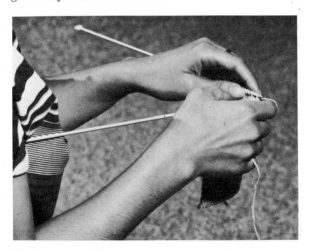

Hold one needle in each hand, as shown in the illustration. Note that both hands rest on top of the needles. The left needle has the stitches of the previous row and the non-working end moves freely. The right needle makes the new stitches and its non-working end is tucked under the arm. The left hand feeds the stitches towards the point of its needle, while the right hand moves like a shuttle, feeding yarn as needed and resting on top of the needle between movements.

This method requires long needles that can be

tucked under the arm, or double-pointed needles of any length plus a belt or stick tied round the waist to secure the end of the right needle.

YARN ON LEFT HAND
Hold yarn as for previous method, but in left hand. Hold needles also in a similar way, but this time leaving both non-working ends to move freely. The stitches on the left needle are fed towards the point of the needle with the left thumb. The right needle is given a rotating movement to bring through the new stitches.

This method can be used with needles of any length, but it is generally considered more comfortable to use the shortest possible needles for the stitches in hand.

When using this method, make sure to give the same tension to knit and purl stitches. See also second paragraph of *Purl* (page 15).

YARN ON BOTH HANDS (Jacquard—see page 78)
Being able to knit with the yarn on either the right or the left hand is a great advantage. In fact, keeping yarn in both hands is the best way to knit Jacquard patterns.

If only one hand is used to hold the yarn, long strands appear on the wrong side which are easily

caught. If both hands are used, each one holds a different colour. The main colour is kept in the right hand, and the stitches are worked once over and once under the yarn held in the left hand. Thus, all the strands are woven in.

When the contrasting colour has no more than two or three stitches together, these are knitted with the left hand, without weaving in the strands. If more than three stitches appear at any one time, the yarns must change hands in order to weave in the strands.

If more than two colours are involved in any one row, keep only one colour in your right hand and weave in all the others.

If you have difficulty working Jacquard on the wrong side of the work, knit it in rounds or use double-pointed needles and go back each time to the beginning of the row. This method has the disadvantage of having to break the yarn each time.

FOUR-NEEDLE KNITTING
This is the best way of working in rounds for knitters who like to keep the yarn in their *right* hand. The stitches are divided in three, roughly equal, groups, and placed on three of the needles. If any corners are to be worked, the stitches should be divided so that two needles meet at the corners. The fourth needle is held in the right hand, its non-working end secured by a stick or belt tied round the waist.

New stitches are worked with the right needle until one of the other three becomes free. The fourth needle is then removed from the belt or stick, and the free needle is put in its place. This change of needles is repeated until the work is finished.

When working with four needles take care to keep the tension correct when changing from one needle to the next.

CIRCULAR-NEEDLE KNITTING
This is the best way of working in rounds—or working flat when many stitches are involved—for knitters who like to keep the yarn in their *left* hand. As in four-needle knitting, the work is kept on the lap.

To work in rounds, hold one metal end in each hand and knit for as long as you need. It is worth placing markers round the needle, between stitches, to pinpoint the beginning of each round and lines of increases, decreases, etc. Such markers can be small rings or safety pins, a tie made out of contrasting yarn, etc.

To knit flat, proceed similarly but turn work at the end of every row.

CASTING ON

The following are a selection of many possible ways to start knitting. Each one has different applications, and it is important to use the right one for the job. Invisible casting on for ribbing is dealt with later in the chapter.

INDEX-FINGER CAST ON (one needle)

This is a variation of the more common 'thumb method', and is a good, all-round cast on. If you have a tendency to cast on too tightly, use a needle one or two sizes larger.

Loop the yarn, leaving a free end about three times the width you intend to knit, and hold the loop up with the index finger of your left hand, so that the free end runs under the other three fingers. Hold the other end of the yarn and the needle in the right hand in the usual way. Pass needle under strand between index and middle fingers, wind right end of yarn round needle, taking yarn first under and then over needle, and draw through a loop. Repeat this action.

LEFT-HAND CAST ON (one needle)

The end result is exactly as for index-finger cast on, but you may prefer this method if you usually hold the yarn in your left hand.

Loop the yarn, leaving a free end about three times the width you intend to knit, and hold the loop up with the index finger of your left hand so that the free end runs under the other three fingers.·Wrap other end round thumb, passing it first under and then over, and secure it with the last three fingers just like the free end. Take needle in right hand, insert it under loop around thumb, catch strand going from thumb to index finger and draw it through loop. Tighten up this first stitch.

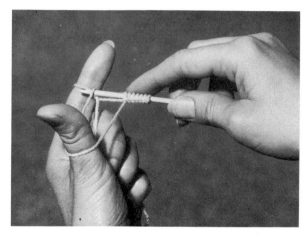

Wind free end of yarn round index finger as before. The other end should now go from needle, over thumb, down between thumb and index finger, and under last three fingers. The needle will now go under the strand between thumb and index finger, before catching the strand between index finger and needle in order to draw through the next loop. Repeat this action.

KNIT-STITCH CAST ON (two needles)

A very loose edge suitable for lace and other stretchy patterns. It can be tightened up somewhat by knitting the first row through the back of the stitches. Make the first stitch using the index-finger or the left-hand methods, but leave only a short free end of yarn.

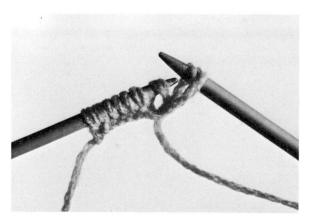

Now, take both needles, keeping the one with the stitch in your left hand. Insert right needle into stitch from front to back, wind yarn round needle taking yarn first under and then over needle, and draw a loop. Transfer loop from right to left needle. Repeat this action.

CABLE CAST ON (two needles)
A very strong and elastic edge, suitable for fabrics other than lace. The first row can be knitted through the back of the stitches if it needs tightening up. Use the cable or knit-stitch methods when extra stitches need to be cast on halfway through knitting, for instance to make buttonholes.

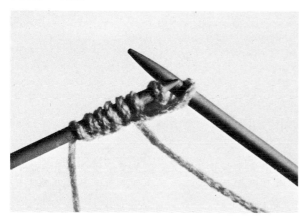

Proceed as for knit-stitch cast on to obtain the first two stitches. From then on, insert right needle between the last two stitches on left needle, instead of through the last stitch.

SINGLE-LOOP CAST ON (one needle)
A very light and loose cast on, suitable for lace and fine knitting. Use it as well in a contrasting yarn when the cast on row will have to be unravelled at a later stage, for instance to continue work in the opposite direction. Its simplicity often deceives beginners, who do not realise it is more difficult to knit the first row after this cast on than after any of the others.

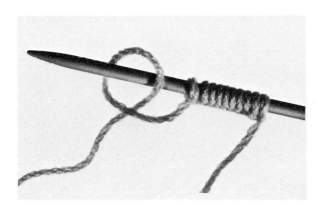

Make a slip knot by the index-finger or left-hand methods, leaving a short free end of yarn. Keep the needle in your right hand. With left hand, make a loop like the one shown in the illustration, slip it around the needle and tighten it up. Repeat this action.

BASIC MOVEMENTS
The parentheses show the abbreviations used in the book.

KNIT (k)
With yarn at back of work, insert right needle into first stitch on left needle, from front to back and under left needle. Wind yarn round right needle, taking it first under and then over needle, draw through a loop and drop stitch on left needle.

If the right needle is inserted through the back instead of through the front of the stitch on left needle, the resulting stitch will be twisted.

PURL (p)
With yarn at front of work, insert right needle into first stitch on left needle, from right to left and in front of left needle. Wind yarn round right needle, taking yarn first over and then under the needle. Draw through a loop and drop stitch on left needle.

Knitters who keep the yarn in their left hand may find it easier to wind the yarn first under and then over right needle. This should only be done when a twisted stitch is desired, or when the process is reversed in the following row by

15

knitting through the back of the stitch. (See Stocking Stitch Variations, page 55.)

OVERS

To work an 'over' means to wind the yarn around the right needle. The precise way of making an over depends on whether the stitches before and after it are both knit, both purl, one knit and one purl or one purl and one knit, and on whether the over itself should be knit or purl, single or double. To avoid confusion, the instructions in this book have adopted four terms which, combined, can describe all possible situations. (The 'front' is the side facing you at any one moment.)

Yarn forward (yf)
Bring yarn from back to front of work, *under* right needle.

Yarn back (yb)
Take yarn from front to back of work, *under* right needle.

Yarn over needle (yon)
Take yarn either from front to back or from back to front of work, *over* right needle.

Yarn round needle (yrn)
Give yarn a complete turn round needle. Your particular situation will tell you whether that should be done clockwise or anticlockwise but always take yarn *first over and then under* the needle.

SLIP STITCH (sl)

Pass a stitch from left needle to right needle without knitting or purling it. Always slip stitches one at a time.

Stitches are most often slipped *purlwise*, that is picking them up as if they were to be purled, in order to avoid twisting them. However, some situations require that the stitches should be slipped *knitwise*, that is, picking them up as if they were to be knitted. When instructions do not specify, slip stitches purlwise.

CABLES (FC and BC)—see also page 64.

A cable is, generally, a group of knit stitches that crosses another group of knit stitches on a purl background at regular intervals.

With right side facing you, slip the stitches to be crossed onto a cable needle. This should be of a smaller diameter than the set used for knitting, in order not to stretch the stitches. Keep cable needle at front of work for a front cross (FC) or at back of work for a back cross (BC). Work as many stitches from left needle as required by your particular cable, avoiding gaps between these stitches and those already on right needle. Now, work stitches on cable needle, starting with the one at the right end, in order to complete the cable.

When the abbreviations are followed by a pair of figures (for instance, FC4–4), the first figure indicates the number of stitches to be slipped

Cables: (*above*) Front cross (FC); (*below*) Back cross (BC)

onto cable needle and the second the number of stitches to be worked from left needle before working the ones on the cable needle. When one of the figures indicates a single stitch (for instance, FC4–1), and the pattern shows the sides of the cable travelling separately over the background, the single stitch is to be purled, not knitted.

When the abbreviations are followed by three figures (for instance, FC4–1–4), the central figure indicates stitches to be *purled* in the middle of the cable. In this case, slip the stitches indicated by the first two figures onto the cable needle (five stitches in the example), knit as many stitches from left needle as indicated by the third figure, slip the central stitch(es) back to left needle and purl them (these should be slipped from the left end of the cable needle), and finally knit the stitches still on the cable needle (this time from the right end).

TWISTED STITCHES (LTw2 and RTw2)
A method of crossing two knit stitches on the right side of the work, without using a cable needle.

For a left twist (LTw2), take right needle behind first stitch on left needle and knit the second stitch. You can knit it through the back of the loop; it is easier and there is less danger of deforming the work through pulling. Without dropping any stitches from left needle, knit the first stitch in the usual way. Drop both the first and the second stitches from left needle.

For a right twist (RTw2), insert right needle purlwise into second stitch on left needle and pull it forward slightly, let it go and then knit it in the

usual way, making sure that the right needle passes *in front* of the first stitch on left needle. Without dropping any stitches from left needle, knit the first stitch in the usual way. Drop both stitches from left needle.

CASTING OFF
To cast off is to work a final row that will secure the stitches, so that no ladders will form. Just as you did when casting on, use the method that best suits the occasion. Cast off either on a right-side or a wrong-side row, but always work the cast-off row in pattern.

Casting-off methods for single and double ribbing are explained on page 18.

ORDINARY CAST OFF
A good method for most purposes.

If you tend to cast off too tightly, use a needle one or two sizes larger than for the rest of the work.

Work two stitches. Insert tip of left needle into the stitch you have worked first, lift it over the second stitch and over the point of the right needle and let it go. Repeat this action, working one extra stitch every time.

SUSPENDED CAST OFF
A much looser cast off, suitable for lace and other stretchy fabrics.

Work as for ordinary cast off, but do not let go the pass-over stitch until another of the stitches on left needle has been worked.

CROCHET CAST OFF

This is an ordinary cast off, but it is worked with the help of a crochet hook. To be used with yarns without much elasticity, ie cotton, linen or silk.

Knit the first stitch using the crochet hook instead of the right needle. Insert hook into second stitch (now the first on left needle), wind yarn round it and draw a loop both through the stitch on left needle and the stitch already on hook. Leave loop on hook. Repeat this action.

PROVISIONAL CAST OFF

To be used when there is a need to remove the needles and stitch holders are not available or would not be adequate.

Thread a tapestry needle with a length of contrasting yarn, and slip all the stitches in the row from the knitting needle to the tapestry needle, one by one, so that the contrasting yarn ends up replacing the knitting needle. Tie both ends of the contrasting yarn, so that it cannot be pulled off inadvertently. When ready to continue work, cut the tie and pick up the stitches, one at a time, with a knitting needle. It is often easier to do this with a needle one or two sizes smaller.

CASTING OFF SHAPINGS

When groups of stitches need to be cast off every two rows for shaping, say, necklines or shoulders, turn the work before knitting last stitch on left needle to ensure a smooth edge.

INVISIBLE CASTING ON AND OFF FOR RIBBING

Ribbing (see page 58) can be cast on and off in the usual way, obviously working in pattern when casting off, but far better results are obtained when using an invisible method. The advantage of this method is that it eliminates the need for folded neckbands and other borders.

CASTING ON SINGLE RIBBING (first method)

Using a contrasting yarn and the single-loop method, cast on half the amount of stitches needed plus one. Continue as follows:

Row 1 *k1, yf, yon*. Repeat from * to *. End k1

Rows 2 and 4 *k1, yf, sl1, yb*, k1
Rows 3 and 5 yf, *sl1, yb, k1, yf*, sl1
Row 6 *k1, p1*, k1
Row 7 *p1, k1*, p1

Unravel cast-on row and continue working in ribbing, that is, repeat rows 6 and 7.

CASTING ON SINGLE RIBBING (second method)

Using a contrasting yarn and the single-loop method, cast on half the amount of stitches needed plus one. Work in stocking stitch (see page 55) for four or six rows. Unravel cast-on row, if necessary cutting contrasting yarn between stitches to facilitate the operation, and at the same time pick up the stitches let free, with a needle one or two sizes smaller. Make sure you work so that the new needle points in the same direction as the one holding the last row. Fold the work in two, right side out, and hold in left hand. With third needle in right hand, continue work in ribbing, alternately working one knit stitch from the left needle at the front, and one purl stitch from the left needle at the back.

CASTING ON DOUBLE RIBBING

Proceed as for single ribbing (second method), but knit two stitches from left needle at the front, and purl two stitches from left needle at the back. The result will have a slight slant to one side.

CASTING OFF SINGLE RIBBING

Cut the yarn at a distance of about three and a half times the width of the work to be cast off, and

thread it through a tapestry needle. Working from right to left, and assuming the first stitch is a knit stitch, insert tapestry needle into first stitch on knitting needle as if to purl it, drop stitch from knitting needle, and pull yarn through. Insert tapestry needle into first stitch on knitting needle (which is now a purl stitch) as if to knit it, drop stitch from knitting needle, and pull yarn through. *Insert tapestry needle into previous knit stitch (which is now off the needle), from front to back, then into first stitch on knitting needle (also a knit stitch) as if to purl it, drop stitch from knitting needle, and pull yarn through. Insert tapestry needle into previous purl stitch (which is now off the needle), from back to front, then into first stitch on knitting needle (also a purl stitch) as if to knit it, drop stitch from knitting needle, and pull yarn through. Repeat from *.

Do not pull yarn too tight; the result must be elastic. If a firmer edge is desired, as for instance for a V-neck, the last two or four rows of ribbing can be worked in tubular stocking stitch:

Row 1 (and 3) *k1, yf, sl1, yb*, k1
Row 2 (and 4) *sl1, yb, k1, yf*, sl1

If a drawstring is required at the end of the ribbing, work more rows in tubular stocking stitch, but remember it must be an even number of rows. This will create a double edge that will have no visible join.

CASTING OFF DOUBLE RIBBING
Cut the yarn, leaving an end about three and a half times the width of the work to be cast off, and thread it through a tapestry needle. Working from right to left, and assuming the first two stitches are knit stitches, insert tapestry needle into first stitch as if to purl it, drop stitch from knitting needle, and pull yarn through. Insert tapestry needle into second stitch left on knitting needle (a purl stitch) as if to knit it, working your way round the back of the knit stitch before it, and pull yarn through. Do not drop any stitches from needle. *Insert tapestry needle into previous knit stitch (which is now off the knitting needle), from front to back, then into first stitch on knitting needle (also a knit stitch) as if to purl it, drop this stitch and the first purl stitch from knitting

needle, and pull yarn through. Insert tapestry needle into previous purl stitch (now off the knitting needle), from back to front, then into first stitch on knitting needle (also a purl stitch) as if to knit it, drop stitch from knitting needle and pull yarn through. Insert tapestry needle into last knit stitch off needle, from front to back, then into first stitch on knitting needle (also a knit stitch) as if to purl it, drop stitch from knitting needle and pull yarn through. Insert tapestry needle into last purl stitch off needle, from back to front, then into second stitch on knitting needle (also a purl stitch) as if to knit it, working your way round the back of the knit stitch before it, and pull yarn through without dropping any stitches from knitting needle. Repeat from *.

Do not pull yarn too tight; the result must be elastic. For a firmer edge, and one that has less of a slant, the last two or four rows of ribbing can be worked, instead, thus:

Row 1 (and 3) *k1, sl1 with yarn at back, p1, sl1 with yarn at front*, k1, sl1
Row 2 (and 4) *p1, sl1 with yarn at front, k1, sl1 with yarn at back*, p1, sl1

These casting off methods look far more complicated on paper than they are in reality. Once the principle is understood, they are a tremendous help to any knitter. If you cannot get them right, check whether you are inserting the needle, not into the *previous knit* (or *purl*) *stitch*, as instructed, but into the stitch *below* that.

INCREASES AND DECREASES
Increases and decreases are used to alter the number of stitches in a row. When a series of consecutive stitches are involved, one of the methods explained for casting on or off should be used, but when only one or two stitches are increased or decreased at a time, there is a tremendous number of techniques which can be used; a fact worth remembering when designing.

Single increases and decreases often have a slant to right or left, and when used in symmetrical situations (for instance to shape the top of sleeves) two with opposing slants should be paired. But it must be pointed out that using a

19

right slant on the right side and a left slant on the left side is far less conspicuous than using a right slant on the left side and a left slant on the right side.

Paired single decreases can be transformed into paired double decreases by working them over three stitches instead of over two. This is not possible with increases. However, it is possible to obtain a non-paired double increase or decrease by working a pair of single increases or decreases next to each other. A stitch or two can be worked between them to form an axis.

As for increases and decreases that are double in their own right, if they have a slant and are paired in the work, follow the advice given for single increases and decreases. Otherwise, use them in any position, paired or not.

All the following increases and decreases are worked on the right side. If they are to be placed at the edges, work them after the selvedge (see next heading) at the beginning of rows, and before the selvedge at the end of rows. For a 'fully fashioned' effect, work them two or three stitches after or before the selvedge.·

SINGLE INCREASES WITHOUT A SLANT

These are all worked over one stitch. Both sides of the illustration have been worked in the same way, leaving a stitch between the increase and the selvedge.

1 Knit through front of stitch in the usual way, but do not drop stitch from left needle. Knit the same stitch again, this time through the back of the loop, and drop it from left needle. In paired increases, work the increase on the left side one stitch further from the edge than the increase on the right side.

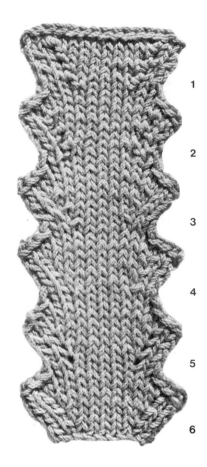

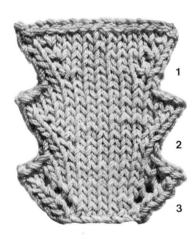

2 With left needle, pick up strand that lies between first stitch on left needle and stitch below last on right needle. Twist the strand and knit it. If you do not twist it, a hole will appear.

3 Work an over (yarn forward, yarn over needle) between two stitches.

SINGLE INCREASES WITH A SLANT

All worked over one stitch, leaving one stitch between the increase and the selvedge.

1a Right side: knit stitch in the usual way but do not drop it from left needle. Purl same stitch and drop it from left needle.

Left side: first purl and then knit the stitch.

1b Right side: like 1a, left side.
Left side: like 1a, right side.

2a Right side: knit through the head of the stitch below the first stitch on left needle, which is behind the needle, then knit stitch on needle in the usual way.

Left side: knit first stitch in the usual way, then the head of stitch below.

2b Right side: like 2a, left side.
Left side: like 2a, right side.

3a Right side: knit into stitch below the first stitch on left needle, then knit the stitch above.

Left side: knit first stitch on needle, then knit stitch below this stitch.

3b Right side: like 3a, left side.
Left side: like 3a, right side.

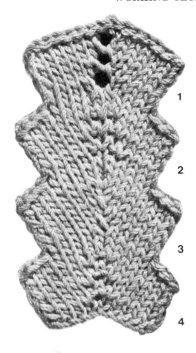

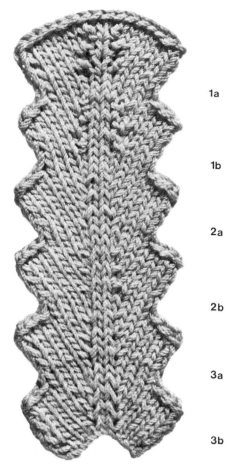

DOUBLE INCREASES OBTAINED BY JOINING A PAIR OF SINGLE INCREASES

The illustration shows the effects achieved when the single increases just explained are worked in the centre instead of at the edges. Here, they have been placed at either side of an axis stitch.

REAL DOUBLE INCREASES

1 This is a double over, worked between the two central stitches thus: yarn forward, yarn round needle, yarn over needle. On the next row (wrong side), twist the second over before purling it.

2 Worked over two stitches, the second being the axis. Knit the stitch before axis first through the front, in the usual way, and then through the back. Do the same with the axis.

3 Worked over one stitch. Knit through the head of the stitch below first stitch on left needle, which is behind the needle, then knit the stitch on needle through the back of the loop. Drop the stitch from left needle. Pick up again the head of the stitch below with left needle and knit it a second time.

4 Worked over one stitch. Knit stitch in the usual way, but do not drop from needle. Purl it, again without dropping it from left needle, and knit it again.

SINGLE DECREASES WITH A SLANT

All worked over two stitches. In the illustration, one stitch has been left between the decrease and the selvedge.

1a Right side (ssk): slip two stitches knitwise, wind yarn round right needle as if to knit, and with left needle pass the two slipped stitches over loop thus formed and over point of right needle, in an action similar to the one used for casting off.

Left side (k2tog): knit two stitches together, inserting right needle first into second stitch, then into first stitch, in the usual way.

1b Right side: like 1a, left side.
Left side: like 1a, right side.

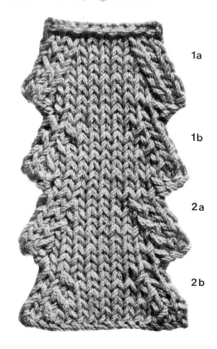

2a Right side (k2tog-b): knit two stitches together, inserting right needle through the back of both loops.

Left side: slip two stitches knitwise, return them twisted as they are to the left needle, one by one, and knit them together inserting right needle first into second stitch, then into first stitch.

2b Right side: like 2a, left side.
Left side: like 2a, right side.

DOUBLE DECREASES OBTAINED BY JOINING A PAIR OF SINGLE DECREASES

The illustration shows the effects which can be achieved when single decreases (2a) are worked in the centre instead of at the edges. In this case, they have been placed at either side of an axis stitch.

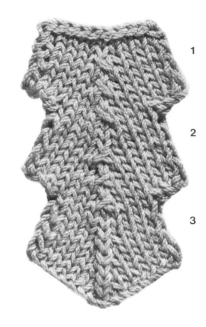

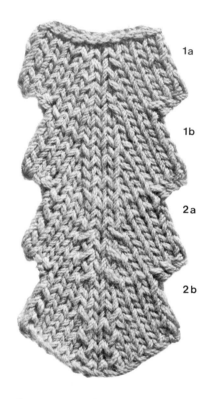

REAL DOUBLE DECREASES

These are all worked over three stitches. The first two could be used paired, one at either side of the work. They could also be used alternately, for a zigzag effect.

1 (sl1, k2tog, psso) Slip one stitch knitwise and knit the next two stitches together, inserting right needle first into second stitch and then into first. With left needle, pass slipped stitch over stitch just made, and over point of right needle, in an action similar to the one used for casting off.

2 Slip one stitch knitwise. Knit a stitch, pass the slipped stitch over it as if casting off, return stitch to left needle, and with right needle pass the following stitch on left needle over it and over

point of left needle. Slip stitch back to right needle.

3 Slip two stitches taking them *together* knitwise. Knit the following stitch, and with left needle pass the two slipped stitches over the stitch just made and over the point of right needle.

SELVEDGES

Always work one or two selvedge stitches at both ends of your flat knitting, either to give it a neat finish or to leave it ready for a join. As with so many things in knitting, there is a selvedge for every job. Therefore, make a point of using the one best suited to the occasion, even if that means working different selvedges at either end.

1 STOCKING-STITCH SELVEDGE
Suitable for invisible seams.

Knit first and last stitches on right side of work, and purl first and last stitches on wrong side of work.

2 CHAIN SELVEDGE
Suitable for neat, strong seams with most stitch patterns. Also suitable when stitches will have to be picked up from the edge.

Slip first stitch knitwise, knit last stitch, on right side of work. Slip first stitch purlwise, purl last stitch, on wrong side of work. If working in garter stitch, slip first stitch purlwise, yarn back, knit to last stitch, on right and wrong sides of work.

3 GARTER-STITCH SELVEDGE
Suitable for joins between garment and borders.

Knit first and last stitch of every row.

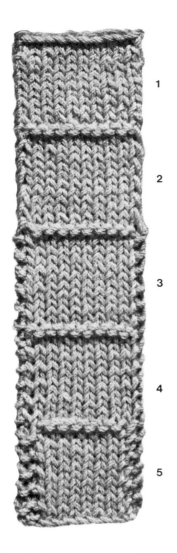

4 SLIPPED GARTER-STITCH SELVEDGE
Suitable for free edges and for joins between garment and borders

Slip first stitch knitwise and knit last stitch, on every row.

5 DOUBLE SLIPPED GARTER-STITCH SELVEDGE
Suitable for free edges.

Slip first stitch knitwise, taking back of loop, and knit second and last two stitches, on every row.

PICKING UP STITCHES
Stitches will need to be picked up when work has to be continued in either the same or a different direction, for instance to knit a border transversely, or when two layers of knitting are needed, for instance for a pocket. Whatever the case, make sure you keep round lines smooth and straight lines straight.

Divide the line where the stitches need to be picked up into sections 5 or 10cm (2 or 4in) wide, and mark the sections with safety pins. Decide how many stitches will be needed in each section

(see page 133), and pick up that number of stitches.

Take a knitting needle of the appropriate size in your right hand, and yarn in your left hand. Working from right to left, on the right side of work, insert needle into work, wind yarn round needle as if to knit, and draw through a loop. Repeat this action.

You may find it easier to use a crochet hook of the same size instead of the knitting needle. When the hook is full of stitches, slip the stitches, one at a time, from the back of the hook onto the knitting needle.

PICKING UP STITCHES ON A HORIZONTAL EDGE
This will either be a cast-on or a cast-off row. The greatest elasticity will be obtained if this row is unravelled and the existing stitches are picked up directly. To facilitate the work, either cast on using the single-loop method and a contrasting yarn, or work a provisional cast off, depending on whether the stitches are to be picked up at the beginning or at the end of work.

If the tension of the work that is to be added has the same tension as the work already in hand, pick up one stitch from every existing stitch. This applies whether the cast-on or cast-off row has been unravelled or not.

If the tension is different, the appropriate number of increases or decreases will have to be introduced.

PICKING UP STITCHES ON A VERTICAL EDGE
The edge should have a chain selvedge, because this makes the operation very easy and looks very neat on the wrong side.

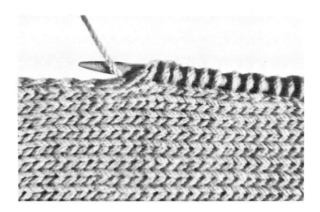

Always work between the selvedge and the last stitch, leaving the whole chain underneath the needle. When more stitches than selvedge chains need picking up, insert needle or hook through tight division between two chains, every time an extra stitch is needed. When the work to be added has the same tension as the work already done, and with most ribbed borders, picking up three stitches every two chains is generally adequate.

23

PICKING UP STITCHES ON A CURVED EDGE

Keep close to the edge, but smooth out any sudden increases or decreases.

PICKING UP STITCHES OTHER THAN AT THE EDGE

If you are working on the right side of the work, keep the yarn underneath the work and the needle or hook on top of it. If you are working on the wrong side, keep both yarn and needle or hook on that side. Draw the loops through wrong-side strands, instead of from one side of the work to the other, making sure none of the picked-up stitches are visible from the right side.

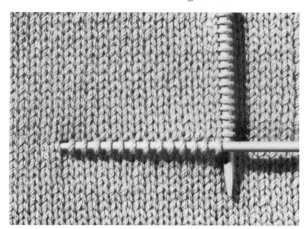

When picking up stitches for a patch or pocket, first pick up, using a short needle, the stitches for one of the sides (one stitch per row), then the stitches for the base with an ordinary needle, and finally the stitches for the other side also with a short needle (and again one stitch per row). Pick up all the stitches from the same length of yarn. Knit across the base, but work the first and the last stitch of each row together with one of the stitches picked up for the sides.

CORNERS

TURNED RIGHT-ANGLE CORNERS

Start work by knitting the horizontal side of the corner, but every other row (either every right-

side or every wrong-side row) do not work the last stitch on the side where the border is going to turn. Put these stitches on a holder. When the border is wide enough, continue work in main stitch pattern, working a chain selvedge on the border side.

To work the vertical side of the corner, pick up the necessary amount of stitches from the edge. Work in border pattern, adding a stitch from the holder every two rows. Cast off immediately after the row in which the last stitch was added.

RIGHT-ANGLE INNER CORNERS

After picking up the stitches from the horizontal and the vertical sides, the corner is worked using double decreases every two rows or rounds. When using a pair of single decreases separated by an axis stitch, the axis should be picked up right from the point where the two sides meet. If the

axis has two stitches, these should be one from the horizontal side and one from the vertical side. Real double decreases should be worked over one stitch from the horizontal side, one from the point where the two sides meet, and one from the vertical side.

ACUTE-ANGLE INNER CORNERS

Work as for right-angle inner corners, but decrease every row or round, instead of every two rows or rounds (see page 24, bottom right).

If the angle is very acute, a few additional single decreases will have to be introduced near the corner, say for about 5–10cm (2–4in), in the cast-off row, to avoid a wavy edge. For ribbed borders being cast off by the invisible method, where these decreases would be awkward to work, pull yarn tight.

WORKING TWO STITCH PATTERNS TOGETHER

It is quite common to have to change pattern in the middle of a row, for instance to work a border or a panel. When this occurs, unless both patterns need the same number of rows to achieve a certain length, one of them will pucker. To avoid this, short rows are introduced at regular intervals to make up the difference.

Calculate the vertical tension given by both patterns (see page 133), and establish the difference between the total number of rows needed to complete a section, for each of the patterns involved. Halve that number, as rows can only be added in pairs, to find the number of times the denser pattern needs row increases. Divide this number into the total length of the section in centimetres (inches). This will tell you for how many centimetres (inches) of the denser pattern you will need two extra rows.

Example: The main pattern needs 78 rows to achieve a length of 24cm (10in), while the border or panel needs 86 rows in order to achieve the same length. The difference in number of rows is:

$$86 - 78 = 8 \text{ rows}$$

Half that number is 4. This means that a pair of extra rows will need adding four times. Dividing this number into the total length:

$$\frac{24\text{cm } (10\text{in})}{4} = 6\text{cm } (2\cdot5\text{in})$$

Therefore, every 6cm (2·5in), a pair of extra rows will have to be added to the denser panel.

If this procedure looks too complicated, or if you are quite good at judging with your eyes, simply knit the section, keeping a close eye on progress. Whenever one part of the work begins to look shorter than the other, increase two rows.

To add the rows, if the denser pattern forms a border, knit first this border, turn work, knit in denser pattern to end of row, turn work and knit denser pattern again, finishing the row this time in the usual way.

If the denser pattern forms a panel, start to apply the above instructions after knitting the stitches to the right of the panel in the usual way.

BIAS FABRICS

These can be worked on most stitch patterns, by simply increasing one stitch at one end and decreasing one stitch at the other end.

Narrow bias bands can be used for ties, borders, and many other purposes. They can be worked so that they form a curve, for instance as borders for round necklines.

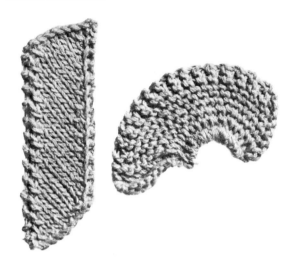

The illustration shows two examples of bias bands. The one on the left is straight, and has been worked in stocking stitch. It has garter-stitch selvedges, an increase on the right side and a decrease on the left side.

The band on the right is curved, and has been worked in garter stitch with slipped selvedges. The increases, also on the right side, have been worked knitting on the head of the stitch *two rows* below the second stitch. A less pronounced curve could be obtained by increasing alternately on the head of the stitch one row below and on the head of the stitch two rows below.

DARTS

Darts are used to make garments longer at the centre than at the seams, for instance when knitting for a woman with a very large bust or for somebody with a stoop.

Decide on the width and the depth of the dart, and convert these measurements into stitches and rows (see page 133). Halve the number of rows and divide the result into the number of stitches. This will tell you how many stitches should *not* be worked at the end of every second row, in order to form the dart.

Example: The dart should have 34 stitches in width and 8 rows in depth. Half the number of rows is 4; that means that the dart will be worked in four right-side or four wrong-side rows. Dividing 4 into 34 stitches gives 8 stitches each time, plus 2 stitches over. The options, then, are to shorten the dart to 32 stitches, or to leave a different number of unworked stitches in two of the rows; for instance, 9, 9, 8 and 8 stitches.

With the right side of work facing you for darts

on the left edge, and the wrong side of work facing you for darts on the right edge, work in pattern until only the stitches that have to be left unworked remain on left needle. Slip the first of these stitches onto right needle, take yarn to opposite side of work, slip stitch back onto left needle, and take yarn back to previous side of work. Turn work and continue knitting, being careful not to pull the yarn too tightly around slipped stitch. Repeat the same process every two rows, each time leaving another group of unworked stitches, until all the stitches that form the dart have been left unworked. Work next row from end to end in the usual way.

The stitches are slipped in order to prevent small holes from appearing in the work.

GATHERINGS
To work gathers, calculate the necessary number of increases or decreases, as appropriate, and distribute them evenly along one row, using either visible or invisible increases or decreases. Alternatively, change to a stitch pattern giving a different tension and keep the number of stitches unaltered.

Bands of gathers are obtained by first increasing and then decreasing the number of stitches.

To calculate the distribution of increases or decreases, find out the difference between the number of stitches in both sections, and divide this difference into the largest of the two figures. The result will tell how often an increase or decrease will have to be worked.

Example: One of the sections has 50 stitches and the other has 75 stitches. The difference is:

$$75 - 50 = 25 \text{ stitches}$$

Dividing 25 stitches into the largest figure:

$$\frac{75}{25} = 3 \text{ stitches}$$

This means that, if the work went from narrow to wide, a single increase would have to be worked on every third stitch. On the other hand, if the work went from wide to narrow, every third stitch would have to be a decrease; that is, every third and fourth stitch of the previous row would have to be knitted together.

To work vertical lines of gathers, apply the principle explained for working two stitch patterns together, but the other way round: to create puckers instead of eliminating them.

BUTTONHOLES
Knitted buttonholes are more elastic than those cut onto cloth, and can therefore be made slightly smaller. However, be careful not to make them too small. If possible, buy the buttons first.

Some buttonholes need to be stronger than others, especially those for children's garments. Reinforced buttonholes can be worked by knitting them in special ways. Avoid reinforcements that mean sewing at a later stage.

1 EYELET BUTTONHOLES
These are mainly used for layette and other delicate work.

Either work an eyelet as explained in Chapter 5 or, for a stronger buttonhole, work as follows:
Row 1 (right side)   Work to buttonhole position in pattern, yf, yon. Continue work in pattern.
Row 2   Work to buttonhole position, sl over, yrn. Continue work in pattern.
Row 3   Work in pattern to stitch before overs, sl this stitch knitwise, k overs together but do not drop them from left needle, pass sl st over new st, k together overs and following st (insert right needle first into st and then into overs).
Continue work in pattern.

2 ORDINARY VERTICAL BUTTONHOLES
At the base of the buttonhole, divide work in two and continue knitting with two balls of yarn, one for each side. Work a slipped garter-stitch selvedge on both sides of the buttonhole. When the top of the buttonhole is reached, discard second ball of yarn and continue work across full width, using only first ball of yarn.

When the work is completed, work a couple of horizontal stitches at top and bottom of buttonhole, using a tapestry needle, before weaving in the ends up and down the sides of the buttonhole.

3 REINFORCED VERTICAL BUTTONHOLES

Proceed as for ordinary vertical buttonholes, but work garter-stitch (non-slipped) selvedges with two strands of yarn. You will need two additional lengths of yarn that will only be picked up when working the selvedges.

4 ORDINARY HORIZONTAL BUTTONHOLES

Row 1 (either side of work) Work in pattern to buttonhole, cast off required number of stitches to form buttonhole (use either ordinary or suspended cast off), and continue work in pattern.
Row 2 Work in pattern to stitch before buttonhole and knit into front and back of this stitch. Cast on one stitch less than was cast off on previous row (use same method used to start work; if this was a two needle method, turn work, bringing yarn forward before slipping last stitch on needle). Continue work in pattern.

5 REINFORCED HORIZONTAL BUTTONHOLES

These are worked in a single row.

Work to buttonhole position in pattern. With yarn in front, slip a stitch, take yarn back and leave it there. Cast off required number of stitches by slipping them, one at a time, from left needle to right needle and passing last stitch on right needle over slipped stitch. It is similar to ordinary casting off but without working the stitches. Slip last cast-off stitch back to left needle and turn work. Pick up yarn and take to back of work. Using cable method, cast on the same number of stitches you have just cast off plus one. Bring yarn to front before placing last loop on left needle, and turn work again. Slip first stitch from left to right needle, knitwise, and pass extra cast-on stitch over it. Continue work in pattern.

6 HORIZONTAL BUTTONHOLES IN RIBBING

Any of the previous methods can be used, but for a really neat buttonhole do not cast off any stitches. Instead, work buttonhole stitches in a contrasting yarn, leaving a long loop of main yarn on wrong side of work. When work is finished, remove contrasting yarn, picking up the stitches on the upper side with a stitch holder and those on the lower side with a needle. Cut the loop in half

and, using one half of the loop and a tapestry needle, tightly cast off the stitches on the knitting needle, by the invisible method. Secure the end stitches to the sides of the buttonhole, weave in and trim yarn.

Now, again with a tapestry needle, pick up, one by one, all the stitches in the holder and draw the other half of the loop through them. Secure yarn at the side with one vertical stitch, to add strength to the buttonhole. Repeat this process three or four times, working alternately from right to left and from left to right, each time securing the yarn to the side with a vertical stitch. Weave in and trim yarn.

HEMS

Hems are typical dressmaking elements that should be avoided whenever possible, because they add unnecessary bulk to knitted garments. Knitters have at their disposal far more interesting and suitable ways of finishing ordinary edges; ways which have been developed by craftsmen working with yarn, not with cloth.

However, there are occasions when hems can prove useful, or when the increased bulk might even be desirable in the design, and therefore it is a good thing to know how to work a hem.

To prevent the hem from stretching, the fold should be knitted using needles one or two sizes smaller than those used for the rest of the garment.

If it blends well with the general design, one or two rows worked in a different stitch pattern can be used to mark the fold line. If working in stocking stitch, knit a wrong-side row or purl a right-side row to obtain a straight edge. If you prefer a picot edge, work thus:
Row 1 (right side) k1, *k2tog, yf, yon*. Repeat from * to *
Row 2 Purl the stitches and the overs from previous row.

HEMS AT THE BEGINNING OF WORK

Cast on with a contrasting yarn, using the single-loop method. After knitting the same number of rows on either side of the fold line, unravel the cast-on row, stitch by stitch, placing the free loops on a spare needle. Make sure this new needle runs in the same direction as the one at the other end of work. Cut contrasting yarn as often as you need to, in order to make the operation as easy as

possible. Now fold the hem and knit next row working together one stitch from each needle. This gives a more elastic and hardwearing hem than sewing up.

HEMS AT THE END OF WORK

Knit the fold, but do not cast off. Cut yarn, leaving a length of about three times the width of the hem. Fold the hem and, with a tapestry needle, sew the stitches on knitting needle, one by one, to the back loop of the stitches opposite. Make sure all the back loops are from the same row, and that each one is on a vertical line with

the stitch it is sewn to. Do not pull the yarn too tight.

JOINING YARN

If you possibly can, add new balls of yarn at the end of rows, not in the middle of them. Leave a length of some 10–20cm (4–8in) of the new yarn before joining it; this will be woven in later. Do not trim any long ends from the old balls until work is finished and is found to be right; if you want to, you can tie them in neat bundles so that they are not in the way.

If you have to join yarn in the middle of a row, or if you are working in rounds, work until some 20cm (8in) of yarn are left, leave end at back of work, and add new ball also leaving a length of it

at back of work. Knit next row with great care, tightening up the two ends of yarn so that the stitches around the join keep the correct tension. When work is finished, weave in the ends, crossing them at the back.

A more professional join in the middle of rows is obtained by *splicing* the yarn. Work until you have enough yarn left to work about six stitches.

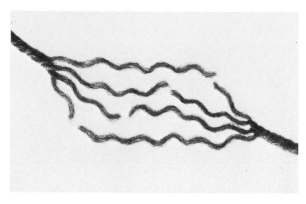

Untwist this length of yarn and a similar length of yarn from the new ball. Cut the strands at different lengths, in such a way that, when both lengths of yarn are put end to end, the overall thickness is maintained. Roll both lengths together, copying as far as possible the original twist of the yarn. Knit with care and trim away any ends that stick out.

Under no circumstances use knots to join yarn.

CHAPTER 2
Finishing Techniques

The most beautifully knitted garment, and the best of designs, can be utterly ruined by a poor finish. Make the most out of your garments by finishing them with a professional touch.

First of all, make sure a garment fits. Either pin it together with safety pins or tack it using a contrasting fine yarn or cotton. If it looks all right, after allowing for the unavoidable curling if the stitch pattern is one that needs blocking, apply any finishes the garment might need. If it does not look right, consult Chapter 9.

Apply finishes in this order, unless special circumstances tell you otherwise:
—weave in yarn ends
—correct uneven stitches
—cold block or press
—join shoulder seams ⎫ either graft
—join sleeves to body ⎬ them or sew
—join sleeve and side seams ⎭ them up
—cold block or press joins
—pick up stitches and work borders, or join individually knitted borders
—sew collar, patch pockets, etc
—work crochet edgings
   fix zips, buttons, elastic bands, etc
—make and fix fringes, tassels, cords, pompons, etc
   comb brushed yarns with a teasel or stiff brush

WEAVING IN YARN ENDS
Any long ends of yarn left when joining in a new ball can now be trimmed, except those at the start of seams that can be used later for sewing up. Never leave less than 10cm (4in) of yarn when trimming the ends.

With the help of a tapestry needle, weave in each one of the yarn ends, darning into the back of the fabric, if possible along the selvedge stitches, for a length of 2–5cm (1–2in), depending on the thickness of the yarn. Pull yarn through and trim off. This is enough to secure the yarn.

To avoid unnecessary weaving, when working narrow stripes carry the colours not in use up the edge, and secure them with the selvedge stitch.

CORRECTING UNEVEN STITCHES
Being a manual process, knitting will always show some degree of unevenness. However, some unevennesses can be corrected easily, and it is worth spending some time just doing that.

Look closely at your work and scan it for anything that does not look quite right. You will probably find whole rows of stitches leaning towards one side, especially in stocking stitch. These are likely to be rows where the work was interrupted. Straighten them up with the help of a cable needle or other short needle.

You might also find odd stitches which look too tight or too loose; they will show less if the change in tension is spread over the stitches at either side. Here, again, gentle pulling with a needle can work wonders.

BLOCKING AND PRESSING
These are both methods of 'setting' knitting. With rare exceptions, for which you should watch, garments knitted with all ordinary yarns look much better after being set even when the stitch pattern itself does not actually require any blocking to remain flat.

Preferably use cold blocking, providing the yarn responds to it. Most yarns will, so long as the garment is sufficiently sprayed; man-made fibres seem to require more wetting than natural fibres.

Always try blocking or pressing first on a sample

COLD BLOCKING
Pin the section to be blocked on a flat surface, such as a table or board covered with a folded blanket, a foam mattress, or a carpet offcut. Use long, glass-headed pins if you can, they are easier to handle. Make sure the surface is dye-fast and clean, and the pins are rust free.

Pin every part of the garment, right side up, making it adopt the right shape and size. Check frequently with a measuring tape. Make sure straight lines are straight and angles are accurate. Pin often, taking care not to pull V-shaped strands with pins. *Slight* variations in size might be corrected at this stage, but do not rely on it.

Now, spray the garment with cold, clean water, and let it dry naturally, preferably overnight, away from direct sun.

When symmetrical shapes are to be blocked, as in the case of sleeves, pin one of them right side down, using only a few pins to give it its general shape. Spray and lay the other one on top, right side up. Pin thoroughly together and spray again.

Cold blocking has tremendous advantages over pressing. No pressure is put on the knitting, and therefore the stitch pattern cannot be unduly

flattened. No accidents with hot irons can occur that might damage the yarn, or might stretch the garment permanently out of shape.

PRESSING

When a yarn does not respond to cold blocking, even after thorough damping, use pressing at the temperature recommended on the yarn label. If there is no recommendation, try a warm iron for cotton, wool and linen, and a cool iron for silk and man-made fibres. (See glossary in Chapter 4 for further details.)

Pin every piece as for blocking, but this time the surface needs to be well padded, and the garment needs to be right side down. Use ordinary pins, because they will interfere less with the iron than those with glass heads. They should be as flat as possible over the surface.

Place a clean cloth between the knitting and the iron, and gently place the iron down on the cloth. Lift iron up again without moving it up and down, as you would in ordinary ironing. Press evenly, but do not let the full weight of the iron rest on the knitting.

If the knitting does not respond to this treatment more than it did to cold blocking, try with a damp cloth or steam iron. In this last case, you could try steaming very close to the dry cloth but without actually touching it. Always experiment with a sample first.

Do not unpin pressed sections until they are cold.

Never press mohair, angora, cashmere or glitter yarns. Try only cold blocking with these fibres.

GRAFTING

This is an invisible way of joining two pieces of knitting together. It has many applications and it

is easy to learn.

If the two sections to be grafted have been blocked or pressed beforehand for convenience, block or press the grafted join afterwards.

For grafting you will need a tapestry needle and a length of yarn three to four times the width of the join. Work is carried out from right to left, and therefore both knitting needles must point to the right.

The key to good grafting is to give the join exactly the same tension as the two sections being put together. This is more easily achieved when both sections are spread flat, one next to the other, on top of a table or other hard surface.

When both sections have been knitted in the same direction, the sides of the join are straight. When they have been knitted in opposite directions, one section will be offset half a stitch from the other.

GRAFTING STOCKING STITCH

Insert tapestry needle into the first of the lower stitches from back to front, drop stitch from knitting needle, and pull yarn through. Insert tapestry needle into the first of the upper stitches from back to front, drop stitch from knitting needle, and pull yarn through. *Insert tapestry needle into previous lower stitch (which is now off the needle), from front to back, then into first lower stitch on knitting needle from back to front in an action similar to slipping the stitch from knitting needle to tapestry needle, drop stitch from knitting needle, and pull yarn through. Insert tapestry needle into previous upper stitch (which is now off the needle), from front to back, then into first upper stitch on knitting needle from back to front, drop stitch from knitting needle, and pull yarn through. Repeat from*.

30

GRAFTING REVERSE STOCKING STITCH

When the whole row is in reverse stocking stitch, you may find it more convenient to turn the work and proceed as has just been explained.

Insert tapestry needle into the first of the lower stitches from front to back, drop stitch from knitting needle, and pull yarn through. Insert tapestry needle into the first of the upper stitches from front to back, drop stitch from knitting needle, and pull yarn through. *Insert tapestry needle into previous lower stitch (which is now off the needle), from back to front, then into first lower stitch on knitting needle from front to back, drop stitch from knitting needle, and pull yarn through. Insert tapestry needle into previous upper stitch (which is now off the needle), from back to front, then into first upper stitch on knitting needle from front to back in an action similar to slipping the stitch from knitting needle to tapestry needle, drop stitch from knitting needle, and pull yarn through. Repeat from*.

GRAFTING RIBBING

Use for each stitch the appropriate method of grafting, stocking stitch for knit stitches and reverse stocking stitch for purl stitches. Only sections knitted in the same direction can be grafted successfully. However, narrow sections of single ribbing knitted in opposite directions, such as two front borders meeting at the back of the neck, can be grafted using a technique that gives a very neat, although not so elastic, join.

Using two knitting needles and two stitch holders, pick up the stitches that need joining in

such a way that the knit stitches are on the needles and the purl stitches are on the holders. Graft stitches on needles as if they were stocking stitch and turn work. Pass stitches on holders onto knitting needles, and graft them also as if they were stocking stitch. Make one or two stitches at the edges with the tapestry needle in order to smooth out the slight offsetting of the two sections

GRAFTING TO A SIDE EDGE

The edge to be grafted must have a chain selvedge.

Place edge section above knitting-needle section.

Make sure they are both flat (unless, of course, you are trying to gather one of them), and secure both ends with safety pins. If necessary, divide both sections into equal parts, counting rows or stitches to make sure the parts are equal, and secure the sections with more safety pins at every division. Use any of the above methods for grafting, but this time catch the strands between selvedge and first stitch from the upper section, instead of stitches.

SEAMS

There are flat seams, invisible seams, and seams

31

that are neither flat nor invisible. Use the most appropriate one for each occasion.

Flat seams may not create thicker lines, but they are certainly visible and they often look messy. Avoid them. If you want a garment not thickened by seams, design it so that it has no seams, making the most of circular knitting, grafting and picking up stitches.

On the other hand, non-flat seams are nothing to be ashamed of. Properly sewn, they will not detract from a garment, neither will they add unnecessary stiffness. They can even help to keep garments in shape.

The illustrations show seams, and later joins, being sewn with contrasting yarn. This is only to demonstrate that the seam or join stitches are invisible from the right side of work. In reality, only matching yarn should be used, with a tapestry needle of the appropriate size.

Weave in the yarn at the beginning and at the end, up and down the edge, but do not make any knots. Pull the yarn gently but firmly and keep checking the right side of work. The result must be strong but elastic. Too many stitches too close to each other should be avoided; they only result in stiff and mis-shapen seams.

The following instructions, if exactly observed, will ensure that when the edges to be sewn together have the same number of rows, both ends of the seam will match perfectly and no puckering will occur, even if the seam has not been pinned or tacked. When the edges are of a different shape (for instance, in the case of set-in sleeves), pin them and tack them carefully before starting the seam.

INVISIBLE SEAM
This is a soft seam, perfectly invisible if used for joining stocking stitch. Do not pull the yarn too tight.

It needs a stocking-stitch selvedge, and is worked on the right side. It can be started at

either end. All you have to do is pick up the strands between the selvedge and the first stitch, one by one, alternating one from each side.

To join reverse stocking stitch, work also on the right side (meaning the right side of the *reverse stocking stitch*). Take the same strands as above, which will now look like loops. The result will only be invisible from a distance; close examination will show a break in the horizontal lines formed by the rows.

Other stitch patterns can be joined by this method. Both sides must match, and in this case should have a chain selvedge. Try a sample first.

BACKSTITCH SEAM
This seam shows a clear but neat line on the right side. It is very strong and very elastic. Use it with any pattern, but always with a chain selvedge. Work is done on the wrong side, having first put both right sides against each other.

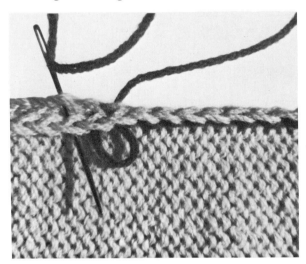

Working from back to front, and from right to left, insert needle through first pair of chains, loop yarn round the end of the seam, insert needle through second pair of chains, also from back to front, and pull yarn through. *Insert needle from front to back into previous pair of chains, then from back to front into following pair of chains, and pull yarn through. Repeat from *.

The back of the stitches will be twice as long as the front. The chains should look flat and tidy; be careful not to catch any other strands when inserting the needle through them. Also, make sure that you catch both sides of both chains every time.

BACKSTITCH SEAM FOR RIBBING
Worked in the following way the seam is almost invisible and from a distance the ribbing looks as if it is unbroken.

For single ribbing, work a knit stitch immediately after the chain selvedge, on both edges.

Polo-neck jumper with chevron design and alpaca waistcoat (see page 154)

For double ribbing, make one side end on two knit stitches and the other on two purl stitches, plus the chain selvedge. If this means that front and back of garment will need a different number of stitches, make the front larger than the back and take that into account when calculating the armholes and other increases or decreases.

Proceed as for ordinary backstitch seam.

HORIZONTAL KNITTED SEAM

A very good seam for shoulders, when grafting is not convenient or adequate. Without casting off any stitches, place right sides of work together, with both needles pointing in the same direction. Cast off, working on the wrong side and knitting together one stitch from each needle.

VERTICAL KNITTED SEAM

A very strong and decorative seam, with a great number of variations.

The first section must be knitted with a chain selvedge. If convenient, cast on all the stitches at the same time, and keep those for the second section on stitch holders.

When the first section is finished, either pick up the stitches on the holders or cast on as needed. Work in pattern until only one stitch is left, then work together this stitch and the two strands of the selvedge chain from the first section. Either

Maroon polo-neck with chevrons on sleeves and blue/grey tweed collared jumper (see page 154)

knit or purl, taking first the stitch or first the chain. The illustration shows:

top—knit, taking first the stitch through the back of the loop, and then the chain

centre—knit, taking first the chain and then the stitch

bottom—purl, taking first the stitch and then the chain. This is also the movement shown by the knitting needles

FIXING BORDERS

Whichever way you choose to fix borders, make sure none of the stitches show on the right side. The general sewing rules explained for seams apply also to fixing borders.

Work always on the right side, starting with the end of the border that has buttonholes, if there are any.

Pin the work carefully, placing small safety pins across the join, and making sure that the border neither puckers nor pulls the rest of the garment. Do not cast off the border until you are sure it is the correct length; wait, if necessary, until it is sewn in place.

It is not often that borders and main sections of garments have the same number of rows. When they do not, pick up two strands instead of one from the side that has the greatest number of rows, as often as necessary for a smooth join.

Avoid, if possible, sewing borders that have been knitted transversely. It is best to pick up the stitches for these borders from the edge of the garment.

All borders worked in ribbing should have a knit stitch on the side of the join, after the selvedge stitch.

FLAT JOIN

This join, being flat, is not invisible, but because of its situation in the garment it can be used as a decorative element. Work a sample first.

The selvedges on both sides should either be ordinary garter stitch or slipped garter stitch.

With a tapestry needle, pick up the grooves that appear on the very edge, one by one, alternately working one from each side.

CHAIN JOIN

The main section should have a chain selvedge, which will show flat on the wrong side of the work. The border should have a garter-stitch or slipped garter-stitch selvedge.

With a tapestry needle, alternately pick up one of the strands between the chain edge and the first stitch of the garment, and one of the grooves at the very edge of the border.

ladder and draw it through the selvedge stitch and through the loop already in crochet hook. Repeat this last movement.

Remember that each one of the loops along the border represents two rungs of the ladder. If the border has more rows than the garment, draw through together the second rung of one loop and the first rung of next loop, as often as necessary for a smooth join.

KNITTED JOIN

Use the same technique as for knitted vertical seam.

FIXING BIAS-BAND EDGINGS

Fix one of the sides of the bias band to the edge of the garment using a backstitch or an invisible seam (make sure that you knit both the bias band and the garment with the right selvedge). Wrap bias band round the edge of the garment, and fix the second side of the bias band to the garment with a slipstitch. Preferably, work the slipstitch under the seam, so that it will not show on the right side. For a thicker effect, fix the bias band a few stitches away from the edge.

CROCHET EDGINGS

Many crochet edgings can be successfully applied to knitting, but crochet is a different craft and therefore beyond the scope of this book. The following crochet technique, however, is so easy and effective that it seems worthwhile to make an exception.

CORDED EDGING

It is worked from left to right. Holding hook in right hand and yarn in left, insert hook into cast-off edge or chain selvedge, and draw a loop. Still with loop on hook, wind yarn round hook, taking yarn first behind and then in front of hook, and draw a new loop through the loop on hook. *Insert hook into next cast-off stitch or chain, catch yarn with hook pointing downwards, and draw a loop. With this and the previous loop on hook, wind yarn round hook, taking yarn first behind and then in front of hook, and draw a new loop through the two loops on hook. Repeat from*. Hold hook as you would a pen.

A variation consists of working a chain selvedge on the border as well as on the main section, and joining both edges with an invisible seam, resulting in a flat, double chain at the wrong side.

LIFTED LADDER JOIN

This join is almost flat, giving a very effective and slightly raised chain on the right side of work.

Work it with a stocking-stitch selvedge on both border and main section of garment. Do not be afraid to unravel the edge.

Drop the last stitch of the border selvedge from knitting needle and let the selvedge ladder down to the cast-on row. You might want to keep the ladder on a vertical knitting needle or stitch holder, to make sure you pick up the strands later in the correct order. Insert a crochet hook into the first selvedge stitch of the main section and catch the first rung of the ladder, drawing the rung through the first selvedge stitch. Insert hook into second selvedge stitch, catch the next rung of the

When drawing the loop through the edge, make it long enough for the hook to be almost parallel to the edge. Use a hook one or two sizes smaller than the knitting needles used for the garment.

If you can crochet, you will find it easier to understand the instructions knowing that they represent nothing more than double crochet (American single crochet), worked from left to right instead of from right to left.

FIXING ZIPS (ZIPPERS)

The stiffness of a zip does not blend particularly well with the elasticity of knitting, which is why they should be fixed with especial care, and why unnecessary zips should be avoided.

One case in which zips are fully justified is casual jackets requiring a fastening that leaves no gaps. In this case, an open-end zip should be purchased before the design is finalized, to ensure that the front opening matches the length of the zips available. As a further precaution, do not cast off any stitches until the zip has been satisfactorily tacked in place.

Before fixing the zip, tack a strip of muslin or other fine fabric on the right side of the garment, to prevent the edge from stretching. Tack and sew the zip on the wrong side, using two strands of matching cotton. First sew the zip near the teeth with a backstitch, then secure the other side with a slipstitch. Make sure none of the stitches show on the right side.

If the zip is to show, the garment should have a

non-curling border or a garter stitch selvedge, and the zip is placed so that only the teeth show on the right side.

Concealed zips without flaps are positioned so that the edge of the garment just overlaps the teeth of the zip.

Concealed zips with flaps should be placed off centre if the flap is to run in a central position. This means that one side of the garment will be wider than the other. On the side that has no flap, the zip is sewn as for non-concealed zips. On the other side, the zip is placed at the start of the flap, and is completely concealed by it.

One problem with zips is to find a colour that perfectly matches the garment. When a good match is not available, a darker colour will show less and, unless a contrasting zip is a design feature, it might be worth concealing the zip.

Even with a matching colour, zips do not look especially tidy on the wrong side, so when knitting really smart garments it is a good idea to conceal the zip on this side. To do this, pick up the necessary number of stitches, working on the wrong side all along the fabric edge of the zip. Knit a few rows and cast off so that the teeth of the zip are not overlapped by the knitting. Using matching cotton, sew the edge of the knitting to the zip with a slipstitch. Alternatively, if the zip is to be placed at the edge of a border worked transversely in ribbing, the last few rows of this border could be worked in tubular stocking stitch. If the knit stitches and the slipped stitches of the last row are then slipped onto two separate needles, and cast off loosely as two separate pieces of stocking stitch, a casing for the zip is automatically obtained.

BUTTONS

When the design calls for it, or when suitable buttons are not available, try making your own.

A simple method is to cover a button mould or an old button with a knitted octagon. The mould or button must be able to withstand the same washing or dry-cleaning processes as the garment. The octagon must be large enough to cover completely the mould or button.

Working in any pattern that will not show the mould when stretched over it, and using needles two or three sizes smaller than those used for the garment, cast on a few stitches, say three to seven depending on yarn and mould. Knit, increasing two stitches at the centre or one at each edge on every row, until the necessary width is obtained. Continue straight for a few rows, then decrease two stitches on every row, until only the same number of stitches as cast on remain. Cast off.

To cover the mould, use a tapestry needle and one of the ends of yarn dangling from the cast-on or cast-off row. Work a running stitch all along the edge of the octagon, place mould inside the octagon, and pull the yarn so that the running stitch is tightened up and the mould is covered.

37

Work a few stitches to secure the yarn.

If the buttons are to be embroidered, do that before covering the mould. If covered buttons seem too harshly shaped, try stuffing the octagon with scraps of the same yarn.

Alternatively, cover a ring with corded crochet edging, and work a decorative centre with the help of a tapestry needle.

The illustration shows:
top left—mould covered with stocking stitch worked in chenille
top right—mould covered with reverse stocking stitch worked in glitter yarn
bottom left—bramble stitch worked in worsted wool, stuffed with scraps of yarn
bottom right—ring covered with corded crochet worked in bouclé cotton

WAISTBANDS
If the top of a skirt ends in ribbing, this can be strengthened by fixing an elastic band to the wrong side. Pin the elastic band carefully, making sure it is evenly distributed, tack it and, before trimming it, wear the skirt for a short time to make sure it feels comfortable. Sew the elastic with two strands of matching cotton, using a herringbone stitch.

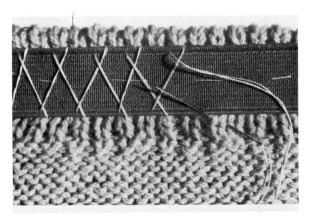

If the skirt waist is non-elastic end with a hem and thread the elastic through using a safety pin. Or, for a less bulky waist, use previous method but fix petersham instead of elastic and leave a

vertical opening at the top of the skirt. Avoid zips to fasten the opening.

Always use elastic that is fairly wide and soft.

FACINGS
Not only should facings be unnecessary, they should be avoided. Facings make for stiff edges that pull the rest of the garment. Edges are best strengthened and kept flat by techniques developed within knitting, not within dressmaking.

LINING
Lining, except perhaps for loose linings in skirts, is another process best avoided in knitting.

A knitted garment, if lined, will lose its elasticity and that degree of comfort associated with knitting, because the lining will stiffen it.

To prevent the need for lining, knit heavy garments such as coats and skirts at a firm enough tension, and allow for the fact that they are likely to increase in length under their own weight. Knit these garments, or at the very least their edges, in flat stitch patterns.

CORDS AND TIE-UP BANDS
With cords, as well as with all the other trimmings, it is best to be bold rather than shy, imaginative rather than conservative.

Always allow plenty of yarn for your trimmings; they all take up tremendous amounts.

TWISTED CORD (*left*)
Cut several strands of yarn, three times the

required length. Knot them together at both ends, making sure none of the strands is tighter or looser than the rest. Give one end to another person to hold, or attach it to a hook, door knob, etc. Insert a pencil or stick into your end, and another pencil or stick at the other end if somebody is helping you. Keep twisting the pencil(s) until the entire length is well twisted. Holding strands taught, fold cord in half. Knot the two ends together, let the cord twist over itself, and even it out.

FAGGOT CORD (centre)

Using one or more strands of yarn, and comparatively fine knitting needles, cast on 2 stitches. Turn work. With yarn at back, insert needle purlwise through both stitches and purl them together. Keep turning the work and repeating this movement.

PLAITED CORD (right)

Cut several strands of yarn one and a half times the required length. The number of strands must be multiples of three. Knot the strands together and divide into three equal parts. Plait the three bundles of strands and tie at the end.

Alternatively, use twisted or faggot cords instead of bundles of strands.

TIE-UP BANDS

Bands can easily be knitted using a flat stitch pattern such as garter stitch or ribbing. Use one or more strands of yarn and comparatively fine needles.

If a non-flat stitch pattern is used, for instance stocking stitch, the band can be rolled up and stitched together with matching yarn to make a cord.

FRINGES

ORDINARY FRINGE

Cut strands of yarn twice the required length. Wrap the yarn round cardboard or a book of the same length as the fringe, and cut along one of the edges. Take a few strands together, fold them in half, and draw this fold through edge of garment with the help of a crochet hook. Pass the yarn

ends through the loop thus formed, and pull tight to fasten. Tidy up the slip knot and trim ends.

For a tufted fringe, brush firmly with a teasel.

For a more elaborate effect, cut longer strands of yarn and, after fastening loops at the edge of the garment, divide the dangling yarn ends in two. Tie two adjoining halves together in a lattice pattern.

LOOP FRINGE

This is worked separately and later sewn up to the edge of the garment. The instructions can be adapted to any needs. For instance, work the top in garter stitch, moss stitch or other flat stitch instead of in faggots. Or make the band of faggots narrower or smaller. Or allow more or less stitches for unravelling instead of the five stitches in the sample.

Using two or more strands of yarn, and comparatively fine needles, cast on 13 stitches by the single-loop method. Work as follows:

Row 1 k2, yf, k2tog, k1, yf, k2tog, k6
Row 2 p5, k2, (yf, k2tog, k1) twice

Repeat these two rows for the required length. Cast off on an odd-numbered row, slipping the first stitch, and drawing yarn through after casting off the next seven stitches. Unravel remaining five stitches to form the loops.

If the loops are curled and you would prefer them straight, cold block the fringe, keeping the loops taut with the help of a knitting needle drawn through and fixed in position with pins.

TASSELS

Cut a piece of cardboard to the length of tassel required, or take a book of the appropriate size. Wrap yarn loosely around the card or book, until

the desired thickness is obtained. Thread a strand of yarn through one of the ends; it must be long enough for later winding around the tassel and sewing it into position. Tie strand firmly to secure the end of the tassel. Cut all the strands at the other end with sharp scissors. Wind the long strand around the tassel, several times, a short way from the tied and folded end. Secure strand, threading it through the tie just made and up, so that it comes out next to the first knot. Trim, if necessary, and fix to garment with long strand.

POMPONS

Pompons can be worked in one or more colours. When working in colours, either wind colours together for a random effect, one after the other for stripes, or in blocks for areas of colour.

Cut two cardboard pieces in the shape of doughnuts. The outer circle should be cut at the size required for the pompon. The inner circle

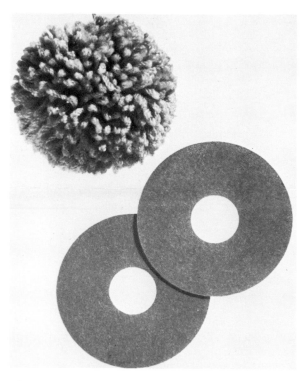

will determine how compact the pompon will be: a diameter of one third that of the outer circle will give a medium pompon (see illustration), while a diameter half that of the outer circle will give a really tight pompon.

Place cards together and wind yarn around the ring until the hole is full. Cut through all the layers of yarn, working around the edge with sharp scissors. Pull cards apart and tie the pompon at the centre, as tightly as possible, leaving one or two long ends for later fixing the pompon to the garment. Remove cards, fluff pompon, trim if necessary and fix.

To make several pompons at once, wrap yarn between two long nails or rods, firmly secured to a workbench, until required thickness is obtained. Tie firmly at intervals slightly longer than needed, each time leaving long ends for later sewing. Cut yarn carefully at midpoint between ties. Fluff and trim.

LOOKING AFTER KNITTING

Keep all your knitted garments carefully folded and protected from dust and strong sunlight. Do not hang them under any circumstances, or they will lose their shape. Wash your garments before storing them for any length of time, and use moth balls if the garments are made of wool.

Clean often, previously turning garment inside out to avoid pilling, and following strictly the instructions given by the yarn manufacturer. If in doubt, first clean a sample, drawing the outline of the sample on a piece of paper before washing or dry-cleaning it, so that it can be checked afterwards for changes in size.

Unless otherwise advised by the manufacturer, if a yarn needs to be hand washed, this should be done in hand-hot or cold water, using a mild cleansing agent. Rinse thoroughly, at the same temperature used for washing. Always lift gently and do not wring, but squeeze dirt and water out. Roll in a towel to remove excess moisture.

Always dry knitting flat, and away from direct heat and sunlight. A good way is to put a clean towel or other absorbent cloth on the floor or on top of a flat surface, and dry the garment on top of that. Shape the garment carefully while still wet. If necessary, check dimensions with a measuring tape before and after washing.

Stains should be treated as soon as possible, and always before the actual washing.

It is a good idea to shake garments occasionally to remove accumulated dust.

If pilling occurs, brush garment with one of the special brushes sold for this purpose, or pick it off with your fingers or a strip of sticky tape.

Snags should never be cut off. Using a short knitting needle or a cable needle, ease the affected stitches so that they recover their previous appearance. If the yarn has actually stretched, draw any remaining loop through the fabric with the help of a crochet hook.

Part Two: Design

To design something, whatever its nature, is to devise a way of putting materials together, so that they will serve exactly a well-defined purpose, in a way that is pleasing to the eye. Obviously, 'pleasing to the eye' does not mean it has to please everybody's eye, because that would be impossible. What it means is that it must conform to the rules, or indeed the anti-rules, of an aesthetic trend. Originality is not essential; the fact that something has not been done before does not make it necessarily good or desirable. However, originality that comes from keeping a very open mind, and not being shy to use something new if it provides the best solution or the best effect, is indeed very valuable.

Knitting design, as a whole, is a fairly straightforward exercise. There are basically three elements to consider: shape, texture and colour. By emphasising one and playing safe with the others, highly different designs can be achieved. If you have never designed before, concentrate on the aspect you think will be easiest for you to start with, and take the other two gently until your confidence grows.

A pitfall to avoid is the temptation to use, in a single design, everything one knows and all the ideas one has. For a design to be of any quality, it is essential that it should have *unity of idea*. This idea can be simple or complex; it can be traditional or innovative. What matters is that it must be there, and it must be consistent all the way through. Give yourself time to think about it but, once it is clear in your mind, stick to it, and do not try to add new elements that do not fit in, no matter how exciting they might be.

Another characteristic of a good knitting design is that it must *speak the language of the knitting craft*. Or, put into plainer words, all aspects must be planned and solved keeping in mind the characteristics of knitted fabrics and the techniques for, say, shaping, strengthening and flattening, at the knitter's disposal. A design that uses hand-knitting just as it would use any other fabric, with hems, lining, interlining and darts everywhere, might be excellent from a dressmaker's point of view, but it is not true knitting because it only uses one of the aspects of this craft: weaving.

A third ingredient is *respect for the natural tendencies*. Yarns, stitch patterns, shapes, they all have, one could say, very strong wills. If they decide to go one way, there is nothing you can do about it. Trying to force them only results in garments that are 'not quite right'. Either they will go limp instead of maintaining a soft fullness, or they will be too stiff for comfort, or the edges will curl instead of staying flat, or many other possibilities that are best avoided.

Finally, to produce good designs there must be an element of *enjoyment* while designing. Of course, it will be hard work, and sometimes you may not feel up to it, or might get discouraged by an early failure. Creating something is often compared to giving birth, and when giving birth to a garment you must expect some labour pains! However, your overall feeling must be one of enjoyment because your imagination can run free, because you can transform ideas into something tangible, because you are playing a big game with colours, textures and shapes.

CHAPTER 3
Defining the Project

If a design must serve exactly a specific purpose, it is obvious that the purpose itself must be defined precisely. In knitting, it is not much good saying 'Oh, I will just knit a cardigan . . .' A casual summer cardigan is not the same as a dressy winter cardigan. And a cardigan for a tall, slim, middle-aged woman with high shoulders is not the same as a cardigan for a chubby young boy.

The following notes will help you define what you want a garment to be. They will also give you general guidelines for achieving your purpose. Make a list of your requirements and, if it is impossible to fulfil all of them, decide which ones should take priority over the others.

THE GARMENT

USE
Should the garment be appropriate for a party, dressing-up, smart everyday wear, casual everyday wear, sports wear, tough indoor or outdoor jobs?

FASHION VALUE
Should it be a timeless classic, a traditional knit, have a discreet but fashionable look, follow the latest and boldest fashion trends, or be fully original and independent from fashion and tradition?

WARMTH
Is the garment intended for winter, for summer, or for mid-season? Must it keep the wind out?

For warm garments use either wool that is not highly twisted or mohair, cashmere, or angora. For medium warmth use highly twisted wool, alpaca, silk, blends or man-made fibres. For cool garments use cotton and linen.

Use close-texture, thick stitch patterns and tight fittings for warmth; openwork and loose fittings for coolness.

To keep the wind out, use really compact stitch patterns, zipped and double-breasted front openings and tight cuffs.

THICKNESS
Does it matter whether the garment is thick or thin?

Thickness should not be taken as equivalent to warmth, because so much depends on the type of fibre used. A thin wool jumper could easily be warmer than a thick acrylic one. Therefore, if a garment must be of a specific thickness, the number of possible yarns will be greatly reduced.

HANDLE
Does it matter whether the garment is rough or soft to the touch? Are there any fibres that you, or the person who is going to wear the garment, dislike the feel of?

Choose soft yarns for garments to be worn next to the skin.

CLEANING
Is it essential that the garment be easily cleaned at home? Is it important that it should be machine-washable?

DURABILITY
Do you want the garment to last a long time, or just one season?

Some fibres last longer than others. Also, good quality yarns last longer than poor quality ones.

Do not put so much effort into garments unlikely to be very hardwearing, or into those that will only be fashionable for a very short time.

WEIGHT
Does the person who is going to wear the garment or you, the knitter, object to heavy garments? Do you object to very light ones?

Some yarns, and thick cotton is a good example, are much heavier than others. A large garment might then prove to be too much for the knitter's arms, or the wearer's shoulders.

Conversely, some people do not like to wear lightweight garments.

PRICE
Does the garment need to be kept within a budget?

Except when durability is not very important, let the price influence only the type of fibre but not the quality of the yarn. For example, if mohair would be right but you cannot afford it, buy the best soft wool your budget allows for, rather than an inexpensive mohair imitation that will soon lose its looks and not keep you as warm.

OTHER CHARACTERISTICS
Should the garment complement or match other clothes? Are pockets necessary?

THE WEARER

PERSONAL PREFERENCES

Does the person who is going to wear the garment like bright or muted colours, discreet or showy clothes, baggy or tight-fitting garments?

When designing for somebody else, try to produce garments that fit his or her personality and needs, not yours. This is especially important when designing for somebody of the opposite sex, or belonging to a different age group.

FIGURE

All styles do not suit all people, and everybody is conscious of certain things he or she should avoid.

Drooping shoulders are emphasized by raglan sleeves, while set-in sleeves emphasize broad, square shoulders. Crew-necks and similar round necklines do not go well with long necks, while high and bulky polo-necks do not go well with short necks. Yokes and square necklines are best avoided for people with broad shoulders. Also avoid belts with a short or heavy waist, sleeveless garments with very thin or very heavy arms, and continuous sleeves with a large bust.

Conversely, some shapes and patterns can improve a figure. Properly fitted set-in sleeves can help drooping shoulders; long tops go well with a short waist, a large bust, or large hips; horizontal stripes or welts will add body to a small frame or shorten a long waist; and vertical stripes will help a large frame or a short waist.

CHILDREN

Some features help a garment last longer, by making it more adaptable to a growing child. For instance, turned-up cuffs that can be unturned, double-breasted fronts that can become single, and seams with large allowances that can be re-stitched nearer the edge.

Loose-fitting styles are obviously more adaptable than tight-fitting ones, and garments simply knitted in one colour will be easier to transform than heavy-patterned ones.

Baby garments should be easy to put on and take off, have few seams, and small and simple fastenings. Unnecessary thickenings should be carefully avoided.

ALLERGIES AND SENSITIVITIES

Both the fibres that make a yarn, and the treatments applied to fibres to improve or alter their properties, can induce allergy symptoms: an itch, a rash, a runny nose . . .

There have always been people sensitive to natural fibres, but with the widespread use of man-made and chemically-treated fibres, the number of those affected by yarns is increasing.

Small children and babies are particularly to be watched, since constant contact with easy-to-wash fibres could cause discomfort now, or prepare the ground for future disorders. It is a serious problem, but one that is not yet well understood, so it is best to play safe and avoid contact with suspect yarns.

CHAPTER 4
Choosing Yarns

Yarn is such an important element of knitting that its choice will either make or break a design. It will also lengthen or shorten the life of a garment, and greatly influence its comfort. For all these reasons, penny-pinching when buying yarn is always a false economy in the long run. Although it must also be pointed out that high prices should never be taken as a guarantee of quality, because they are greatly influenced by production, country of origin, fashion and novelty value.

Knitting yarns are generally bought at specialised shops. Well-run shops are invaluable sources of advice for knitters; indeed, in some countries they even adapt designs to your own measurements, and teach you how to knit them, as an inclusive part of their service. But, for obvious reasons, these shops can only stock a limited range of all yarns produced, and to find the yarn you want you might have to go to several shops. If you feel adventurous, it is also possible to obtain more unusual varieties by mail, often direct from the manufacturers. Craft magazines often advertise firms selling by mail. A small payment might be asked for the shade cards but, even if that is not refunded with your first order, it is generally worthwhile.

Most often, yarns come in balls or in skeins (also called hanks). Skeins need winding into balls. If you do that by hand, always hold the ball in the palm of your hand and wind the yarn around your four fingers; every so often, disentangle your fingers from the ball and continue winding in a different position, so that the ball becomes round. Winding around the fingers stops the yarn from stretching.

Machine-wound balls should always be started from the inner end of the yarn, in order to avoid unnecessary twisting. If the ball does not carry a tag that makes it easy to pull out the inner end, put your fingers right inside the centre of the ball in order to find it. Removing the paper band usually helps the operation.

Yarns can also come in cones. These are mainly intended for machine knitting, where they are fixed to a spindle that allows the cone to rotate when the yarn is pulled horizontally. In hand knitting, if the cone is left upright on the floor, the yarn being pulled from the top may get twisted and become difficult to work with. To avoid this, place the cone on its side inside a large enough box, and leave the box on the floor. When you pull the yarn, the cone will roll on its side and the yarn will not tangle.

Practically all the yarns sold in shops carry a label or band indicating composition, cleaning instructions, pressing temperatures, shade reference, dye-lot reference and recommended needle size. Follow carefully the instructions for cleaning and pressing, but only use the recommended needle size as a guide, which is what it really is. The actual needles you will need will depend both on the stitch pattern used and on your own way of knitting. (See also Appendix.) Always keep a band or label for future reference.

When buying yarn, make sure you buy enough for the whole garment (see page 139 for how to calculate amount needed), making sure that all of it has been dyed in the same batch. This is easily checked by looking at the dye-lot reference on the band or label. Small differences between batches are unavoidable, and these would later show in the finished garment. Shops normally offer a 'lay-by' service, by which they reserve extra yarn of the same batch for a few days or weeks, or they take back any left-over yarn within a reasonable period of time.

Different dye lots, however, can prove an asset when fully integrated in the design. Jacquard and striped patterns can look more subtle if worked in slightly different shades, providing, obviously, that these are evenly distributed throughout. A cheap way of buying good yarn is to purchase remnants of several batches of the same colour, to knit a garment in carefully worked out stripes. A thin line in a contrasting colour could be added to separate the stripes.

YARN TYPES
Yarns come in a variety of thicknesses, fibres, colours and textures. A guide to these is given later in the chapter, in the form of a Glossary.

There are two main types of yarn, natural and man-made, and a large number of blends that combine both types. They all have advantages and disadvantages, which the Glossary should help you to discover. In general terms, man-made fibres can be more easily and cheaply produced (which does not mean they are always more cheaply sold), are easier to clean than untreated natural fibres, and do not shrink, although they can stretch. On the other hand, natural fibres

44

'breathe', have a much pleasanter feel, are generally more comfortable, and pill noticeably less.

Whatever their type, to obtain good results only *honest* fibres should be used, meaning by honest those that look what they really are: cool if they are cool, soft if they are soft, etc. And here is where man-made fibres can be a problem, because they often imitate the natural look but not the natural qualities. Two bitter experiences of mine might help illustrate this point.

One is a very long, extremely thick jacket that in cold weather always prompts envious looks, knitted in what looks like wool slub. It is, in fact, an acrylic blend so uninsulating that the jacket can only be worn in warmer weather, when what you want is something far less cumbersome.

The other is a sleeveless top knitted in what a Spanish shop sold as 'summer yarn', which is too stifling to wear in a not-so-hot English summer. The yarn, this time, is acrylic imitating mercerised cotton.

TEXTURE
Yarns give garments their basic texture, although texture is also achieved with stitch patterns. There is no set rule as to whether the pattern or the yarn should be chosen first, but different yarns make the same stitch pattern look so different, that it is always worthwhile knitting a few samples before going any further with the design. Buying a single ball of the yarn you have in mind to knit these samples is often a good investment.

When clarity of stitch is important, use smooth and well-twisted yarns. Fancy-textured yarns such as gimp or chenille are best worked in straightforward stitch patterns. One of the simpler knit and purl combinations, or perhaps a cable or a few bobbles, is the most they can take without looking fussy. If a complex stitch pattern is used, the yarn's own texture will not allow it to show properly. Untwisted or hairy yarns will also detract from the clarity of the stitch pattern. This is clearly shown by the illustration, where exactly the same sample appears knitted in well-twisted worsted (top left), lopi (top right), chenille (bottom left) and loop (bottom right).

The thickness of the yarn will obviously have an effect on the final size of the stitch. A stitch pattern so small that it will hardly be noticeable in a fine yarn can look very dramatic if the yarn is really thick. Conversely, and this applies most especially but not exclusively to lace, the most beautiful of the large stitch patterns can look clumsy and out of proportion in thick yarn.

Some yarns will simply make it difficult to work some types of stitch pattern. This is the case with patterns including pass-slipped-stitch-over instructions and mohair or other brushed yarns: the hairs get caught and are difficult to pull. When a yarn makes it particularly difficult to work a certain pattern, either change the yarn or the pattern. Otherwise, you will be putting a lot of effort into something that almost certainly will not look right.

COLOUR
Yarns also give garments their colour, but this is something you will have to consider very care-

45

fully, unless you are one of those lucky people that instinctively know how to use colour. If you are not, do not worry; it can be learnt.

The first thing to remember is that yarns very often look duller before they are knitted. If you have doubts as to whether a certain green might be 'just a trifle bright', the odds are that the first time you wear it you will develop a parrot complex! Also make sure that the shade you choose suits your complexion, eye and hair colour by placing a ball or skein under your chin and looking at yourself in a mirror.

Remember, as well, that colours play optical tricks. Dull colours or subtle combinations will make you look small, while bright colours and bold contrasts will make you look larger. Cool shades of blue, green and violet will also make you look smaller than warm shades of red, orange or yellow.

If you are going to mix colours, at first you will probably get better results with muted shades rather than with bright, contrasting colours, as these are more difficult to combine successfully. The safest combinations are those that use shades of a single colour; for example, cream, beige, medium brown and dark brown.

Smooth yarns will always produce much sharper colour breaks than yarns with some degree of fluff or texture. The illustration shows two extremes: wool crêpe (top) and brushed mohair combed with a teasel after knitting (bottom).

An easy way of introducing colour in a garment is to use a multicoloured yarn. These yarns, however, will change the appearance of stitch patterns in similar ways to fancy-textured yarns. The illustration on page 47 shows samples in the same stitch as those illustrating texture, but knitted this time in ombré (top left), random-dye slub marl (top right), splash-dye (bottom left) and twist (bottom right).

If a suitable mixture of colours cannot be found, two or more fine yarns can be knitted together. In this way, it is possible to create tailor-made combinations of colour and texture. The strands may or may not be twisted together before being knitted.

When working with ombré or random-dye yarns, make sure that you are not changing the colour sequence when joining a new ball, or colour blobs will appear in the work. Also, start symmetrical sections, such as sleeves, at the same point in the sequence.

GLOSSARY OF TERMS RELATING TO KNITTING YARNS

Acetate A **Natural polymer fibre** obtained from cellulose acetate. It is fairly strong and elastic, but not especially so. Does not absorb much water, and does not show a marked tendency to shrink or stretch. Does not burn readily; melts and drips. It is moderately low priced. Available mainly in blends with more expensive yarns.

Disadvantages: Not very strong or hardwearing. It is easily damaged by heat, and therefore great care should be taken if pressing it.

Acrylic fibres These are **Synthetic fibres** whose main component is a substance called *acrylonitrile*. They are elastic, moderately expensive, warmer than other synthetic fibres, and can be made to resemble wool in appearance. They absorb little moisture and therefore dry quickly. Their affinity to dyes varies with specific brands, and for this reason some offer a good colour range whilst others do not. They are all lightweight, and that makes a ball go a long way. They are not dangerously inflammable.

Disadvantages: Despite their relative warmth they are not as insulating as wool, nor do they 'breathe', so they can be uncomfortable in warm weather. They stretch when in warm, wet conditions, which means that washing must be carefully controlled, and that the garments must always be dried flat. They can pill and/or develop static electricity. To avoid distortion and glazing, any pressing must be done with great care and at a cool setting.

Alpaca Long hairs (white, grey, fawn, brown or black) grown by two very similar members of the camel family, the alpaca and the llama, that live in the South American Andes. In softness and durability both fibres stand halfway between mohair and cashmere. They are fairly warm and have a nice lustre. Generally available in their natural shades, but availability depends on fashion.

Disadvantages: Fairly expensive. Limited supply because of conservation measures to avoid extinction.

Angora Hairs of the Angora rabbit. It is lustrous, extremely soft and warm. To facilitate spinning, it is generally blended with wool. Its availability depends on fashion. It must not be pressed.

Disadvantages: The short hairs shed easily, covering your clothes and those of the people that come near you. They can also irritate nose and throat, and small children can choke on them.

Aran A type of **Wool**. It is a thick ('triple knitting'), strong, hardwearing, four-ply yarn, used for traditional knitting in the Irish islands of the same name. It used to be left undyed or coloured with natural dyes. The name is now applied to all yarns of similar appearance, whether wool or man-made, off-white or brightly coloured.

Blends Yarns obtained by mixing two or more types of fibre, either before or during spinning. There are three reasons for blending fibres: economy, combination of properties when no single fibre is ideal, and texture or colour effects. Irrespective of whether the added fibre is of higher or lower quality than the main fibre, less than ten per cent of it will generally make little difference to the way a yarn feels to the touch.

Less than 15 per cent will rarely show a marked difference in economic terms, texture or appearance. If over 20 per cent is added it will begin to be noticeable, and above 50 per cent it will gradually dominate the characteristics of the yarn.

Bouclé This is a **Fancy-textured yarn**, giving an unevenly knobbly fabric.

Brushed yarn This is a **Fancy-textured yarn**. The fibres have been brought out to produce a furry effect. This can be accentuated if, after finishing it, the garment is firmly brushed with a teasel. Brushed yarns can be knitted with thick needles, letting the hairs fill the gaps, or with finer needles, to obtain a much warmer and furrier garment. If thick needles are used, care must be taken not to stretch the garment, especially when washing it.

Cashmere Short hairs (white, grey or tan) that form the undercoat of the Cashmere goat. It is produced in Northern India and other parts of Asia. It is beautifully soft, lustrous, smooth and light. It is also extremely warm. Its availability depends on fashion.

Disadvantages: Production is low, and obtaining the fibre is a lengthy process, which means that it is very expensive. It is not very hardwearing. Blends with wool make it cheaper and stronger, but detract from its softness.

47

Chenille This is a **Fancy-textured yarn**, giving a velvety fabric. When knitting it, make sure it is not twisted; otherwise the pile will keep changing direction and the result will be uneven.

'Chunky' see **Thickness**.

Coloured yarns Yarns that have been dyed in one or more colours, before or after spinning. See also **Mixture**, **Ombré**, **Solid colour**, **Spiral marl**, **Splash dye**, **Random dye** and **Twist**.

Cotton White staple fibres from the seed of the cotton plant. The length of the fibre determines the quality and the price of cotton, its strength and softness increasing with length. Best cottons come from Egypt and Sea Island (long staple), followed by America (medium staple) and India, at the lower end of the market (short staple). Cotton is a cool, comfortable fibre, ideal for hot weather. It is cheap and can be dyed in a wide range of shades. It has a good resistance to laundering and pressing, and can take a variety of finishes. Both plain and *mercerised* (treated to give it a permanent lustre) cottons can come in different textures.

Disadvantages: Cotton is a comparatively heavy fibre, with poor elasticity and readily inflammable. Poor-quality cottons may shrink when first washed. Not all textures are easily available through retailers.

Crêpe A highly twisted and smooth yarn, with a characteristic crinkle, made out of **Wool** or a man-made fibre imitating wool. It is hardwearing, but considerably heavier than less twisted yarns of similar fibre content.

'Double-double knitting' see **Thickness**.

'Double knitting' see **Thickness**.

From left to right: Slub, Spiral 1, Spiral 2, Bouclé, Gimp, Loop, Chenille, Glitter

Fancy-textured yarns Any yarn that will give a special texture or effect to knitting. See illustration below and individual entries.

Filaments Fibres of enormous length used in the manufacture of yarns.

Fold Another name for **Ply**.

Gimp This is a **Fancy-textured yarn**, giving an evenly knobbly fabric.

Glitter yarns Filaments made out of a thin strip of aluminium foil covered with clear plastic film. Colour is incorporated in the adhesive used to glue the two together. They are fairly flexible, but cannot be pressed.

Disadvantages: They are not very strong. Garments close to the skin might need lining. Care must be taken when dry-cleaning, as unsuitable solvents might cause delamination.

Heather Mixture Another name for **Mixture**.

Linen Long staple fibres extracted from the stalks of the flax plant. Yarns made out of the best fibres are called *line*, and those obtained from shorter and broken fibres are called *tow*. Linen is cool, lustrous, strong and hardwearing. It usually comes in an uneven texture and a wide range of shades.

Disadvantages: Although comparatively cheap, it is more expensive than cotton. It may shrink the first time it is washed, although good linen should not. Not easily available through retailers.

Loop This is a **Fancy-textured yarn**, giving a fabric full of little loops. When knitting it, care must be taken not to catch the loops with the needles.

Lopi A type of **Wool**, used in traditional Icelandic knitting. It is very thick ('double-

double'), warm and fairly light. It is a single, untwisted yarn, that easily breaks. Available mainly in natural colours, but can also be obtained dyed.

Lurex   A trademark for **Glitter yarn**.

Marl   see **Spiral marl**.

Mixture   A subtly **Coloured yarn**, obtained by spinning together staple fibres dyed in more than one colour.

Modacrylic fibres   Modified **Acrylic fibres** with flame resistant properties. They need more care than acrylics when washing because they are more sensitive to heat.

Mohair   White, long hairs of the Angora goat. It is lustrous, smooth, elastic, and stronger than fine wools. It is very warm, very light and very hardwearing. Mohair is difficult to spin, and comes mainly from Turkey. It is usually available brushed, in a wide range of bright colours. See also **Brushed Yarns**.

Disadvantages: Mohair is expensive, and for this reason it is often blended with cheaper fibres. However, before buying, it is worth the effort to compare prices carefully. Blends can be heavier, and therefore a ball of mohair blend may not go as far as a ball of pure mohair.

Natural fibres   Filaments or staple fibres of animal or vegetable origin.

Natural polymer fibres   Filaments or staple fibres manufactured from materials, such as cellulose, which can naturally form fibres.

Noil   The short or knotted fibres separated from the staple fibres by combing.

Nylon   Generic name for a type of **Synthetic fibre** with a high degree of strength, elasticity and toughness. Nylon absorbs very little moisture and, therefore, dries very quickly. It is moderately expensive to produce, and can be spun like wool, being used in blends to improve the strength and durability of this fibre. Not dangerously inflammable; it melts and drips.

Disadvantages: Unpleasant to handle, can irritate the skin, has a 'glassy' appearance (it shines when by itself or when blended with wool), pills and develops static electricity that attracts dirt. It is difficult to dye, and therefore the colour range is limited and not very subtle. Hot in summer, because it does not 'breathe', and cold in winter because it is a bad insulator.

Ombré   This is a **Coloured yarn**, dyed in such

a way that different shades of the same colour appear, one after the other, at regular or irregular intervals.

Pilling   Little balls that form on the surface of a garment, caused by friction.

Ply   Every one of the strands that form a yarn. Amongst knitters, two-ply, three-ply and four-ply have become indications of **Thickness**, but this is a misuse of the expression. A four-ply yarn made out of four fine strands can be far thinner than a two-ply yarn made out of two very thick strands.

Polyamide fibre   Another name for **Nylon**.

Polyester fibres   Synthetic fibres, similar to nylon in general properties but better in appearance. They are less glassy, more pleasant to handle, and do not shine when mixed with wool.

'Quick knit'   see **Thickness**.

Random dye   This is a **Coloured yarn**, dyed in such a way that different colours appear one after the other at regular, or irregular, intervals.

Rayon   Another name for **Viscose rayon**.

Shetland   Originally, it was only the light weight yarn spun from the soft **Wool** of the Shetland Islands sheep, but the term is now applied also to yarns that imitate it with different degrees of success, including man-made fibres. It has a slight fluff, and is available in many colours. The most common real Shetland wool has two plies but knits as 'Four-ply'; imitations often knit as 'Double knitting'.

Silk   The only natural filament, produced by the silkworm to build a cocoon around itself before becoming a chrysalis. To obtain the silk, the cocoons need to be unwound, a tedious and highly skilled operation. Most silk comes from China and Japan. Silk is warm, has a very high lustre and is soft, fine, strong and fairly elastic. Broken lengths of filament are converted into *spun silk*, and the shortest, knotted fibres that form the *noil* are also made into yarn. *Tussah silk* is produced by an undomesticated Indian silkworm. It is brownish, strong, coarse and naturally uneven.

Disadvantages: It is very expensive, especially as filament. Silk noil is comparatively cheap, but it is a tough yarn, without much lustre. Not easily available through ordinary retailers.

Single   A yarn made out of one single **Ply**.

Slub   This is a **Fancy-textured yarn**, that is

From left to right: Two-ply, Three-ply, Four-ply,
Quick knit, Double knitting, Triple knitting,
Double-double Knitting or Chunky, Extra chunky

fine in some places and has big lumps in others.
Knit it with fairly large needles.

Solid colour   Yarns dyed in one single and even
colour.

Spiral   Two types of **Fancy-textured yarns**.
The first type is an untwisted strand winding
itself very closely around a central, hidden
strand. The second type is an untwisted strand
winding around a very fine, visible and twisted
strand.

Spiral marl   This is a **Coloured yarn** which is
a spiral yarn of the second type, in which the
untwisted strand and the fine strand have
different colours. The untwisted strand can also
be multicolour.

Splash dye   This is a **Coloured yarn** that has
irregular marks in one or more colours over a
solid-colour background.

Staple   Fibres of short length used in the
manufacture of yarns.

Synthetic fibres   Filaments manufactured
from substances (mainly oil), that neither suggest nor produce fibres in nature. They are
usually cut into staple fibres and bulked, in order
to imitate wool.

Thickness   Yarn manufacturers use methods
of sizing yarns based on weight and length. These
systems, for there are more than one, are far too
complicated for amateur knitters, and somehow a
practice has evolved of giving names to thicknesses. Some of these names are arbitrary, and
others are even misleading (see **Ply**), but its use is
so widespread that it cannot be ignored. The
illustration above shows full-size samples of

yarns and their common names. See Appendix for
a rough guide of what size needles to use with each
thickness.

Triacetate   Modified **Acetate**, more resistant
to heat. It can be made to absorb very little
water, thus drying as quickly as synthetic fibres.
It is, however, considerably cheaper to produce
than these.

'Triple knitting'   see **Thickness**.

Tweed   Thick, lumpy, woollen-spun **Wool**,
made out of strong quality fibres. Somewhat
coarse. It generally has speckles in other colours.

Twist   This is a **Coloured yarn**, the plies of
which are of different colours, or of different
intensities of the same colour.

Unst   Very thick ('Double-double' or 'Extra
chunky') **Wool**, produced by the sheep of the
Shetland Island of that name.

Vicuña   Finest, softest and most rare animal
hair. The vicuña is the smallest type of llama, and
has not yet been domesticated. It is extremely
expensive.

Viscose rayon   A **Natural polymer fibre**, formed by the regeneration of cellulose extracted
from wood pulp. When dry, it is reasonably
strong and elastic. It is limp, cool to the touch and
highly absorbent of water. It can be made to look
superficially like wool, and in this way it is used in
blends because of its cheapness.

Disadvantages: When wet, it loses half its strength
and can be easily stretched out of shape. Inflammable.

Baby briefs and matinee jacket and toddler's chenille top
(see page 155)

Wool Staple fibres (off-white, grey, tan or brown) that form the fleece of sheep. The length of the fibre determines the quality and the price of wool, its warmth and softness increasing, but its strength and elasticity decreasing as the fibre gets shorter. The best wool is *merino*, also called *botany*, of Spanish origin but now mainly produced in Australia. *Lambswool* comes from the first clipping of baby merino lambs, and is very fine. Second comes the wide range of *crossbred* wools, produced all over the world, and finally the *carpet* or *rug* types, produced by Asiatic and mountain sheep. Only the first two types are suitable for knitwear. See also: **Aran, Brushed yarns, Crêpe, Lopi, Shetland, Single, Tweed, Unst, Woollen** and **Worsted**.

Wool is a warm fibre that will absorb excess moisture, such as perspiration, without feeling cold and clammy. It can take a certain degree of shaping through blocking, but this must be done with great care. It comes in a very wide range of shades, and in almost any texture, but the availability of specific textures depends on fashion and demand. Well-twisted wool is stronger than wool with a minimum of twist, but you will find that it is not as soft and warm. It is not inflammable.

Wool can be treated to make it shrink resistant, and machine-washable wool is becoming increasingly popular. When using it, knit it slightly tighter than you would ordinary wool.

Disadvantages: Some types of crossbred wool are too rough for direct contact with the skin, and should be kept for outer wear. Wool is sensitive to heat, moisture and chemicals, and has to be washed with care in order to avoid felting. Relaxation shrinkage might also occur, unrelated to washing, if wool is knitted loosely; this means that the fibres can shorten spontaneously, because the tension given is not enough to keep them in shape. Untreated wool can be attacked by moths when stored for any length of time; make a point of using mothballs as a prevention.

Woollen wool Fibrous yarns, produced from haphazard bundles of fibres.

Woollen-spun A yarn, made out of any fibre, processed and spun like **Woollen wool**.

Worsted Smooth yarns, produced after eliminating the short fibres, and making the ones that are left parallel to each other. Most ordinary knitting wool is worsted.

Yarn A continuous strand of natural or man-made filaments or staple fibres twisted together.

Camisole evening top with Jacquard motif and mohair cardigan (see page 155)

CHAPTER 5
Choosing Stitch Patterns

Together with yarns, stitch patterns are means of achieving texture. Few movements need to be known to knit the vast majority of patterns and some, despite a complex appearance, are very easy to learn. Therefore, even if you are not experienced, you will not need to stick to garter stitch or stocking stitch for your first designs.

The patterns in this chapter are only a very small selection of what can be done with needles and yarn. There is, in fact, an infinite number of patterns you can use, and you must not feel restricted to just copying what you see in print. Experiment, try any combination that occurs to you, alter and adapt to suit your own needs and—above all—knit, knit, knit.

THE TEST SWATCH

Before using a stitch pattern it is essential to make a sample, called a swatch, in the yarn that will actually be used. The importance of this sample cannot be stressed enough. At a later stage it will be used to calculate the stitches and rows a garment will have, and therefore it must be knitted in the right tension and with the same yarn that will be used for the garment. You should also knit in the same shade; because of the dyeing process pale-coloured yarns, especially white, are often slightly thicker than darker yarns and this affects the tension.

Never rely on a swatch you have not knitted yourself; the tension will never be exactly the same. And do make a swatch for every pattern used in a garment, as two patterns will rarely give the same count. The swatch will allow you to find out how a particular pattern looks in a particular yarn. As the previous chapter has shown, the yarn used can transform the appearance of the pattern, and care should be taken not to knit in unsuitable yarns.

The size of the swatch will vary with the type of yarn and pattern, but as a rule it has to be big enough to show a few repeats of the pattern. With fine yarns, a swatch 6–7cm square ($2\frac{1}{2}$in square) might be enough, while for thicker yarns it needs to be at least 11–12cm square ($4\frac{1}{2}$in square). These dimensions will allow you to measure the number of rows and stitches per 5cm (2in), or 10cm (4in), once the swatch has been blocked.

TENSION

A pattern will only look right if knitted at the correct tension for the yarn. Therefore, if in doubt, knit another swatch with different size needles and compare the two. The yarn label and the Appendix will both give you an idea of needle size, but do not follow this advice blindly. The size you will actually need will depend on the way you knit and the pattern you choose.

To know whether the tension is right, feel the swatch. A good swatch is elastic, and when pulled sideways and released will immediately regain its original shape. If it is too tight, it will be stiff, the stitches will look very close to each other, and when pulled sideways it will not stretch easily. If it is too loose it will be flabby, the stitches will be uneven and spreading, and when pulled sideways it will stretch easily and remain stretched.

Garments knitted too tightly lack elasticity, while garments knitted too loosely will become baggy and shapeless in next to no time. For this reason, you should never repeat a design on needles one size larger or smaller to obtain a garment slightly bigger or smaller than the original. This practice is often recommended but only results in garments with the wrong tension that do not wear properly.

There are two exceptions to the rules on tension. Borders, cuffs and other elements requiring firmness must be knitted at a tighter tension than the rest of the garment, in order to help them keep their shape. This is especially true of ribbing. If your ribbed borders stretch with wear, they are almost certainly too loose (or you are using a stretchy yarn). The second exception is scarves, stoles and loose-fitting garments such as bed jackets which can be knitted looser providing the pattern has tight points that keep it in shape.

To end a swatch, cast off or cut the yarn (not too near the last stitch!) and thread it through the last row with a sewing needle.

Always keep all your swatches, noting the type of yarn and needles used. They are invaluable for future reference, and for checking how the garment will respond to blocking and washing.

CIRCULAR KNITTING

The following instructions are all for flat knitting. Patterns only involving knit and purl stitches, however, can be easily adapted to circular knitting. Just knit the purl stitches and purl the knit stitches on those rounds that take the place of wrong-side rows.

ABBREVIATIONS
(See Chapter 1 for details of instructions)

...	Repeat instructions between asterisks as many times as necessary to complete row
(...)	Repeat instructions in brackets as many times as indicated immediately after the brackets
BC	Back cross a cable
FC	Front cross a cable
k	Knit
k-b	Knit back of stitch
k2tog	Knit two stitches together
k2tog-b	Knit two stitches together inserting needle through the back
LTw2	Twist two stitches to the left
p	Purl
p-b	Purl back of stitch
p2tog	Purl two stitches together
p3tog	Purl three stitches together
p2tog-b	Purl two stitches together inserting needle through the back
psso	Pass slipped stitch(es) over any stitches worked after slipping it/them, and draw needle through
RTw2	Twist two stitches to the right
sl	Slip specified number of stitches onto right needle, without working them; unless otherwise instructed, pick the stitches as if they were to be *purled*
ssk	Slip, slip, knit. Slip two stitches as if they were to be *knitted*, then insert tip of left needle through them and knit them together
st, sts	Stitch, stitches
yb	Yarn back
yf	Yarn forward
yon	Yarn over needle
yrn	Yarn round needle

KNIT AND PURL COMBINATIONS

These are the most elementary of all stitch patterns, requiring only two movements; knit and purl. When changing from one to the other, pass yarn from right to wrong side of work, or vice versa, under the needles.

Embossed effects can easily be obtained because knit stitches tend to stand up from purl stitches on vertical lines, and purl stitches tend to stand up from knit stitches on horizontal lines. Motifs can be worked either in reverse stocking stitch, garter stitch or moss stitch on a stocking-stitch background, or vice versa; fairly solid cross-stitch designs may be used. Designs with many fine lines will not show up well, but can be improved by enlarging them so that each cross-stitch square is transformed into a larger one measuring two stitches by two rows. The result will be four times bigger than the original, and may be drawn on graph paper before knitting it.

Other possible motifs are diagonal stripes, chevrons and simple geometric shapes, such as rectangles, triangles or diamonds. When working oblique lines, make the contrasting stitch-pattern travel one stitch further *every row* for a flatter slant, and *every two rows* for a steeper one.

STOCKING-STITCH VARIATIONS

Stocking stitch is the most widely used of all knitting stitches. It requires careful blocking because of a strong tendency to curl.

The twisting of the stitches in the second and third variations gives a tighter fabric. To obtain similar tensions, needles one size larger will be required for twisted stocking stitch than for plain stocking stitch. Crossed stocking stitch can be worked with different size needles; one size larger for the purl rows.

Another effect of the twisting is a tendency of the fabric to slant towards the left. This is especially noticeable in the last variation, and should be corrected when blocking.

Plain Stocking Stitch (*top*)
Any number of stitches
Row 1 (right side) knit
Row 2 purl

Crossed Stocking Stitch (*centre*)
Any number of stitches
Row 1 (right side) knit into back of loop
Row 2 purl
Alternatively:
Row 1 (right side) knit
Row 2 purl passing yarn *under* needle

Twisted Stocking Stitch (*bottom*)
Any number of stitches
Row 1 (right side) knit into back of loop
Row 2 purl into back of loop
Alternatively:
Row 1 (right side) knit passing yarn *over* needle
Row 2 purl passing yarn *under* needle
Repeat rows 1 and 2 of any one pattern

Tubular Stocking Stitch (*not illustrated*)
Plain stocking stitch can be worked in the form of a tube either by knitting in the round in the usual way or by using the following two-needle method:

Multiple of 2 stitches
All rows *k1, yf, sl1, yb*

GARTER STITCH AND REVERSE STOCKING STITCH
These two stitches are closely related in appearance but behave very differently. Garter stitch is a reversible and very flat stitch that requires little or no blocking, while reverse

stocking stitch tends to curl and has to be well blocked. Furthermore, garter stitch 'takes up', making a thick fabric that is elastic sideways, while stocking stitch is elastic vertically. The taking-up effect can be fully appreciated in the sample; both bands have the same number of rows.

Garter Stitch (*top*)
Any number of stitches
All rows knit

Reverse Stocking Stitch (*bottom*)
Any number of stitches
Row 1 (right side) purl
Row 2 knit
Repeat rows 1 and 2

WELTING
Welts are formed by alternating knit and purl rows and offer the beginner great scope for experimenting. Try any combination you like.

Welts extend the fabric horizontally and compress it vertically, giving a shorter length than stocking stitch for the same number of rows. Stocking stitch welts corrugate the fabric far more than the others and can either be blocked flat or left unblocked. Garter stitch welts need some blocking because the fabric tends to curl.

Reverse Stocking Stitch Welt (*top*)
Any number of stitches
Rows 1, 3, 5, 6 and 8 (right side) knit
Rows 2, 4 and 7 purl

Garter Stitch Welt (*bottom*)
Any number of stitches
Rows 1, 3, 5, 6, 7, 9, 11, 12, 13, 14, 15 and 16 (right side) knit
Rows 2, 4, 8 and 10 purl
Repeat rows 1 to 16

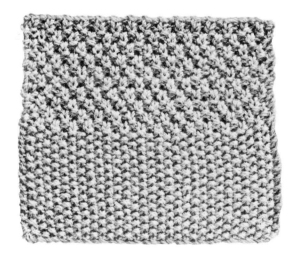

MOSS-STITCH VARIATIONS

Moss stitch gives a very flat, reversible fabric. It literally stands up from stocking stitch if the two are combined. Irish moss stitch compresses the fabric slightly sideways. Blocking may not be necessary.

Irish Moss *or* **Corn Stitch** *(top)*
Multiple of 2 stitches plus 1
Rows 1 and 4 *k1, p1*, k1
Rows 2 and 3 *p1, k1*, p1
Repeat rows 1 to 4

Moss, Rice *or* **Seed Stitch** *(bottom)*
Multiple of 2 stitches plus 1
All rows *k1, p1*, k1

Tumbling Blocks
A reversible pattern that looks the same on both sides. Needs thorough blocking.

Multiple of 12 stitches
Rows 1 and 2 *k6, p6*
Rows 3 and 4 *p1, k5, p5, k1*
Rows 5 and 6 *k1, p1, k4, p4, k1, p1*
Rows 7 and 8 *p1, k1, p1, k3, p3, k1, p1, k1*
Rows 9 and 10 *(k1, p1)twice, k2, p2, (k1, p1)twice*
Rows 11 and 12 *p1, k1*
Rows 13 and 14 *k1, p1*
Rows 15 and 16 *(p1, k1)twice, p2, k2, (p1, k1)twice*
Rows 17 and 18 *k1, p1, k1, p3, k3, p1, k1, p1*
Rows 19 and 20 *p1, k1, p4, k4, p1, k1*
Rows 21 and 22 *k1, p5, k5, p1*
Rows 23 and 24 *p6, k6*
Rows 25 and 26 *p5, k1, p1, k5*
Rows 27 and 28 *p4, (k1, p1)twice, k4*
Rows 29 and 30 *p3, (k1, p1)3 times, k3*

Rows 31 and 32 *p2, (k1, p1)4 times, k2*
Rows 33 and 34 *p1, k1*
Rows 35 and 36 *k1, p1*
Rows 37 and 38 *k2, (p1, k1)4 times, p2*
Rows 39 and 40 *k3, (p1, k1)3 times, p3*
Rows 41 and 42 *k4, (p1, k1)twice, p4*
Rows 43 and 44 *k5, p1, k1, p5*
Repeat rows 1 to 44

Welted Brickwork *or* **Welted Basketweave**
Also a reversible pattern, but with very different sides. It can be slightly stretched, like the sample, or left unblocked.

Multiple of 8 stitches
Rows 1 and 3 k3, *p2, k6*, p2, k3
Rows 2 and 4 p3, *k2, p6*, k2, p3
Rows 5, 7, 13 and 15 purl
Rows 6, 8, 14 and 16 knit
Rows 9 and 11 p1, *k6, p2*, k6, p1
Rows 10 and 12 k1, *p6, k2*, p6, k1
Repeat rows 1 to 16

Seaweed
If left unblocked, this stitch will produce an interesting, fluttering effect. If you decide to block it, do not attempt to flatten it completely.

Multiple of 6 stitches
Row 1 (wrong side) *p4, k2*

Row 2 (and all subsequent right-side rows) k the k stitches and p the p stitches
Row 3 *p3, k3*
Row 5 *p2, k4*
Row 7 p1, *k4, p2*, k4, p1
Row 9 p1, *k3, p3*, k3, p2
Row 11 p1, *k2, p4*, k2, p3
Row 12 as row 2
Repeat rows 1 to 12

Ruffled Edging

A very easy edging, worked transversely. The number of stitches can be varied to make wider or narrower bands. Cold block only.

13 stitches
Row 1 (right side) knit
Row 2 p10; turn, looping yarn around next st (thus: yb, sl1, turn, yb, sl1), k10
Row 3 p10, k3
Row 4 k3, p10
Row 5 k10; turn, looping yarn around next st (thus: yf, sl1, turn, yf, sl1), p10
Row 6 knit
Repeat rows 1 to 6

RIBBINGS

Ribbings are fabrics of great horizontal elasticity. The most elastic make good cuffs and borders for garments, while the less elastic are more suitable as an all-over pattern. However, all ribbings can be used for one or other purpose, if their degree of elasticity is kept well in mind and cuffs and borders are knitted with needles one or two sizes smaller than those used for the main stitch pattern.

Ribbed borders or gathers must not be blocked, or elasticity will be lost for ever.

BASIC RIBBING VARIATIONS

Basic ribbings are probably the most elastic of all ribbings, and also the most often used. For a different effect, try twisting the stitches as explained for stocking stitch. Either twist all the stitches or only every other stitch. These ribbings are reversible.

Single Ribbing (top)
Multiple of 2 stitches plus 1
Row 1 *k1, p1*, k1
Row 2 *p1, k1*, p1
Repeat rows 1 and 2

Double Ribbing (bottom)
Multiple of 4 stitches plus 2
Row 1 *k2, p2*, k2
Row 2 *p2, k2*, p2
Repeat rows 1 and 2

Brioche Rib
Very elastic. The two sides are very different, but

both can be used as the right side of work. The pattern will not form until a few rows have been knitted.

Multiple of 2 stitches plus 1
Row 1 knit
Row 2 *p1, k into st below next st and drop next st from needle*, p1
Repeat rows 1 and 2

CROSS-STITCH RIBBINGS
Fairly elastic. The two ribbings shown in the sample can be combined, for instance introducing a false cable every two or three twisted ribs, or alternating one of each.

Twisted Rib (*top*)
Multiple of 4 stitches plus 2
Row 1 (right side) *p2, RTw2*, p2
Row 2 *k2, p2*, k2
Repeat rows 1 and 2

False Cable Rib (*bottom*)
Multiple of 5 stitches plus 2
Row 1 (right side) *p2, k3*, p2
Rows 2 and 4 *k2, p3*, k2
Row 3 *p2; RTw3 (thus: k through back of loops, first the 3rd st on left needle, then the 2nd st and then the 1st st, dropping the 3 sts at the same time once they have all been knitted)*; p2
Repeat rows 1 to 4

Lace Rib
Not very elastic. Either side can be used as the right side of work.

Multiple of 5 stitches plus 2
Rows 1 and 3 (wrong side at top of sample)
k2, p3, k2
Row 2 *p2, k1, yf, yon, ssk*, p2
Row 4 *p2, k2tog, yf, yon, k1*, p2
Repeat rows 1 to 4

BROKEN RIBBING
Not elastic enough for cuffs and borders, the following are very successful as all-over patterns. The fabric is flat and soft.

Hurdles (*top*)
Multiple of 2 stitches
Rows 1 (right side) **and 2** knit
Rows 3 and 4 *k1, p1*, k1
Repeat rows 1 to 4

Staggered Rib (*bottom*)
Multiple of 2 stitches
Rows 1 and 5 (right side) knit
Rows 2, 3 and 4 *k1, p1*
Rows 6, 7 and 8 *p1, k1*
Repeat rows 1 to 8

FALSE RIBBINGS
These two patterns do not possess the elasticity of true ribbings, but they are related to them by the presence of ribs.

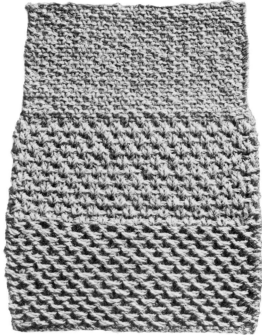

Shadow Rib (*top*)
Multiple of 3 stitches plus 2
Row 1 (wrong side) knit
Row 2 *p2, k1–b*, p2
Repeat rows 1 and 2

Corded Rib (*bottom*)
Multiple of 3 stitches plus 2
Row 1 (right side) *p2, k1*, p2
Row 2 *k2, yf, sl1, yon*, k2
Row 3 *p2, k2tog–b (the sl st and the yon of the previous row)*, p2
Repeat rows 2 and 3

SLIP-STITCH PATTERNS

Very interesting and diverse textures can be achieved with the slip-stitch technique, which consists of slipping one or more stitches at a time, *always purlwise*, keeping the yarn either at the front or back of the work. When the created strands show on the right side the fabric acquires a woven look.

These patterns often have a very close texture because the slipped stitches tend to pull the rest. Consequently, more rows and stitches are likely to be needed than for stocking stitch, as well as more yarn. Some patterns will have to be worked on larger needles to obtain the correct tension.

FABRIC STITCH PATTERNS

The sample clearly shows the pulling effect of the slipped stitches: all three patterns have been knitted over the same number of stitches, but the one at the top is denser than the others because twice the amount of stitches have been slipped. The fabric itself has hardly any elasticity, and closely resembles cloth. For a less dense texture use larger needles with this particular stitch. All three patterns are very flat and can be left unblocked.

Close Woven Stitch (*top*)
Multiple of 2 stitches

Row 1 (right side) *k1, yf, sl1, yb*
Row 2 *p1, yb, sl1, yf*
Repeat rows 1 and 2

Woven Check *or* **Hopsack Stitch** (*centre*)
Multiple of 2 stitches
Row 1 (right side) *k1, yf, sl1, yb*
Rows 2 and 4 purl
Row 3 *yf, sl1, yb, k1*
Repeat rows 1 to 4

Wasp's Nest (*bottom*)
Multiple of 2 stitches
Rows 1 and 3 (right side) knit
Row 2 *k1, sl1*, k2
Row 4 k2, *sl1, k1*
Repeat rows 1 to 4

LIGHT-TEXTURE STITCH PATTERNS

Just a hint of texture in two patterns closely

related to stocking stitch. They both need blocking because of a slight tendency to curl.

Raised Rib (*top*)
Multiple of 2 stitches
Row 1 (right side) *k1, sl1*
Row 2 purl
Repeat rows 1 and 2

Bird's Eye (*bottom*)
Multiple of 2 stitches
Row 1 (right side) *k1, sl1*
Rows 2 and 4 purl
Row 3 *sl1, k1*
Repeat rows 1 to 4

Woven Herringbone
Another dense stitch pattern with a cloth-like texture. The bands can be made as narrow or as wide as required. Needs some blocking.

Slant to the left:
Multiple of 4 stitches plus 2
Row 1 (right side) k2, *yf, sl2, yb, k2*
Row 2 p1, *yb, sl2, yf, p2*, p1
Row 3 yf, sl2, yb, *k2, yf, sl2, yb*
Row 4 p1, *p2, yb, sl2, yf*, p1
Repeat rows 1 to 4

Slant to the right:
Multiple of 4 stitches plus 2
Row 1 (right side) as row 3 above
Row 2 as row 2 above
Row 3 as row 1 above
Row 4 as row 4 above
Repeat rows 1 to 4

Scallop Stitch
One of the less dense of the slip-stitch patterns. Use it for baby wear, yokes, bed jackets and other garments that will not be subjected to heavy use, as the loose strands catch easily. Needs light blocking.
Multiple of 5 stitches plus 2
Row 1 (wrong side and all subsequent wrong-side rows) purl

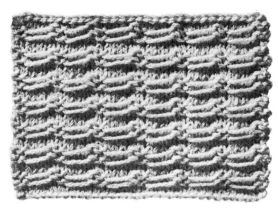

Row 2 knit
Rows 4 and 6 p2, *sl3, p2*
Repeat rows 1 to 6

Ladder and Rope
This pattern has a thick texture, requiring little blocking. It successfully combines the taking-up effects of both slip stitch and garter stitch.

Multiple of 10 stitches plus 5
Row 1 (right side) knit
Row 2 purl
Row 3 *sl1, (k1, sl1)twice, k5*, sl1, (k1, sl1)twice
Row 4 *(yf, sl1, yb, k1)twice, yf, sl1, yb, k5*, (yf, sl1, yb, k1)twice, yf, sl1, yb
Repeat rows 1 to 4

Bead Stitch *or* Mock Smocking
Both sides of this pattern can be used as the right side of work, and they both look very effective. The pattern will need some blocking, but be careful not to flatten it.

Multiple of 6 stitches plus 5
Rows 1, 3 and 5 (right side) k5, *sl1, k5*
Rows 2, 4 and 6 p5, *sl1, p5*
Row 7 k5; *secure sl-st (thus: sl1 knitwise, pass needle under 6 strands behind sl-st and draw a tight loop, pass sl-st over loop), k5*
Rows 8 and 16 purl

61

Rows 9, 11 and 13 k2, *sl1, k5*, sl1, k2
Rows 10, 12 and 14 p2, *sl1, p5*, sl1, p2
Row 15 k2, *secure sl-st, k5*, secure sl-st, k2
Repeat rows 1 to 16

Scattered Oats
A rather dense pattern that requires blocking. Do

not be afraid to drop the long stitch off the needle; it will not unravel.

Multiple of 4 stitches plus 1
Row 1 (wrong side) p1, *p1 wrapping yarn twice round needle, p3*
Row 2 *k3, sl1 letting extra loop drop*, k1
Row 3 p1, *sl1, p3*
Row 4 k1, *sl2, drop sl-st from previous row off needle, sl the 2 sl-sts back onto left needle, pick up dropped st and k it, k3*
Row 5 p4, *p1 wrapping yarn twice, p3*, p1
Row 6 k4, *sl1 letting extra loop drop, k3*, k1
Row 7 p4, *sl1, p3*, p1
Row 8 k4, *drop sl-st off needle, k2, pick up dropped st and k it, k1*, k1
Repeat rows 1 to 8

Quilted Lattice
Not a particularly dense pattern. Needs only slight blocking.

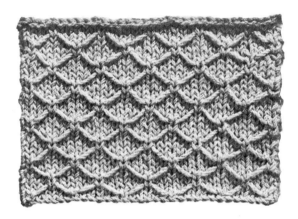

Multiple of 6 stitches plus 3
Row 1 (wrong side and all subsequent wrong-side rows) purl
Row 2 k2, *yf, sl5, yb, k1*, k1
Row 4 k4, *k1 under strand (pass right needle under loose strand in row 2 and k next st bringing it out under strand), k5*, k1 under strand, k4
Row 6 k1, yf, sl3, yb, *k1, yf, sl5, yb*, k1, yf, sl3, yb, k1
Row 8 k1, *k1 under strand in row 6, k5*, k1 under strand, k1
Repeat rows 1 to 8

TWIST-STITCH PATTERNS
The technique for twisting stitches is explained on page 17. You might find it slightly awkward to begin with, but with practice you will soon get used to it. It is certainly worth knowing, as otherwise the stitches would have to be crossed with the help of a cable needle, and when a pattern has many twists the cable-needle method is slower and more tedious.

When two stitches are crossed the fabric is

pulled in horizontally, thus producing a fairly close texture. It will sometimes be necessary to use larger needles than usual to obtain the correct tension.

Twisted diagonals

A very subtle pattern. The instructions appear lengthy but, in fact, the same sequence is followed row after row; it is the starting point of each sequence which differs. Needs slight blocking.

The sample shows a slant to the right. For a slant to the left, work right twists and move the pattern one stitch to the left instead of to the right on every even-numbered row.

Multiple of 9 stitches plus 3
Row 1 (wrong side and all subsequent wrong-side rows) purl
Row 2 k3, *(LTw2)3 times, k3*
Row 4 k2, *(LTw2)3 times, k3*, k1
Row 6 k1, *(LTw2)3 times, k3*, LTw2
Row 8 *(LTw2)3 times, k3*, LTw2, k1
Row 10 k1, (LTw2)twice, *k3, (LTw2)3 times*, k3, (LTw2)twice
Row 12 (LTw2)twice, *k3, (LTw2)3 times*, k3, (LTw2)twice, k1
Row 14 k1, LTw2, *k3, (LTw2)3 times*
Row 16 LTw2, *k3, (LTw2)3 times*, k1
Row 18 k4, *(LTw2)3 times, k3*, (LTw2)3 times, k2
Repeat rows 1 to 18

Ears of Corn

This is one of those Austrian patterns so clearly inspired by nature. To show it at its best it needs to be slightly stretched during blocking.

Multiple of 10 stitches plus 1
Rows 1, 3, 5, 7 and 9 (wrong side) p1–b, *k2, p5, k2, p1–b*

Rows 2, 4, 6, 8 and 10 k1–b, *p2, RTw2, k1, LTw2, p2, k1–b*
Rows 11, 13, 15, 17 and 19 p3, *k2, p1–b, k2, p5*, k2, p1–b, k2, p3
Rows 12, 14, 16, 18 and 20 k1, *LTw2, p2, k1–b, p2, RTw2, k1*
Repeat rows 1 to 20

Honeycomb

This is an easy-to-follow pattern, good for practising the twist-stitch technique. It needs slight blocking, taking great care not to flatten the 'cells'.

Multiple of 4 stitches plus 2
Rows 1 and 5 (right side) knit
Row 2 (and all subsequent wrong-side rows) purl
Row 3 k1, *LTw2, RTw2*, k1
Row 7 k1, *RTw2, LTw2*, k1
Repeat rows 1 to 7

63

TWIST-STITCH PANELS

Because the pulling-in effect of the twisted stitches is mainly horizontal, not vertical, the number of rows in any one length of stocking stitch and a fancy twist-stitch pattern will be basically the same. This allows for the easy introduction of vertical fancy panels on an otherwise plain background.

The hearts panel will need some blocking; the zigzag and bobbles pattern can be cold-blocked but not pressed.

Hearts
Panel of 10 stitches
Row 1 (wrong side and all subsequent wrong-side rows) purl
Row 2 k3, RTw2, LTw2, k3
Row 4 k2, RTw2, k2, LTw2, k2
Row 6 k1, RTw2, k4, LTw2, k1
Row 8 RTw2, k6, LTw2
Row 10 as row 2
Row 12 LTw2, RTw2, k2, LTw2, RTw2
Row 14 k1, k into back loop of st *below* next st to make a stitch, k2tog-b, k4, k2tog, increase as before, k1
Row 16 knit
Repeat rows 1 to 16

Zigzag and Bobbles
Panel of 11 stitches
Row 1 (wrong side) p1, *k1, p1*
Row 2 (LTw2)3 times, p5
Row 3 k5, (p1, k1)3 times
Row 4 p1, (LTw2)3 times, p2; make bobble (thus: k1, p1, k1, p1, k1 in next st, turn work, k5, turn work, p5, pass 4th, 3rd, 2nd and 1st sts over last st); p1
Row 5 k4, (p1, k1)3 times, k1
Row 6 p2, (LTw2)3 times, p3

Row 7 k3, (p1, k1)3 times, k2
Row 8 p3, (LTw2)3 times, p2
Row 9 k2, (p1, k1)3 times, k3
Row 10 p1, make bobble, p2, (LTw2)3 times, p1
Row 11 k1, (p1, k1)3 times, k4
Row 12 p5, (LTw2)3 times
Repeat rows 1 to 12
For a panel with the slant to the right: RTw2 instead of LTw2, and work rows in this order: 1, 12, 11, 10, 9, 8, 7, 6, 5, 4, 3 and 2

CABLES

The cable technique is really quite easy and very effective. See page 16 for full details.

Cables are usually worked in stocking stitch on a reverse stocking-stitch background. They can be used singly, in groups, or as an all-over pattern. The same cable can be repeated throughout, or several can be combined. Any number of stitches can be used both for the cables and for the background between adjacent cables. Cables can be well twisted, elongated or can have a varying pattern of twists. In other words, they are one of the most flexible of stitch patterns and you should feel free to use them as you choose.

Cables are usually blocked but care must be taken not to flatten them excessively; how much you stretch the pattern laterally depends on both the garment and your personal preferences.

BASIC CABLES

The following instructions are general and apply only to the cables, excluding the background fabric. In this way, they can be used to knit *any* cable, whether it is illustrated here or not. All cables are crossed on right-side rows. On wrong-side rows, knit the knit stitches and purl the purl stitches.

To obtain a well-twisted cable, cross it frequently. To obtain an elongated cable, cross it sparingly.

Right-twist Cable (*top section, left*)
Multiple of 2 stitches (minimum 4 sts)
Back cross (BC) half the stitches on a right-side row, not more often than every 4 rows. The sample shows a 4-stitch cable crossed every 6 rows.

Left-twist Cable (*top section, centre*)
Multiple of 2 stitches (minimum 4 sts)
Front cross (FC) half the stitches on a right-side row, not more often than every 4 rows. The sample shows a 6-stitch cable crossed, alternately, every 4 and 8 rows.

Open Cable (*top section, right*)
Multiple of 2 stitches plus 1 (minimum 7 sts)
This cable consists of a pair of 2-stitch 'cords' that travel across the background, crossing each other

Wave Cable (*middle section, left*)
Multiple of 2 stitches (minimum 4 sts)
FC and BC half the stitches, alternately, not more often than every four rows. The sample shows a 6-stitch cable crossed every 4 rows.

Double Cable (*middle section, centre*)
Multiple of 4 stitches (minimum 8 sts)
Imagine that the cable is divided into four equal sections. BC first and second sections, FC third and fourth sections, not more often than every four rows. The sample shows an 8-stitch cable crossed every 8 rows.

Inverted Double Cable (*middle section, right*)
As for double cable, but FC instead of BC and BC instead of FC.

Plait (*bottom section, left*)
Multiple of 3 stitches (minimum 6 sts)
Imagine that the cable is divided into three equal sections. At regular intervals, which should be multiples of 4 rows, BC first and second sections. Then, exactly halfway through each interval, FC second and third sections.

The sample shows a 6-stitch plait crossed every 4 rows. That is to say, the first and second sections are crossed in rows 1, 5, 9, etc and the second and third sections in rows 3, 7, 11, etc.

Inverted Plait (*bottom section, centre*)
As for plait but FC instead of BC and BC instead of FC.

Braid (*bottom section, right*)
Braids differ from plaits in that the cords travel across the background, instead of being close to each other. The following instructions refer to the smallest braid (the one shown in the sample). Once you are familiar with the technique you will be able to knit larger braids by simply increasing the panel by 2, 4, 6, 8, etc stitches, making the braids travel inwards and outwards until they reach the edges of the panel; this will automatically increase the length. Just remember that when two cords cross, the third is at its furthest point away; therefore, to set a large braid correctly, *k2* in row 1 should be increased by half the amount of stitches added to the smallest braid.

Panel of 9 stitches (minimum)
Row 1 (wrong side) k1, p4, *k2*, p2
Row 2 FC2–1, BC1–2, FC2–1
Row 3 (and all subsequent wrong-side rows) k the k sts and p the p sts
Row 4 p1, BC2–2, p2, k2
Row 6 BC1–2, FC2–1, BC1–2
Row 8 k2, p2, FC2–2, p1
Repeat rows 1 to 8

always in the same direction plus a central purl stitch.
To cross the cords: FC2–1–2 or BC2–1–2.
To make cords travel outwards: starting at the purl st just before first cord, BC1–2, p to second cord, FC2–1.
To make cords travel vertically: k the k sts and p the p sts.
To make cords travel inwards: starting at first cord, FC2–1, p to stitch before second cord, BC1–2.
The sample shows a 9-stitch cable travelling twice outwards, once vertically and twice inwards.

Short and Long Cable

Multiple of 20 stitches plus 12

Rows 1, 3, 7, 11, 15, 17, 19, 21, 23, 27, 31, 35, 37 and 39 (right side) *p2, k8*, p2

Row 2 (and all subsequent wrong-side rows) k the k sts and p the p sts

Rows 5, 9 and 13 *p2, k8, p2, FC4–4*, p2, k8, p2

Rows 25, 29 and 33 *p2, FC4–4, p2, k8*, p2, FC4–4, p2

Repeat rows 1 to 40

Rib and Braid

Multiple of 18 stitches plus 12

Row 1 (wrong side) k3, *p2, k2, p2, k3*

Rows 2 and 18 p3, *BC1–1, p2, BC1–1, p3*

Row 3 (and all subsequent wrong-side rows) k the k sts and p the p sts

Rows 4 and 12 *p2, (BC1–1, FC1–1)twice, (p2, k2)twice*, p2, (BC1–1, FC1–1)twice, p2

Rows 6 and 14 *p2, k1, p2, FC1–1, p2, k1, (p2, k2)twice*, p2, k1, p2, FC1–1, p2, k1, p2

Rows 8 and 16 *p2, (FC1–1, BC1–1)twice, (p2, k2)twice*, p2, (FC1–1, BC1–1)twice, p2

Row 10 p3, *BC1–1, p2, BC1–1, p3, k2, p2, k2, p3*, BC1–1, p2, BC1–1, p3

Rows 20 and 28 p3, *(k2, p2)twice, (BC1–1, FC1–1)twice, p2*, k2, p2, k2, p3

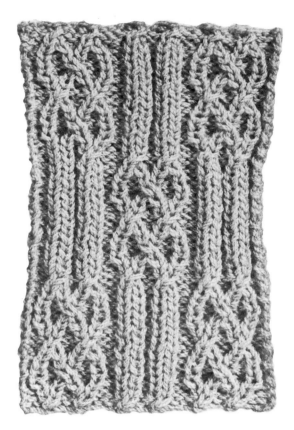

Rows 22 and 30 p3, *(k2, p2)twice, k1, p2, FC1–1, p2, k1, p2*, k2, p2, k2, p3

Rows 24 and 32 p3, *(k2, p2)twice, (FC1–1, BC1–1)twice, p2*, k2, p2, k2, p3

Row 26 p3, *k2, p2, k2, p3, BC1–1, p2, BC1–1, p3*, k2, p2, k2, p3

Repeat rows 1 to 32

This pattern can also be worked using the twist-stitch technique. RTw2 instead of FC1–1 and LTw2 instead of BC1–1.

Tracery

In this pattern the number of stitches is increased in certain rows to correct the pulling-in effect of the cables.

Multiple of 10 stitches plus 2 (minimum 22 sts)

Rows 1, 3, 5 and 7 (right side) p5, *RTw2, p8*, RTw2, p5

Row 2 (and all subsequent wrong-side rows, except rows 8 and 20) k the k sts and p the p sts and the twisted sts

Row 8 k5, *p into front and back of each of next 2 sts, k8*, p into front and back of each of next 2 sts, k5

Row 9 p5, *BC2–2, p8*, BC2–2, p5

Row 11 p3, *BC2–2, FC2–2, p4*, BC2–2, FC2–2, p3

Row 13 p1, *BC2–2, p4, FC2–2*, p1

Row 15 p1, k2, *p8, BC2–2*, p8, k2, p1

Row 17 p1, *FC2–2, p4, BC2–2*, p1

Row 19 p3, *FC2–2, BC2–2, p4*, FC2–2, BC2–2, p3

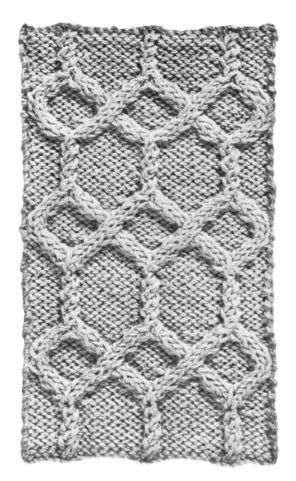

Row 20 k5, *(p2tog)twice), k8*, (p2tog)twice, k5

Repeat rows 1 to 20

FANCY PATTERNS

This category includes stitches worked in a variety of techniques impossible to classify under any main grouping.

Vertical Herringbone

A very neat, no-fuss pattern. Needs to be blocked.

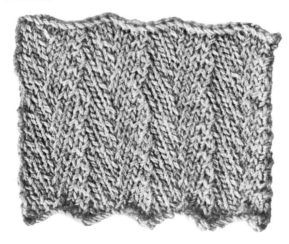

Multiple of 7 stitches plus 1
Row 1 and 3 (wrong side) purl

Row 2 *k2tog, k2; increase thus: k purl head of st *below* next st, then k st above; k2*, k1
Row 4 k1, *k2, increase, k2, k2tog*
Repeat rows 1 to 4

ELONGATED STITCH

A very easy and very effective technique. The stitches are knitted in the usual way, except that the yarn is wound two or more times round the needle instead of only once; in the next row the first loop of the group is worked and the rest left

to unravel. Several backgrounds can be used for this kind of stitch: stocking and reverse stocking stitch, garter stitch, moss stitch, etc. The fabric will need more or less blocking depending on the background.

Simple Elongated Stitch (*top*)
Either on a right-side or on a wrong-side row: wind yarn twice round needle. On next row, drop extra loop.

Twisted Elongated Stitch (*centre*)
On a right-side row: wind yarn first round both needles, then just round right needle in the usual way. Draw through the second loop only, being careful to maintain an even tension all along the row.

Waves (*bottom*)
Multiple of 8 stitches plus 2
Rows 1 (right side), **2, 3, 4, 6, 7 and 8** knit
Row 5 *k2; k(2)2 (thus: k next 2 sts winding yarn twice round needle); k(3)2 (thus: k next 2 sts winding yarn 3 times round needle); k(2)2*, k2
Row 9 *k(3)2, k(2)2, k2, k(2)2*, k(3)2
Repeat rows 2 to 9

Fish Scales

This pattern has a certain tendency to curl and therefore needs blocking, but be careful not to flatten the scales.

Multiple of 4 stitches
Rows 1 and 3 (right side) knit
Row 2 p1, *yrn, p2, pass yrn over these 2 sts, p2*, yrn, p2, pass yrn over, p1
Row 4 p1, *p2, yrn, p2, pass yrn over*, p3
Repeat rows 1 to 4

BERRY STITCHES

Both patterns are very knobbly, but at the same time slightly lacy. They are quite dense, requiring large amounts of yarn, but can be knitted on thick needles if a soft and more lacy fabric is desired, because the tightening effect of the three stitches purled together keeps the rest in place. They are very flat and pressing should be avoided.

Bramble *or* **Trinity Stitch** *(top)*
Multiple of 4 stitches
Rows 1 and 3 (right side) purl
Row 2 *(k1, p1, k1) in same st, p3tog*
Row 4 *p3tog, (k1, p1, k1) in same st*
Repeat rows 1 to 4

Raspberries *(bottom)*
Multiple of 4 stitches
Row 1 (wrong side) *(k1, p1, k1) in same st, p3tog*
Row 2 *k1, p3*
Row 3 *k3, p1*
Row 4 *p1, k3*
Row 5 *p3tog, (k1, p1, k1) in next st*
Row 6 *p3, k1*
Row 7 *p1, k3*
Row 8 *k3, p1*
Repeat rows 1 to 8

TUFTS AND BOBBLES

These can be knitted in a variety of ways and sizes. It is best to experiment with the number of stitches and rows until the best combination is found for a particular project. Tufts and bobbles can be placed in rows, in columns, in groups, or

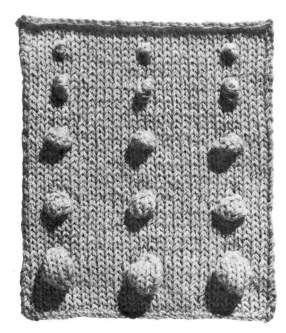

just scattered all over. At least one stitch or one row should be left between two bobbles. Large white bobbles tend to look dirty very quickly because they pick up dust. Tufts and bobbles should not be pressed; if the background pattern needs blocking, use the cold-water spray method. The following variations are illustrated from top to bottom, always working over 1st.

Small Tuft
(k1, p1)twice in same st, pulling up sts loosely, then pass 1st, 2nd and 3rd sts, *in this order*, over 4th st.

Large Tuft
(k1, p1)4 times in same st, then pass 1st, 2nd, 3rd, 4th, 5th, 6th and 7th sts, *in this order*, over 8th st.

Camel-coloured V-neck with striped borders and green cotton twin-set (see pages 155 and 156)

Knobbly Bobble

(k1, p1, k1, p1, k1) into same st, turn work, k5, turn, p5, pass 4th, 3rd, 2nd and 1st st, *in this order*, over 5th st.

Bubble Bobble

(k1, p1, k1, p1, k1) into same st, pulling up sts loosely, turn work, sl1, p4, turn, sl1, k4, turn, p2tog, p2, p2tog, turn, sl1 knitwise, k2tog, psso.

Balloon Bobble

(k1, p1, k1, p1, k1, p1, k1) into same st, (turn work, sl1, p6, turn, sl1 knitwise, k6)twice, turn, sl1, p6, turn, k2tog-b, k3, k2tog, turn, p2tog, p1, p2tog, turn, sl1 knitwise, k2tog, psso.

FLORAL MOTIFS

Like bobbles these can be combined in numerous ways with the same or different backgrounds to the ones shown. They will need more or less blocking depending on the background pattern, but be careful not to flatten the raised motifs. The following are illustrated from top to bottom.

Meadow Flower

3 stitches

P3tog, but do not drop sts from left needle, k3tog again without dropping sts from needle, p3tog and then drop sts from needle.

Rosebud

1 stitch

Row 1 (right side) k into front and back of same st to make 5 sts

Peach mohair jacket and bouclé cardigan with eyelets (see page 156)

Row 2 p5 wrapping yarn twice round needle every time
Row 3 sl5 dropping extra loops
Row 4 sl5
Row 5 sl3, k2tog, psso

Daisies

7 stitches

Row 1 (right side) k1, insert right needle in st 5 rows beneath the 4th (central) st of the group and draw a loop, k5, draw another loop from same st below, k1
Row 2 p2tog-b, p5, p2tog
Row 3 k3, draw a third loop from st below, place it on left needle and k2tog (through back of loop and front of st), k3

Peonies

11 stitches

Rows 1, 3 and 5 (right side) p5, k1-b, p5
Rows 2, 4, 6 and 8 k5, p1-b, k5
Row 7 p1, insert right needle in st to the right of twisted st in row 1, yb, draw a long loop, k1 and pass loop over this st, p3, k1-b, p3, draw a second loop from st to the left of twisted st in row 1, k1 and pass loop over this st
Row 9 p5, k into front and back of next st to make 7 sts, p5
Row 10 k5, p7, k5
Row 11 p5, k2tog-b, k3tog b, k2tog, p5
Row 12 k5, p3tog, k5

Fur Stitch

This is a good pattern both for thick garments and for trimmings. Knit row 6 carefully and as tightly as possible. If any one of the stitches of the previous row becomes loose, tighten it by pulling the corresponding loop. Do not press.

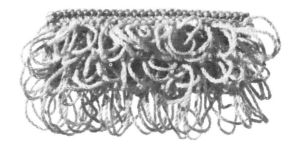

Any number of stitches

Rows 1 (right side) **to 4** knit
Row 5 *k1 wrapping yarn around 3rd finger of left hand to make a loop (hold the finger always in the same position); transfer new st back onto left needle, k2tog-b dropping loop around finger and *first* st from left needle*
Row 6 knit back of loops
Repeat rows 1 to 6

OPENWORK PATTERNS

All openwork patterns use the technique of increasing the number of stitches by means of 'overs', while at the same time decreasing it by knitting two or more stitches together. The difference between eyelets and lace patterns is only a matter of quantity; in the first case the openwork is merely perforations in a dense fabric, while in the second the actual structure of the fabric is perforated.

Eyelet patterns require more or less blocking depending on the background. Lace patterns not only need blocking, they also need to be thoroughly stretched in order to show the openwork at its best. Blocking the swatches prior to calculating stitches and rows for a garment is therefore especially important.

Only fine yarns should be used to knit large lace patterns, as otherwise these lose their daintiness. If you are using a thickish yarn, stick to simple eyelets or faggoting stitches. The need to use fine yarns and the often lengthy instructions are compensated for by the fact that fewer stitches and rows are required for a similar area than in most other patterns.

EYELET VARIATIONS

With the exception of the two lower examples, which are always knitted in rows to allow for the threading of ribbons, all the other eyelets in the sample can be distributed to suit your needs and preferences. It is not necessary to leave extra

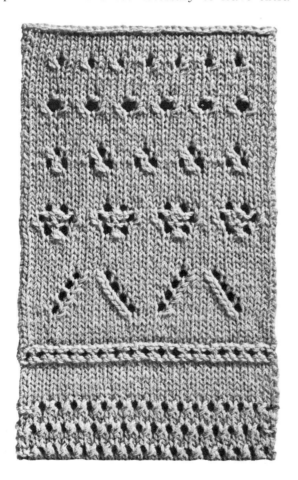

stitches between two eyelets if a close arrangement is desired. The different eyelets are illustrated from top to bottom.

Simple Eyelet
3 stitches
Row 1 (right side) either k2tog, yf, yon, k1 *or* k1, yf, yon, ssk (the first method has been used to knit the four right-hand eyelets, and the second to knit the three left-hand eyelets)
Row 2 purl

Double Eyelet
4 stitches
Row 1 (right side) k2tog, yf, yon, ssk
Row 2 p1, (p1, k1) into yon from previous row, p1

Cloverleaf Eyelet
5 stitches
Row 1 (right side) k1, yf, yon, sl1 knitwise, k2tog, psso, yf, yon, k1
Rows 2 and 4 purl
Row 3 k2, yf, yon, ssk, k1

Flowerhead Eyelet
7 stitches
Rows 1 and 5 (right side) k2, yf, yon, sl1 knitwise, k2tog, psso, yf, yon, k2
Rows 2 and 6 purl
Row 3 k2tog, yon, p3, yon, ssk
Row 4 p1, k5, p1

Diagonal Eyelets
6 stitches
Slant to the right:
Row 1 (right side) k3, k2tog, yf, yon, k1
Row 2 (and all subsequent wrong-side rows) purl
Row 3 k2, k2tog, yf, yon, k2
Row 5 k1, k2tog, yf, yon, k3
Row 7 k2tog, yf, yon, k4

Slant to the left:
Row 1 (right side) k1, yf, yon, ssk, k3
Row 2 (and all subsequent wrong-side rows) purl
Row 3 k2, yf, yon, ssk, k2
Row 5 k3, yf, yon, ssk, k1
Row 7 k4, yf, yon, ssk

Ribbon Eyelet
Multiple of 2 stitches plus 1
Rows 1 (right side), **2 and 4** knit
Row 3 *k2tog-b, yf, yon*, k1

Dimple Eyelet
Multiple of 2 stitches
Row 1 (right side) p1, *yb, yon, p2tog*, p1
Rows 2 and 6 p (purl back of loop of yons)
Row 3 knit
Row 4 purl

Row 5 p2, *yb, yon, p2tog*
Repeat rows 1 to 6

VERTICAL INSERTIONS
Three closely related vertical panels worked in eyelets on a reverse stocking-stitch background.

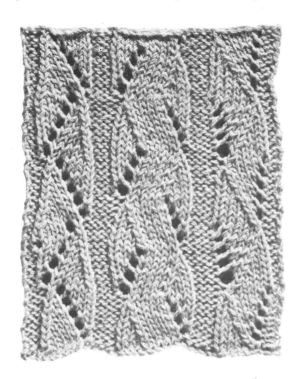

Comb Stitch (*left*)
Panel of 6 stitches
Row 1 (wrong side and all subsequent wrong-side rows) purl
Row 2 yon, k4, k2tog
Row 4 k1, yf, yon, k3, k2tog
Row 6 k2, yf, yon, k2, k2tog
Row 8 k3, yf, yon, k1, k2tog
Row 10 k4, yf, yon, k2tog
Row 12 ssk, k4, yf, yrn
Row 14 ssk, k3, yf, yon, k1
Row 16 ssk, k2, yf, yon, k2
Row 18 ssk, k1, yf, yon, k3
Row 20 ssk, yf, yon, k4
Repeat rows 1 to 20

Track of the Turtle (*centre*)
Panel of 9 stitches
Row 1 (wrong side and all subsequent wrong-side rows) purl
Row 2 yon, k4, ssk, k3
Row 4 k1, yf, yon, k4, ssk, k2
Row 6 k2, yf, yon, k4, ssk, k1
Row 8 k3, yf, yon, k4, ssk
Row 10 k3, k2tog, k4, yf, yrn
Row 12 k2, k2tog, k4, yf, yon, k1
Row 14 k1, k2tog, k4, yf, yon, k2
Row 16 k2tog, k4, yf, yon, k3
Repeat rows 1 to 16

Folded Ribbon (*right*)
Panel of 6 stitches
Row 1 (wrong side and all subsequent wrong-side rows) purl
Row 2 yon, ssk, k4
Row 4 yon, k1, ssk, k3
Row 6 yon, k2, ssk, k2
Row 8 yon, k3, ssk, k1
Row 10 yon, k4, ssk
Row 12 k4, k2tog, yf, yrn
Row 14 k3, k2tog, k1, yf, yrn
Row 16 k2, k2tog, k2, yf, yrn
Row 18 k1, k2tog, k3, yf, yrn
Row 20 k2tog, k4, yf, yrn
Repeat rows 1 to 20

ONE-ROW FAGGOTING VARIATIONS
In these, the most elementary of lace patterns, the same row is repeated throughout, thus creating a fabric with two identical sides. The variations are illustrated from top to bottom.

Basic Faggoting
Multiple of 2 stitches
k1, *yf, yon, ssk*, k1

Feather Faggoting
Multiple of 4 stitches plus 2
k2, yf, yrn, p2tog, k2

Purse Stitch
Multiple of 2 stitches
p1, *yrn, p2tog*, p1

Turkish Stitch
Multiple of 2 stitches
k1, *yf, yon, k2tog*, k1

73

MORE FAGGOTING VARIATIONS

Here two or more rows are needed to create a pattern, and therefore the two sides of the work are different. The following are illustrated from top to bottom.

Rickrack Faggoting
Multiple of 3 stitches plus 1
Row 1 (right side) k1, *yf, yon, ssk, k1*
Row 2 k1, *yf, yrn, p2tog, k1*
Repeat rows 1 and 2

Feathered Ladder
Multiple of 4 stitches
Row 1 (right side) *k2tog, yf, yrn, yon, ssk*
Row 2 *p1, (p1, k1) into double over, p1*
Repeat rows 1 and 2

Vandyke Faggoting
Multiple of 3 stitches
Row 1 (right side) *k1, yf, yrn, yon, k2tog*
Rows 2 and 4 purl, dropping second loop in double over
Row 3 *k2tog, yf, yrn, yon, k1*
Repeat rows 1 to 4

Zigzag Trellis
Multiple of 2 stitches
Slant to the left:
Row 1 k1, *ssk, yf, yon*, k1
Row 2 purl

Slant to the right:
Row 1 k1, *yf, yon, k2tog*, k1
Row 2 purl
Repeat rows 1 and 2

Madeira Mesh
This very old Spanish pattern is very easy to follow. Both sides are identical.

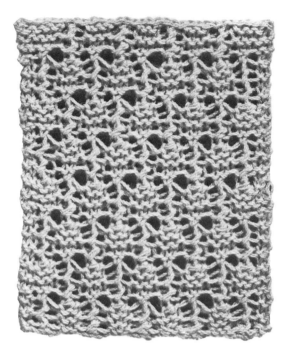

Multiple of 6 stitches plus 7
Rows 1 to 6 k2, *yf, yrn, p3tog, yon, k3*, yf, yrn, p3tog, yon, k2
Rows 7 to 12 k2, *k3, yf, yrn, p3tog, yon*, k5
Repeat rows 1 to 12

Peacock Feathers
Despite its intricate appearance, this is another relatively easy pattern. It derives from traditional Shetland lace.

Multiple of 16 stitches plus 1
Row 1 (wrong side and all subsequent wrong-side rows) purl
Rows 2, 6, 10, 14, 18, 22, 26 and 30 knit
Rows 4, 8, 12 and 16 (k1, yf, yon)3 times, *(ssk)twice, sl2 knitwise, k1, p2sso, (k2tog)twice, (yf, yon, k1)5 times, yf, yon*, (ssk)twice, sl2 knitwise, k1, psso, (k2tog)twice, (yf, yon, k1)3 times
Rows 20, 24, 28 and 32 (k2tog)3 times, *(yf, yon, k1)5 times, yf, yon, (ssk)twice, sl2 knitwise, k1, psso, (k2tog)twice*, (yf, yon, k1)5 times, yf, yon, (ssk)3 times
Repeat rows 1 to 32

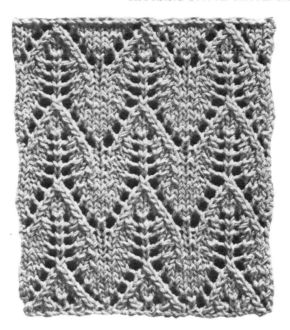

Tudor Brickwork
Multiple of 14 stitches plus 6
Row 1 (wrong side and all subsequent wrong-side rows) purl
Row 2 k2, *k2tog, yf, yon, k1, yf, yon, ssk, k3, k2tog, yf, yon, k4*, k2tog, yf, yon, k2
Row 4 k1, *k2tog, yf, yon, k3, yf, yon, ssk, k1, k2tog, yf, yon, k4*, k2tog, yf, yon, k3

Row 6 k2tog, yf, yon, ˣk5, yf, yon, sl1 knitwise, k2tog, psso, yf, yon, k4, k2tog, yf, yon*, k4
Row 8 k2, *yf, yon, ssk, k4, yf, yon, ssk, k3, k2tog, yf, yon, k1*, yf, yon, ssk, k2
Row 10 k3, *yf, yon, ssk, k4, yf, yon, ssk, k1, k2tog, yf, yon, k3*, yf, yon, ssk, k1
Row 12 k4, ˣyf, yon, ssk, k4, yf, yon, k3tog, yf, yon, k5*, yf, yon, ssk
Repeat rows 1 to 12

Arrowheads
Multiple of 10 stitches plus 1
Row 1 (wrong side and all subsequent wrong-side rows) purl
Row 2 k1, *yf, yon, ssk, k2tog, yf, yon, k1*
Row 4 k2, *yf, yon, ssk, k3, k2tog, yf, yon, k3*, yf, yon, ssk, k3, k2tog, yf, yon, k2
Row 6 k3, *yf, yon, ssk, k1, k2tog, yf, yon, k5*, yf, yon, ssk, k1, k2tog, yf, yon, k3
Row 8 k4, *yf, yon, sl1 knitwise, k2tog, psso, yf, yon, k7*, yf, yon, sl1 knitwise, k2tog, psso, yf, yon, k4
Rows 10, 12 and 14 k1, *ssk, k2, yf, yon, k1, yf, yon, k2, k2tog, k1*
Repeat rows 1 to 14

Scrolls
Light coming from a certain direction makes this pattern look like a delicately woven trellis.

Multiple of 10 stitches plus 2
Row 1 (right side) k1, *yf, yon, k8, k2tog*, k1
Row 2 p1, *p2tog, p7, yrn, p1*, p1
Row 3 k1, *k2, yf, yon, k6, k2tog*, k1
Row 4 p1, *p2tog, p5, yrn, p3*, p1
Row 5 k1, *k4, yf, yon, k4, k2tog*, k1
Row 6 p1, *p2tog, p3, yrn, p5*, p1
Row 7 k1, *k6, yf, yon, k2, k2tog*, k1
Row 8 p1, *p2tog, p1, yrn, p7ˣ, p1
Row 9 k1, *k8, yf, yon, k2tog*, k1
Row 10 p1, *yrn, p8, p2tog-b*, p1

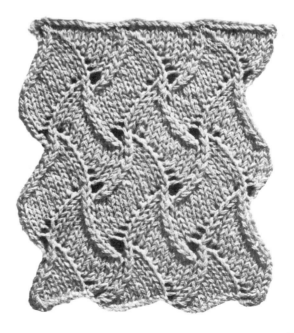

Row 11 k1, *ssk, k7, yf, yon, k1*, k1
Row 12 p1, *p2, yrn, p6, p2tog-b*, p1
Row 13 k1, *ssk, k5, yf, yon, k3*, k1
Row 14 p1, *p4, yrn, p4, p2tog-b*, p1
Row 15 k1, *ssk, k3, yf, yon, k5*, k1
Row 16 p1, *p6, yrn, p2, p2tog-b*, p1
Row 17 k1, *ssk, k1, yf, yon, k7*, k1
Row 18 p1, *p8, yrn, p2tog-b*, p1
Repeat rows 1 to 18

Oriel

Multiple of 12 stitches plus 1
Rows 1, 3 and 5 (right side) p1, *ssk, k3, yf, yrn, p1, yon, k3, k2tog, p1*
Rows 2, 4, 6 and 8 k1, *p5, k1*
Row 7 p1, *yon, k3, k2tog, p1, ssk, k3, yf, yrn, p1*
Row 9 p2, *yon, k2, k2tog, p1, ssk, k2, yf, yrn, p3*, yon, k2, k2tog, p1, ssk, k2, yf, yrn, p2
Row 10 k2, *p4, k1, p4, k3*, p4, k1, p4, k2
Row 11 p3, *yon, k1, k2tog, p1, ssk, k1, yf, yrn, p5*, yon, k1, k2tog, p1, ssk, k1, yf, yrn, p3
Row 12 k3, *p3, k1, p3, k5*, p3, k1, p3, k3
Row 13 p4, *yon, k2tog, p1, ssk, yf, yrn, p7*, yon, k2tog, p1, ssk, yf, yrn, p4
Row 14 k4 *p2, k1, p2, k7*, p2, k1, p2, k4

Rows 15, 17 and 19 as row 7
Rows 16, 18, 20 and 22 as row 2
Row 21 as row 1
Row 23 p1, *ssk, k2, yf, yrn, p3, yon, k2, k2tog, p1*
Row 24 k1, *p4, k3, p4, k1*
Row 25 p1, *ssk, k1, yf, yrn, p5, yon, k1, k2tog, p1*
Row 26 k1, *p3, k5, p3, k1*
Row 27 p1, *ssk, yf, yrn, p7, yon, k2tog, p1*
Row 28 k1, *p2, k7, p2, k1*
Repeat rows 1 to 28

Thistle

A very delicate Victorian pattern.

Multiple of 10 stitches plus 1
Row 1 (and all subsequent wrong-side rows) purl
Row 2 (ssk)twice, *(yf, yon, k1)3 times, yf, yon, k2tog, sl1 knitwise, k2tog, psso, ssk*, (yf, yon, k1)3 times, yf, yon, (k2tog)twice
Row 4 ssk, *k3, yf, yon, k1, yf, yon, k3, sl1 knitwise, k2tog, psso*, k3, yf, yon, k1, yf, yon, k3, k2tog
Row 6 ssk, *k2, yf, yon, k3, yf, yon, k2, sl1 knitwise, k2tog, psso*, k2, yf, yon, k3, yf, yon, k2, k2tog

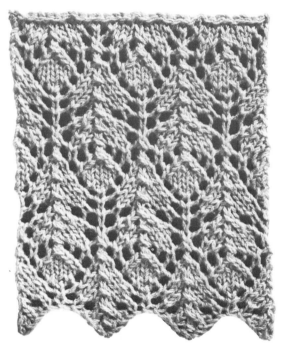

Row 8 ssk, *k1, yf, yon, k5, yf, yon, k1, sl1 knitwise, k2tog, psso*, k1, yf, yon, k5, yf, yon, k1, k2tog
Row 10 ssk, *yf, yon, k1, yf, yon, ssk, k1, k2tog, yf, yon, k1, yf, yon, sl1 knitwise, k2tog, psso*, yf, yon, k1, yf, yon, ssk, k1, k2tog, yf, yon, k1, yf, yon, k2tog
Row 12 ssk, *yf, yon, k2, yf, yon, sl1 knitwise, k2tog, psso*, yf, yon, k2, yf, yon, k2tog
Row 14 k1, *yf, yon, k3, sl1 knitwise, k2tog, psso, k3, yf, yon, k1*
Row 16 k1, *yf, yon, k1, yf, yon, k2tog, sl1 knitwise, k2tog, psso, ssk, (yf, yon, k1)twice*
Row 18 as row 14
Row 20 k2, *yf, yon, k2, sl1 knitwise, k2tog, psso, k2, yf, yon, k3*, yf, yon, k2, sl1 knitwise, k2tog, psso, k2, yf, yon, k2
Row 22 k3, *yf, yon, k1, sl1 knitwise, k2tog, psso, k1, yf, yon, k5*, yf, yon, k1, sl1 knitwise, k2tog, psso, k1, yf, yon, k3
Row 24 k1, *k2tog, yf, yon, k1, yf, yon, sl1 knitwise, k2tog, psso, yf, yon, k1, yf, yon, ssk, k1*

Row 26 as row 12
Row 28 as row 4
Repeat rows 1 to 28

Cobweb Edging

This edging is worked from bottom to top, the top having one third less stitches than the bottom. *Cast on by the single-loop method.* Block it with great care if any blocking is necessary.

Multiple of 3 stitches plus 1
Row 1 k1–b, *p2, k1–b*
Row 2 p1, *k1–b, k1, p1*
Repeat rows 1 and 2 for desired length of frill
Row 3 k1–b, *drop next st off needle, p1, k1–b*
Rows 4, 6 and 8 p1, *k1–b, p1*
Rows 5, 7 and 9 k1 b, *p1, k1–b*
Unravel dropped stitches all the way down

COLOUR PATTERNS

There are four ways of introducing colour to knitting: working single-colour patterns in stripes; combining colours while knitting to create motifs (Jacquard); embroidering; and dividing the garment into large colour areas (mock patchwork and picture knitting).

Whatever the system used, the distribution of colour has a strong effect on the pattern, to the point that the overall impression can be totally different. It is therefore essential to carry out a study of colour before starting to knit, unless you are copying motifs which are already presented in colours you can match. Copy the design several times on the appropriate sheet of graph paper, using crayons or felt-tip pens. Change the colours around until you find a combination you like. For straightforward stripes, if you already have the yarn, cut small lengths and combine them on a white sheet of paper or twist them round a finger, trying to keep the relative widths in the right proportion.

STRIPES

A number of patterns can be worked in stripes without any problems. Some will change colour in continuous lines, others in broken lines, and others in zigzags. Try, for example, stocking and reverse stocking stitch, garter and reverse garter stitch, weltings, ribbings, woven and vertical herringbones, scallop stitch, scattered oats, the light texture stitches and the fabric stitches.

When working out stripes in several colours, either make them all have an even number of rows, so that all the colours start at the same edge of the work, or combine them so that stripes with an odd number of rows start at the same edge of the work where the colour was last left. Otherwise, you will have to break the yarn.

INTERLOCKING STRIPES

Changes of colour in stocking stitch can be made softer if the first one or two rows of the new colour are worked in slip stitch. The stripes can be of any width. Instructions are for colours D (dark) and L (light) as shown in illustration.

Sawtooth
Multiple of 2 stitches plus 1
Row 1 (last row of D stripe, wrong side) with D, purl
Row 2 with L, *k1, sl1*, k1
Continue with L in stocking stitch, beginning with a purl row

Rabbit Ears
Multiple of 12 stitches plus 3
Row 1 (last row of L stripe, wrong side) with L, purl
Row 2 with D, k1, *sl1, k5*, sl1, k1
Row 3 with D, p1, *sl1, p11*, sl1, p1
Continue with D in stocking stitch, beginning with a knit row

Waves
Multiple of 4 stitches plus 1
Row 1 (last row of D stripe, wrong side) with D, purl
Row 2 with L, *k1, sl3*, k1

Row 3 with L, p2, *sl1, p3*, sl1, p2
Continue with L in stocking stitch, beginning with a knit row

JACQUARD

There are two types of Jacquard. The first type is always knitted in stocking stitch and uses more than one colour in the same row, following charts to build up colour motifs. It is often known as Fair Isle knitting, but strictly speaking this name refers only to a particular type of design and should not be used as a generic term. As well as on Fair Isle, this type of Jacquard has been used for centuries in every country that has developed traditional colour motifs, from Scandinavia to South America.

Any design that can be charted and does not consist of large, solid areas of colour can be

knitted this way. Cross-stitch and tapestry patterns are ideal for copying (each cross or petit-point becomes a stitch), providing you remember that knitting stitches are elongated and, therefore, the result will be squatter than the chart. To see exactly how your chosen design will look when knitted up, copy it onto a tension diagram (see Chapter 8). (The technique for working with more than one yarn is explained in Chapter 11.)

The second type of Jacquard has the advantage of needing only one colour in any one row. It can be based on different techniques, but the most common of these is slip stitch (all the stitches are slipped purlwise). The resulting fabric is often rather dense, and therefore should be knitted with needles larger than usual for a softer texture. The following patterns all use this type of Jacquard. Instructions are for colours D (dark), L (light), B (black) and W (white), as shown in illustrations. Jacquard patterns of either type need careful blocking.

Pin Stripes
Multiple of 2 stitches plus 1 (colours D and L)
Row 1 (right side) with D, *k1, sl1*, k1
Row 2 with D, *p1, sl1*, p1
Row 3 with L, *sl1, k1*, sl1
Row 4 with L, *sl1, p1*, sl1
Repeat rows 1 to 4

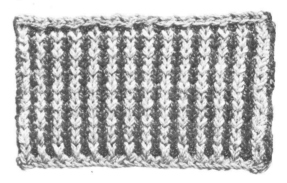

Pin Checks
Multiple of 2 stitches plus 1 (colours D and L)
Row 1 (right side) with D, knit
Row 2 with D, purl
Row 3 with L, *k1, sl1*, k1
Row 4 with L, *k1, yf, sl1, yb*, k1
Repeat rows 1 to 4

Zebra Chevron
Multiple of 18 stitches plus 1 (colours D and L)
Row 1 (wrong side) with D, purl
Row 2 with L, *sl1, k2*, sl1
Row 3 (and all subsequent wrong-side rows) using same colour as previous row, sl the sl sts and p the rest

Row 4 with D, *k1, sl1, (k2, sl1)twice, k3, (sl1, k2)twice, sl1*, k1
Row 6 with L, *k2, (sl1, k2)twice, sl1, k1, sl1, (k2, sl1)twice, k1*, k1
Row 8 with D, repeat row 2
Row 10 with L, repeat row 4
Row 12 with D, repeat row 6
Repeat rows 2 to 12

Chequers
Multiple of 10 stitches plus 2 (colours D and L)
Rows 1 and 13 (right side) with L, knit
Rows 2 and 14 with L, *p2, k1, p1, k1*, p1, k1
Rows 3, 7 and 11 with D, k1, *k5, (sl1, k1)twice, sl1*, k6
Rows 4, 8 and 12 with D, k6, *(yf, sl1, yb, k1)3 times, k4*, k1
Rows 5 and 9 with L, k2, *sl1, k1, sl1, k7*, sl1, k1, sl1, k2

Rows 6 and 10 with L, k1, (k1, yf, sl1, yb)twice, *(k1, p1)3 times, (k1, yf, sl1, yb)twice*, k2
Rows 15, 19 and 23 with D, k1, *(sl1, k1)twice, sl1, k5*, (sl1, k1)3 times
Rows 16, 20 and 24 with D, k1, *(yf, sl1, yb, k1)3 times, k4*, (yf, sl1, yb, k1)3 times
Rows 17 and 21 with L, *k7, sl1, k1, sl1*, k7
Rows 18 and 22 with L, k1, *(p1, k1)3 times, (yf, sl1, yb, k1)twice*, (p1, k1)3 times
Repeat rows 1 to 24

Three–colour Tweed
Multiple of 3 stitches plus 1 (colours D, L and B)

Row 1 (wrong side) with L, knit
Row 2 with D, k3, *sl1, k2*, k1
Row 3 with D, k3, *yf, sl1, yb, k2*, k1
Row 4 with B, *k2, sl1*, k1
Row 5 with B, k1, *yf, sl1, yb, k2*
Row 6 with L, k1, *sl1, k2*
Row 7 with L, *k2, yf, sl1, yb*, k1
Repeat rows 2 to 7

Chains
Multiple of 8 stitches plus 6 (colours D, L and B)

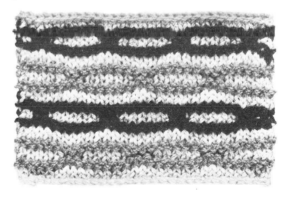

Rows 1 and 9 (right side) with L, knit
Rows 2 and 10 with L, purl
Rows 3 and 4 with D, knit
Row 5 with L, k6, *sl2, k6*
Row 6 with L, p6, *sl2, p6*
Row 7 with D, repeat row 5
Row 8 with D, knit
Rows 11 and 12 with B, knit
Row 13 with L, k2, *sl2, k6*, sl2, k2

Row 14 with L, p2, *sl2, p6*, sl2, p2
Row 15 with B, repeat row 13
Row 16 with B, knit
Repeat rows 1 to 16

Tutti-frutti
Multiple of 4 stitches plus 3 (colours D, L, B and W)

Row 1 (wrong side) with D, purl
Row 2 with B, k2, *sl1, k1*, k1
Row 3 with B, p2, *sl1, p1*, k1
Row 4 with L, k1, *sl1, k1*
Row 5 with L, purl
Row 6 with W, k1, *sl1, k3*, sl1, k1
Row 7 with W, p1, *sl1, p3*, sl1, p1
Row 8 with B, k2, *sl3, k1*, k1
Row 9 with B, *p3, sl1*, p3
Row 10 with D, k1, *sl1, k3*, sl1, k1
Repeat rows 1 to 10

EMBROIDERY
Motifs can be embroidered on a garment either by trying to imitate knitting stitches (Swiss darning) or by using conventional embroidery stitches.

Swiss darning is most often used on a stocking-stitch background, but can also be used on other stitch patterns. In its traditional form it is used for motifs similar to the ones obtained with the first type of Jacquard, and therefore both methods can be combined. Jacquard is best for

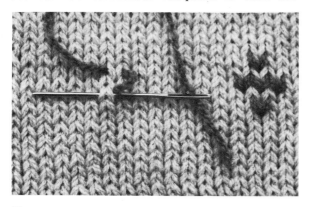

frequent changes of colour, while Swiss darning is most suitable when there are long gaps between stitches of the same colour in any one row, for example with widely spaced little motifs or vertical lines.

To work Swiss darning, move from right to left and from top to bottom, following the steps shown in the illustration. If there are more than two or three stitches, instead of going back to the far right at the end of a row, turn the work upside down. This will allow you to work from right to left without leaving long strands at the back of the work.

Use either the same type of yarn you used for the background or one that is not too thick but thick enough to cover the stitch underneath. Because of the double thickness of the embroidered stitches, these will tend to stand up from the rest.

Details on how to work other embroidery stitches are outside the scope of this book, but many can be used for motifs that may either take advantage of the framework given by the knitted background, or flow freely over it. For this type of embroidery any yarn or thread can be used. French knots and blanket, chain, running, satin, stem, cross, feather or couching stitches are just a few of the stitches that can be used to decorate a garment.

MOCK PATCHWORK AND PICTURE KNITTING
This type of knitting is used to divide a garment into well-defined colour areas, or to create a picture effect. The picture could be anything from an abstract arrangement of colours to a well-defined landscape, a face, some flowers, a sailing boat (see diagram opposite), a cartoon character or an object.

Most commonly these arrangements are worked in plain stocking stitch, but there is no reason why different colour areas should not be treated in different ways, providing the broken colour lines between two areas are closely studied and any differences in tension carefully worked out. Both stitch patterns and yarns could be used to change the texture of the colour areas or a Jacquard design could be used in places instead of a solid colour.

To plan your picture, draw a tension diagram of your garment (see Chapter 8) and mark the different colour areas carefully in pencil. With a thicker pencil or a felt-tip pen, retrace the outline, following the graph-paper lines closest to the original drawing. You now have a graph showing colour areas in stitches and rows.

To knit the picture, you will need a separate ball of yarn for each colour area. Therefore, if the same colour appears more than once in any one row, you might need to split a ball or skein of that colour into several small balls. A neat way of doing this is to wind the yarn round bobbins.

When changing colour, make sure you twist the two yarns around each other; otherwise you will end up with two or more pieces of knitting instead of one.

The main problem with mock patchwork is that the little balls or bobbins tend to get tangled, especially when there is a large number of them, and this slows down progress.

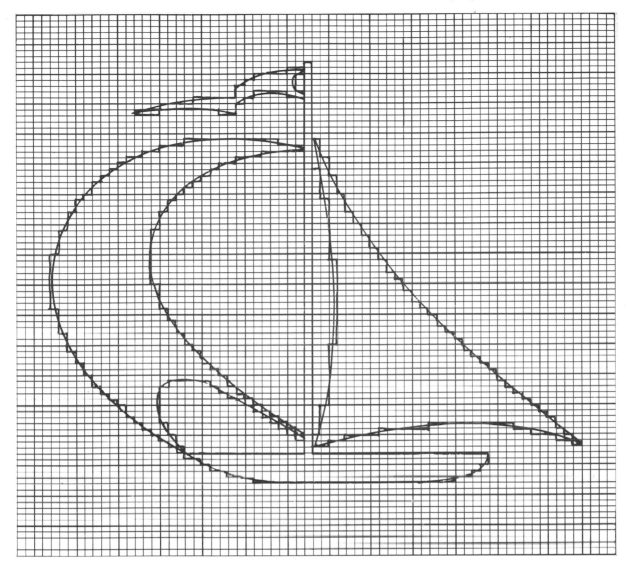

CHAPTER 6
Choosing Shapes

Garments can be knitted as a single piece but usually they are worked in sections which are later put together. The shape of these sections can easily be reduced to essentials and the design generally benefits from simplicity. This makes shape far easier to understand and master in knitting than in dressmaking. How different shapes are put together, and how they are constructed are matters of style.

Four techniques are used to give shape to knitting: increasing, decreasing, gathering and darting. Increases are used for widening, decreases for narrowing, gatherings for sudden changes in width within given edges, and darts for three-dimensional shapings.

The following notes explain in general terms what shapes can be used and how they can be knitted. No actual measurements are given for any of the shapes; these can only be fixed once the style has been decided (Chapter 7), and once the body measurements of the wearer are known (Chapter 8). When specific body measurements are relevant, these are indicated in the illustrations. In such cases, the cross indicates the bone at the top of the spine (see page 121).

The illustrations show how different shapes look once they are finished. In some cases, this is complemented by diagrams showing the open, flat shape. This is how your knitted sections should look if you are working them flat.

If you prefer to work in rounds, cut the shapes out of paper and stick them together to give a three-dimensional effect. If you end up with a funnel-shaped paper and you are working a sleeve, place a marker at the beginning of the rounds to pinpoint a line of double increases or decreases, which would correspond to the seam of a flat sleeve. If you are working the body you will have two lines of double increases or decreases, corresponding to the two side seams; place your markers, one at the beginning of the rounds, and the other by the central stitch.

BODY
The body of a garment is the section that starts at the hips and ends underneath the arms. It can either be worked in rounds, or flat. If worked flat it is most often knitted as a back and a front joined with side seams. Front and back generally have the same width, but should one of them need to be wider it should be the front.

The base of the body must be flat. Therefore, if the main stitch pattern has a tendency to curl, the base will need a border worked in a different pattern.

The same shape can often be adapted to two or three of the following styles: loose, gathered at the waist, or gathered at the base. The length of the shape can also vary; the illustrations show a medium-length garment, but this could be altered by shortening or lengthening the piece below the waistline.

Although the rest of the body might be tapered, the base must always be straight, even if it is only for a short length. In those garments with borders, the tapering could start just after the border.

STRAIGHT BODY
This is a simple rectangle. It is suitable for medium-length and short garments for women with no figure problems, and for any length of garment for children and men. Women's longer garments will generally fit tightly at the hips and loosely at the bust. It is easy to work and widely used.

TAPERED BODY
This is narrower at the top than at the base. It is suitable for people with large hips and a small chest or bust, and for pregnancy smocks. It is also good for onion-shaped, highly gathered fashion garments. It can be gathered at the waist.

INVERTED TAPERED BODY
Wider at the top than at the base. Suitable for fashion garments, clinging at the hips but otherwise very loose. Also good for people with narrow hips and a large chest or bust.

MIXED BODY
Wide at the base, getting narrower, and straight at the top. It follows the most common feminine figure: wider below the waist than above it. Useful for designs that emphasize the natural line.

INVERTED MIXED BODY
Straight at the base and widening at the top. Good for fashion garments, for women with large busts, and for increased ease at the underarm.

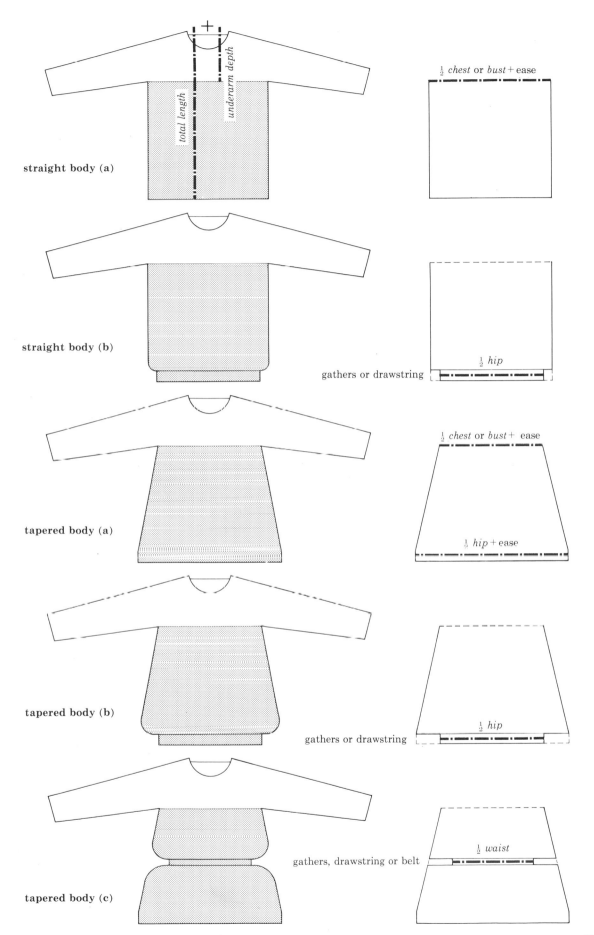

straight body (a)

total length

underarm depth

½ *chest* or *bust* + ease

straight body (b)

gathers or drawstring

½ *hip*

tapered body (a)

½ *chest* or *bust* + ease

½ *hip* + ease

tapered body (b)

gathers or drawstring

½ *hip*

tapered body (c)

gathers, drawstring or belt

½ *waist*

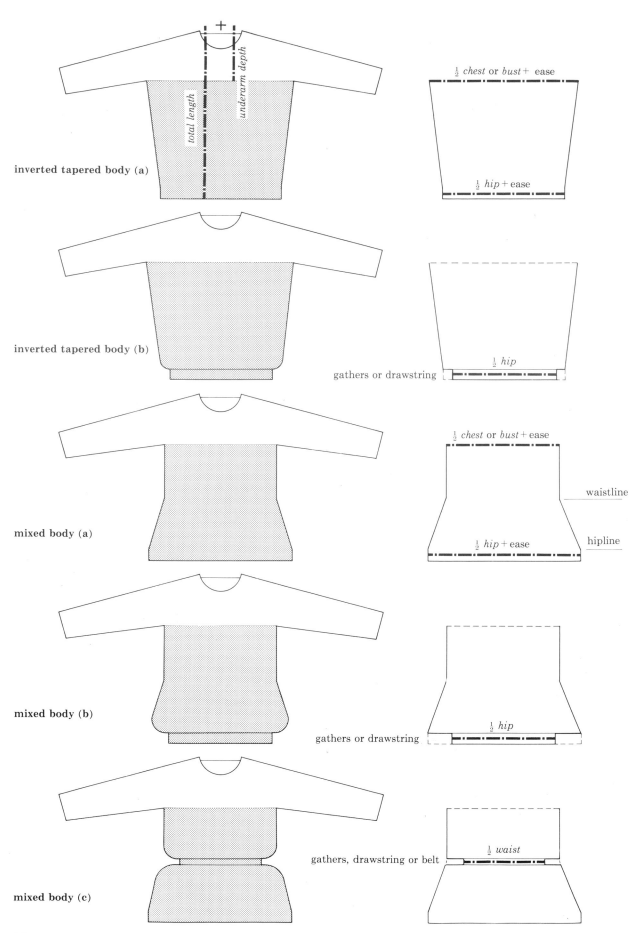

inverted tapered body (a)

½ *chest* or *bust* + ease

½ *hip* + ease

total length

underarm depth

inverted tapered body (b)

gathers or drawstring

½ *hip*

mixed body (a)

½ *chest* or *bust* + ease

waistline

½ *hip* + ease

hipline

mixed body (b)

gathers or drawstring

½ *hip*

mixed body (c)

gathers, drawstring or belt

½ *waist*

84

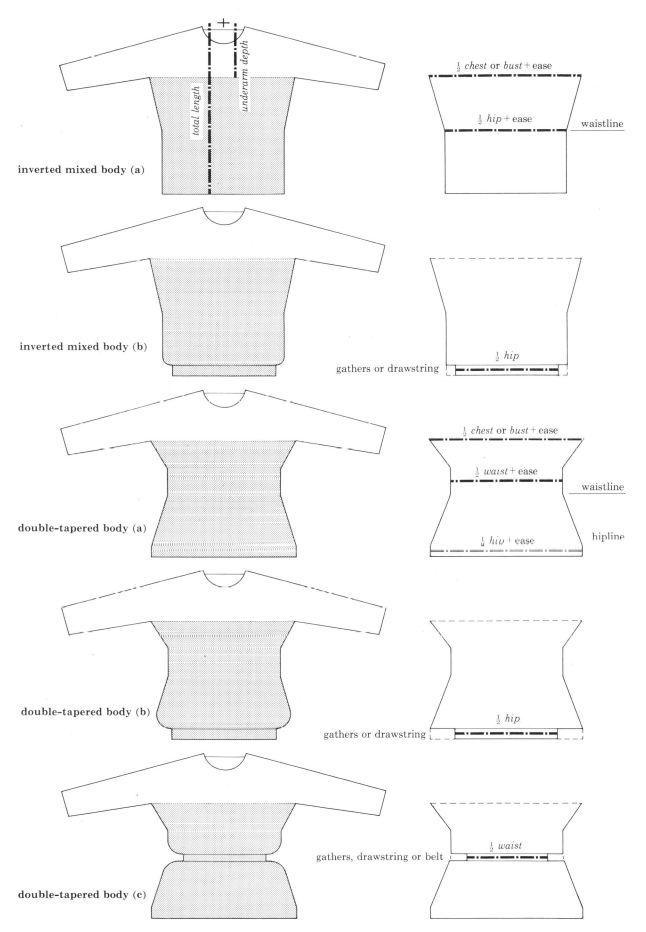

inverted mixed body (a)

total length

underarm depth

½ *chest* or *bust* + ease

½ *hip* + ease — waistline

inverted mixed body (b)

gathers or drawstring

½ *hip*

double-tapered body (a)

½ *chest* or *bust* + ease

½ *waist* + ease — waistline

½ *hip* + ease — hipline

double-tapered body (b)

gathers or drawstring

½ *hip*

double-tapered body (c)

gathers, drawstring or belt

½ *waist*

85

DOUBLE-TAPERED BODY

Wide at the base, it narrows, continues straight, and widens again at the top. The lower section follows the most common feminine figure, whilst the top allows for fashion shapings, increases in underarm ease, and large busts.

SLEEVES

These are usually worked flat but can also be knitted in rounds. They can be left loose at the bottom, or gathered in a cuff. The top can end in a shoulder cap or in a straight line. The length can also vary: short, above-elbow, three-quarter, seven-eighths or long. The illustrations show long sleeves; to shorten them, use only as much of the upper part of the diagram as needed to give the required length (see pages 89 and 90).

Most often, cuffed sleeves are knitted in a single piece, starting with the cuff and simply changing needles, if necessary, to work the sleeve. If the sleeve is to be gathered, work the increases on the first row of the sleeve. Sometimes, though, sleeves are worked from the top, ending with the cuff. In this case, any gatherings have to be worked as decreases.

If the sleeve is to be worked transversely, but the cuff is not, knit the sleeve separately, with a chain selvedge at the base. The stitches for the cuff can then be picked up from the selvedge, or the cuff can be worked separately and be grafted to the selvedge.

If the cuff is to be worked transversely, but the sleeve is not, knit them separately, and then attach the cuff to the sleeve in any of the ways suggested for fixing borders, gathering the sleeve if necessary.

If both the sleeve and the cuff are to be worked transversely, knit them separately if they require different size needles. Otherwise, follow the instructions for working two stitch patterns together or follow those for working vertical lines of gathers.

Sleeves without shoulder caps that are to be worked in rounds, can be picked up from the edge of the armhole after finishing the body.

NARROW STRAIGHT SLEEVE

This clings at the top of the arm, but is loose at the wrist. The cuffs will produce a gathered sleeve.

MEDIUM STRAIGHT SLEEVE

Fairly loose at the top of the arm and very loose at the wrist. Cuffs will produce a well-gathered sleeve.

WIDE STRAIGHT SLEEVE

Very loose at the top of the arm, and even more so at the wrist. It is generally used without cuffs or shoulder caps. Cuffs are only advisable in fine yarns and supple stitches; otherwise they would be too heavy and cumbersome.

NARROW-TAPERED SLEEVE

This clings along the length of the arm, and is most frequently used with a cuff. Turned-up cuffs might need to take the tapering into account.

MEDIUM-TAPERED SLEEVE

This is fairly loose along the length of the arm. It is often gathered at the wrist, ending in a cuff, but if the tapering is not very steep it can successfully be left loose.

WIDE-TAPERED SLEEVE

Fairly loose at the wrist and very loose at the top. The sleeve seam may end as far down as the waist, becoming a *batwing sleeve* if the tapering is steep enough. It almost always ends gathered in a cuff.

MIXED SLEEVE

It has a medium or wide, straight top, and a tapered base. It is used to reduce the gathering at the base of a straight sleeve (a), or to give more ease at the top of a narrow-tapered one (b). In the latter case, the width required for the top of the arm has to be reached before starting the straight section.

DOUBLE-TAPERED SLEEVE

It has a much sharper tapering at the top than at the wrist. It is used when a quick increase in width is required at the top of the sleeve, usually to give more ease at the underarm. It generally has a cuff.

INVERTED DOUBLE-TAPERED SLEEVE

It has a slight tapering at the top and a much sharper tapering at the wrist. Used for *angel sleeves* with wide, hanging bases, or for *bishop sleeves* with very full bases gathered at the wrist.

CUFFS

Cuffs may or may not be elastic—elastic cuffs being tighter fitting. However, whatever the type of cuff, to prevent stretching it should be knitted with needles one or two sizes smaller than those used for the rest of the garment.

Turned-up cuffs, if worked flat, should have a seam that is partly on the wrong-side of work, as all the other seams, and partly on the right-side of work, so that when the cuff is turned up the seam will not show.

Some cuffs with fasteners might require a slit at the base of the sleeve, similar to those found in shirts, if there is any danger that the join between cuff and sleeve will be too narrow for the hand to go comfortably through.

(*opposite*) Girl's cardigan in blue and white and boy's jumper with diagonal stripes on front (see page 156)

(*overleaf*) Purple tunic with Jacquard design and man's grey waistcoat (see page 157)

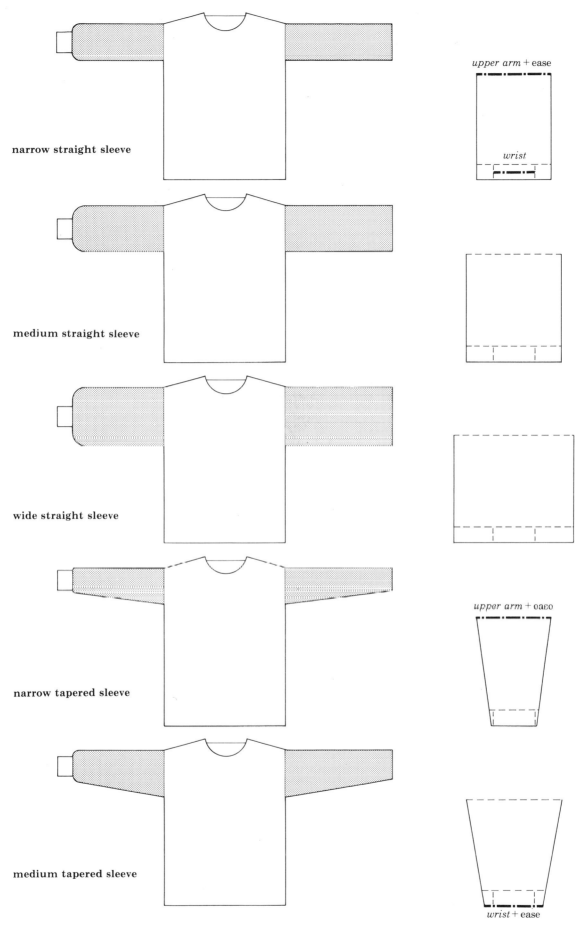

narrow straight sleeve

upper arm + ease

wrist

medium straight sleeve

wide straight sleeve

narrow tapered sleeve

upper arm + ease

medium tapered sleeve

wrist + ease

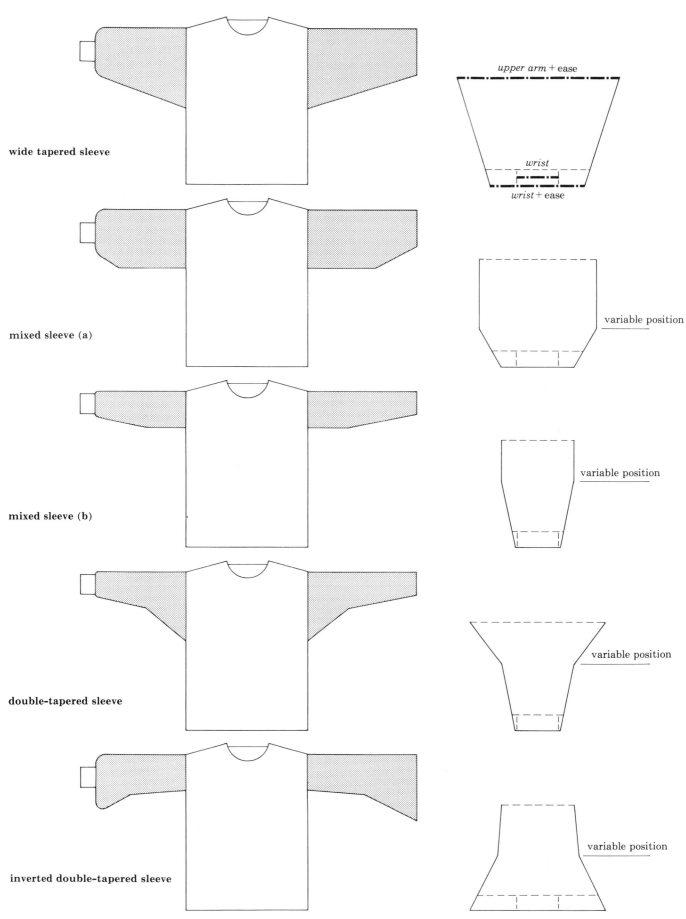

wide tapered sleeve

upper arm + ease

wrist

wrist + ease

mixed sleeve (a)

variable position

mixed sleeve (b)

variable position

double-tapered sleeve

variable position

inverted double-tapered sleeve

variable position

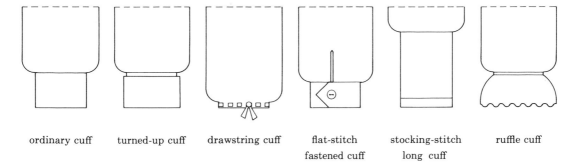

ordinary cuff   turned-up cuff   drawstring cuff   flat-stitch fastened cuff   stocking-stitch long cuff   ruffle cuff

ORDINARY RIBBED CUFFS
The most commonly used of all cuffs. Both single and double ribbing can be used.

DECORATIVE RIBBED CUFFS
A more interesting cuff can be achieved by using a more elaborate but elastic stitch pattern, instead of ordinary ribbing. Use, for instance, one of the fancy ribs or a series of small cables separated by one or two stitches in reverse stocking stitch.

DRAWSTRING CUFFS
Just the minimal expression of a cuff, but a good way to secure the base of a sleeve. The cord is drawn through eyelets worked near the edge, or through tubular stocking stitch cast off as ribbing (invisible method).

FLAT-STITCHED CUFFS
These can be worked in any flat stitch pattern, such as garter stitch or moss stitch. They are not really elastic, and unless they are fastened or one is very careful, they can easily be stretched out of shape.

STOCKING-STITCH CUFFS
These are not very common but can be used to great effect. They are generally longer than ordinary cuffs, and can either have two thicknesses—like a sort of very wide hem—or have a small border in another stitch pattern to keep the edge flat. They can be plain, or pick up a colour motif.

RUFFLE CUFFS
These are most often found in fine, lacy garments. The finer the work is, the more gathers there can be.

SHOULDERS
Shoulders affect both the sleeves and the body of a garment, and so they play an important role in the definition of its character.

Whether the body has been worked flat or in rounds, both front and back need to be independent once the underarm is reached, otherwise, the garment would have no armholes! The general idea with shoulders is that front and back can be made narrower above the underarm, providing shoulder caps are worked above the sleeves. The smaller the front and back become, the bigger the shoulder caps will have to be. If front and back have different widths, add these, divide by two, and calculate shoulders as if front and back were equal. Adjust shapings to real front and back by working those decreases that fall short of the narrow section as part of the wider one.

Shoulders are worked in three parts: one is a continuation of the front, another is a continuation of the back, and the third is a continuation of the sleeves. To finish the garment, these three parts are put together with seams or grafting. Sleeveless garments might still have shoulders, although not necessarily the three parts of a shoulder. A halter top for instance, will have the front shaped as for raglan and nothing else.

Another way of working shoulders, which avoids part or all of the seams, is to knit the sleeves as an integral part of the body. These 'continuous' sleeves give very soft lines, and make easy work of finishing the garment. Their main drawbacks are the length of some of the rows, and the weight of the garment in the last stages of knitting.

DROPPED SHOULDERS
The finished sleeves form a right angle with the rest of the garment. They are the easiest of all shoulders and their fitting is foolproof, but the top of the sleeve needs to be as large as the *round shoulder* measurement. For this reason, sometimes one stitch is increased on either side, every row or every other row, when working the last few rows of the sleeves, as shown by the dotted lines in (a). The seam between sleeve and body falls down the upper arm of the wearer.

Front and back are continued straight, although one or two stitches can be cast off at either side if the beginning of the armhole needs to be clearly marked (a). At the top, they can be cast off in a straight line (a), or at a slant (b); the first way is more appropriate for baggy garments and people with high or broad shoulders, while the second is best for fitted garments and people with low shoulders.

The sleeves have no shoulder cap; they are either cast off and sewn to front and back, or grafted to them. This means that the height

91

worked for the armhole in both the front and the back must be half the width of the top of the sleeve.

A variation, which makes the sleeves reach further up the arms, consists of casting off several stitches on either side of front and back, instead of just one or two (b). The sleeves are made longer accordingly, and are then fixed in such a way that the stitches cast off at front and back are joined to the sides of the sleeves, while the top is fixed to the vertical edges of front and back.

RAGLAN SHOULDERS
The finished sleeves form a gentle acute angle with the rest of the garment. Their fitting is generally very good, providing the decreases have been properly calculated, and the *round-shoulder* or the *underarm-depth* measurements have been taken into account. People with very high shoulders might need a dart at the top of the shoulder caps; this is worked as a series of double decreases placed in the centre of the cap, starting at mid-height between underarm and top of cap.

Two to four stitches, depending on the thickness of the yarn, are cast off at either side of front and back to mark the beginning of the armholes. Paired single or double decreases are then worked at *regular* intervals, one at each end of front and back, until the neckline is reached. Most necklines will be first reached at the front rather than at the back, and this will have an effect on the shoulder cap.

The sleeves are decreased so that one side of the shoulder cap is exactly like the front of the garment, and the other side exactly like the back. They must be symmetrical; that is, the long side must be to the right of one sleeve, and to the left of the other. The top of the cap, for an adult, is usually betwen 4–8cm (1½–3in) in width, and is cast off at a slant.

A good way to calculate raglan sleeves is to first calculate the decreases for front and back, and then the number of stitches needed at the top of the shoulder cap. Adding these stitches to the decreases on one side of the front and one side of the back, gives the number of stitches at the top of the sleeve. Check this number against the width you want to obtain, and alter any of the previous calculations if necessary. Do not forget to add the dart as well, if there is one.

SET-IN SHOULDERS
The finished sleeves form a sharp acute angle with the rest of the garment. These shoulders are best with medium-wide or tight sleeves, but they only look good when their fitting is perfect. This, added to the complex curves of the shoulder caps used in dressmaking, and to the difficulty of obtaining a good fit from standard knitting patterns, has understandably put off many knitters. A different approach to set-in shoulders, however, proves that there is no need to feel

intimidated by them. The following simplified version, where the curves have been transformed into straight lines, gives consistently good results, provided that the garment is made-to-measure and the measurements are correctly taken.

Front and back must be exactly as wide as the *shoulder-to-shoulder* measurement of the person who is going to wear the garment. This means there will have to be some fairly sharp decreases at the beginning of the armholes. To calculate these decreases, work out the number of stitches needed to give the shoulder-to-shoulder measurement, and subtract them from the number of stitches the front or the back have before the armhole. Cast off one quarter of the resulting number at either side, all in one row, and cast off another quarter of the same number on either side, one by one, every two rows. Continue straight until the edge of the armhole, measured as shown in the illustration, gives half the *round shoulder* measurement. Cast off for the top shoulder seam at a slant, more or less pronounced depending on whether the wearer has high or low shoulders.

The sleeve caps are shaped by casting off on the first row of the cap the same number of stitches that were cast off at front and back on the first row of the armhole. After that, one stitch is cast off on either side, every two rows, until the edge of one side of the cap plus half the row still on the needle, measured as shown in the illustration, gives half the *round shoulder* measurement. For an adult, the row still left on the needle should be between 6–9cm (2½–3½in). Cast off straight. When sewing up, take in the edge of the corners at either end of the cast-off row.

PUFF SHOULDERS
A variation of set-in shoulders. Make the sleeves wider and the caps longer than required by the armhole; gather the excess fabric at the top of the cap when sewing up.

LEG-OF-MUTTON SHOULDERS
Another variation of set-in shoulders. The sleeve starts as narrow, but a row of gathers somewhere between the elbow and the underarm makes it suddenly wider. The rest is as for puff shoulders.

EPAULETTE SHOULDERS
Front, back and sleeves are shaped, to start with, either as ordinary set-in (a) or as steep raglan (b) shoulders. When the shoulder cap reaches the width required for the epaulette, the decreases are stopped and the cap is continued straight until the neck is reached. The cap is then cast off at a slant, making the back longer than the front, as for raglan shoulders, except for a narrow band that is continued until the centre of the back is reached (a). The decreases at front and back are stopped when the length of the

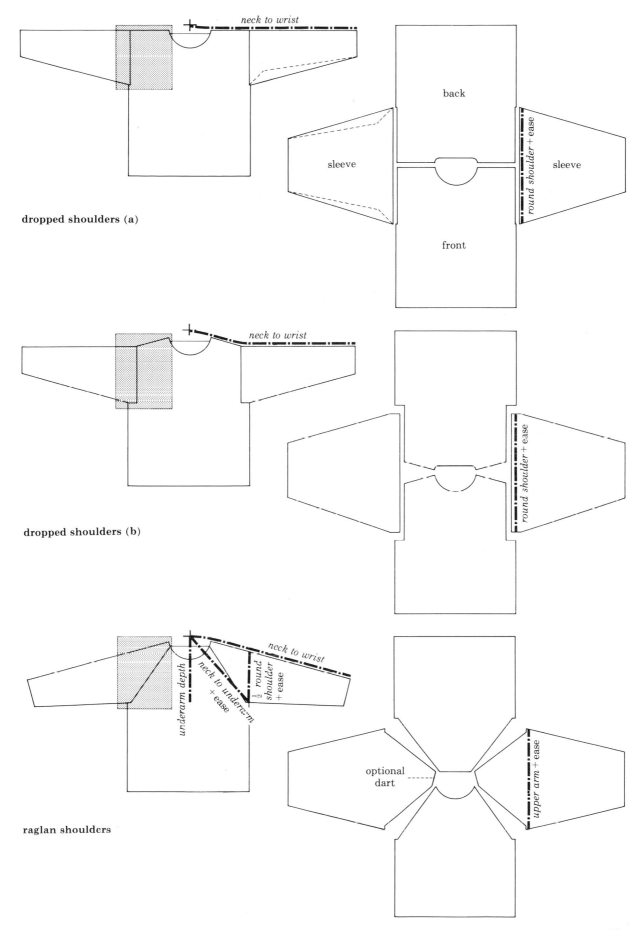

dropped shoulders (a)

neck to wrist

back

sleeve

sleeve

round shoulder + ease

front

dropped shoulders (b)

neck to wrist

round shoulder + ease

raglan shoulders

neck to wrist

underarm depth

neck to underarm + ease

½ round shoulder + ease

optional dart

upper arm + ease

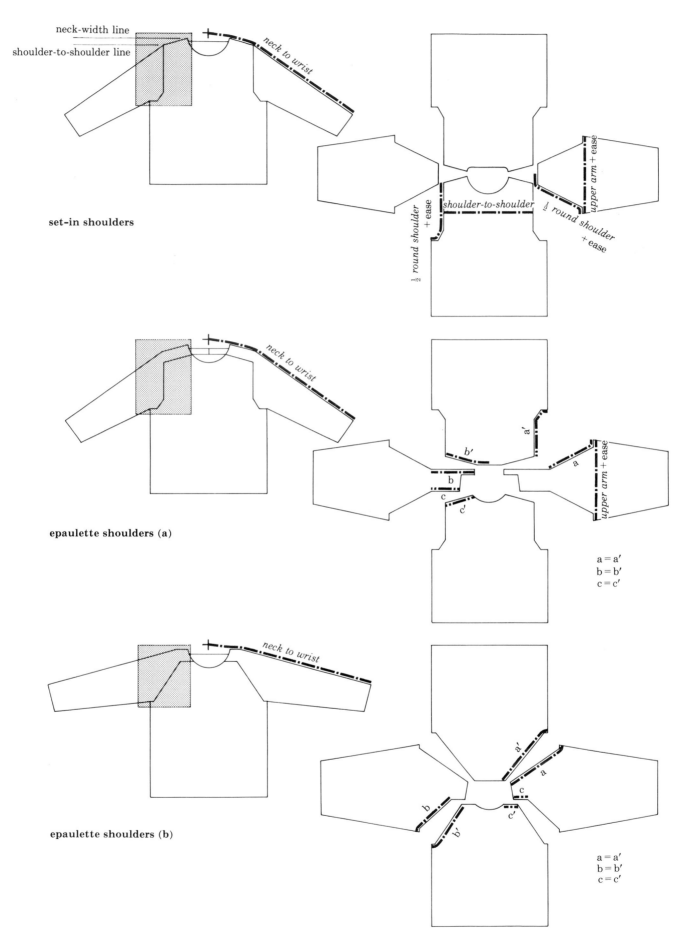

neck-width line

shoulder-to-shoulder line

neck to wrist

set-in shoulders

½ round shoulder + ease

shoulder-to-shoulder

½ round shoulder + ease

upper arm + ease

neck to wrist

epaulette shoulders (a)

b′

a′

b

a

c

c′

upper arm + ease

a = a′
b = b′
c = c′

neck to wrist

epaulette shoulders (b)

a′

a

b

c

c′

b′

a = a′
b = b′
c = c′

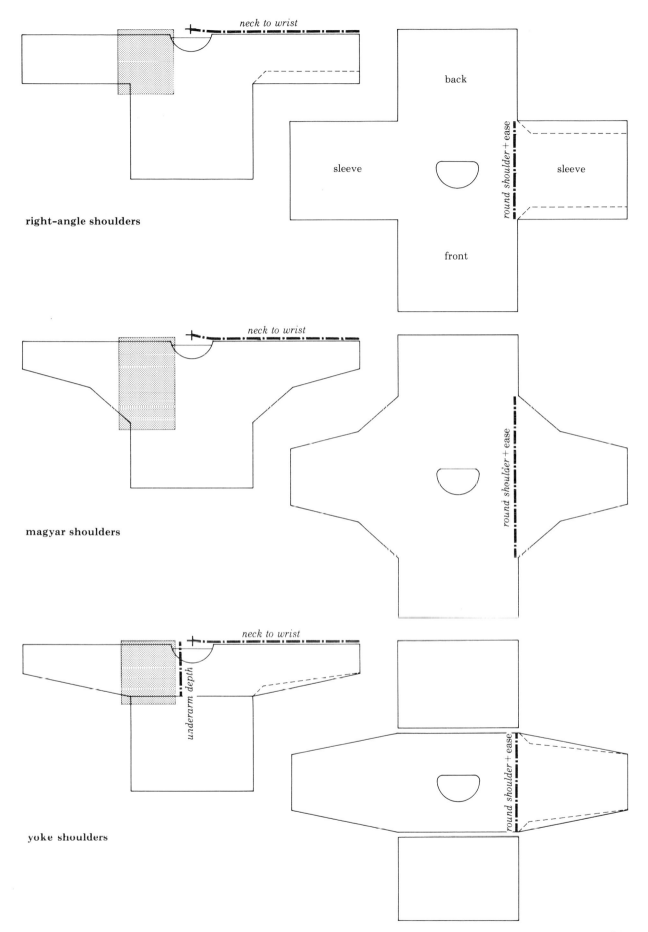

right-angle shoulders

magyar shoulders

yoke shoulders

neck to wrist

back

sleeve

sleeve

front

round shoulder+ease

underarm depth

armhole edge is equal to the length of the shoulder-cap edge, up to the beginning of the epaulette. They can then be cast off in a straight line, if the garment is for a person with high shoulders, or giving a slant to the sides, as for set-in shoulders, if the person has low shoulders. Sometimes, epaulettes are only worked at the front of the garment, in which case the back is treated as an ordinary raglan (b).

RIGHT-ANGLE SHOULDERS
The simplest of all continuous sleeves. They can be worked in three ways. Start with the back, increase all the stitches needed for the sleeves, on either side, when the armhole is reached; work across full width until half the sleeve is complete; proceed similarly for the front; graft both sections together, or cast off and sew. Alternatively, work the front as a continuation of the back, remembering to work a hole for the head. Or, if you prefer to work transversely, start at the base of one of the sleeves, work the sleeve, increase at either end for front and back, decrease the same number of stitches that you increased when the body is finished, and end with the other sleeve. What was said about *round shoulder* measurement when dealing with dropped shoulders also applies here.

MAGYAR SHOULDERS
Similar to right-angle shoulders, but the sleeves are double-tapered instead of straight. This means that the increases and decreases have to be worked in groups, every two rows (either every right-side or every wrong-side row), instead of all at once.

YOKE SHOULDERS
Front and back are cast off in a straight line as soon as the armhole is reached. The sleeves, which can be of any medium or wide shape, are worked as a long strip: first one sleeve, then a straight section, as long as the body is wide, for the yoke, then the second sleeve. What was said about *round shoulder* measurement when dealing with dropped shoulders also applies here.

OPENINGS
Garments which have some openings other than a hole for the head, are most frequently opened at the front, but back, side and shoulder openings are not uncommon.

The illustrations show garments open all the way down. To obtain all possible openings, combine those illustrated with different types of neckline (see below), or start them higher up: work the lower part of the garment in one piece, and divide the work to form the opening at the appropriate height. If the opening has an overlap, this will involve picking up or casting on a few extra stitches to work a double thickness, or

casting off a few stitches for later application of a border.

WIDE OPENING
The two edges do not meet, although ties might be used for fastening. It can also have a lower border spanning the full width of the garment, and any fastenings can then be attached to this border.

EDGE-TO-EDGE OPENING
The two sides meet but do not overlap. The two lower corners can be mitred or rounded. It may or may not have fasteners, but suitable ones are: ties, large hook-and-eyes of the type used for fur coats, buttons and loops, toggles, bands and buckles, cords ending in pompons or tassels, laces drawn through eyelets, and zips.

ZIP-AND-FLAP OPENING
This is similar to an edge-to-edge opening fastened with a zip, but has an added flap that conceals the zip. See Chapter 2 for details of how to work the flap.

OVERLAPPING OPENING
The edges overlap and are most commonly fastened with buttons and buttonholes, although belts and other fastenings can also be used. The most common type of overlap is a border, and especially a ribbed border. However, if the garment is knitted in a flat, strong stitch pattern, it may be possible to avoid using the border.

ASYMMETRICAL OPENING
The aperture can run in any direction, not just the one illustrated. It may or may not overlap, and may or not have fastenings.

DOUBLE-BREASTED OPENING
The edges have a large overlap and are fastened with two lines of buttons and buttonholes. They are very good when extra warmth is required around the chest.

DOUBLE-FLAP OPENING
This is a version of a double-breasted opening that can be worn open or buttoned up. The flaps have a line of buttonholes near the edge, and a line of buttons further in. The garment is buttoned up normally unless an open garment is required, in which case the flaps are turned and the buttons fastened to the buttonholes of the same side.

WRAPOVER OPENING
Both sides have a diagonal edge, and at their base they completely cross the front. The ends can be fastened with buttons or ties, or they can have long ties which are taken round the waist and then knotted together.

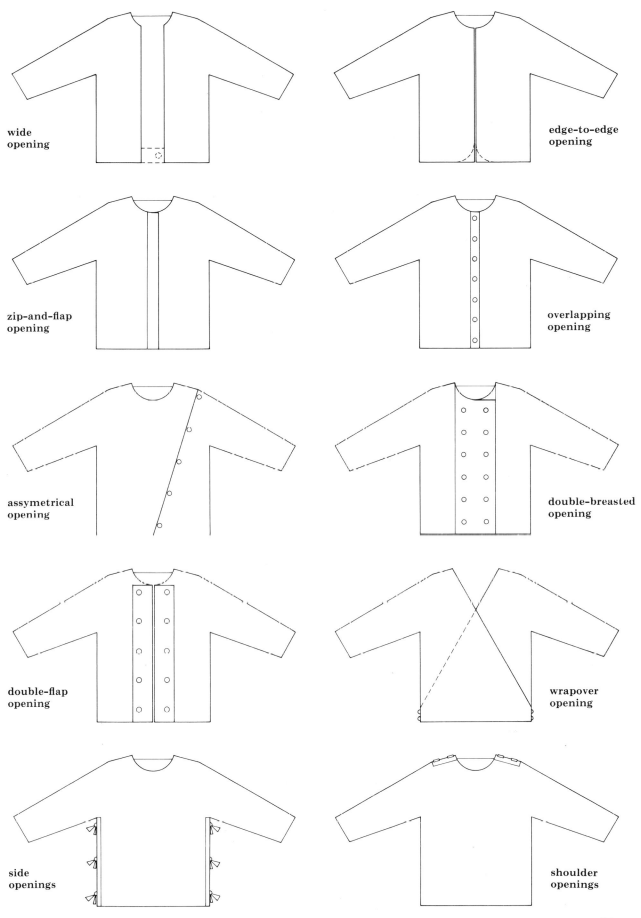

wide
opening

edge-to-edge
opening

zip-and-flap
opening

overlapping
opening

assymetrical
opening

double-breasted
opening

double-flap
opening

wrapover
opening

side
openings

shoulder
openings

97

SIDE OPENINGS

In general, both sides are open. They may or may not overlap, and may be fastened all the way down, or only in part. Any type of fastening can be used.

SHOULDER OPENINGS

One or both shoulders might be open. They are generally fastened with buttons, but any other fastening could be used

NECKLINES

Necklines delineate the opening left at the top of a garment for the head to go through. Their shape is very important because not all necklines suit all people. They are often finished with a border or collar.

Necklines that come close to the base of the neck can have a narrow or a wide fit. Those that fit narrowly, with a border actually standing upright against the neck, are best for overcoats and garments to be worn next to the skin. When a shirt or scarf is to be worn underneath, a slightly wider neckline is more suitable.

To vary a neckline, work a slit at its centre or at the sides.

ROUND NECK

This fits round the base of the neck, leaving a hole just large enough for the head to go through comfortably. The front is cast off like a flattened semicircle, and the back is basically a straight line curving gently upwards at the ends. When finished with a ribbed border, it is called a *crew-neck*.

U-NECK

The back is like that of a round neck. The front is also similar, but much lower. After the original shaping, the sides of the front are worked straight.

SCOOP NECK

A neckline with many variations. It can be wide or narrow, high or small, the front and the back might be the same, or one might be lower than the other. A scoop back, in fact, can go as low as the waist.

SQUARE NECK

All four angles are straight but, again, it can be of any height and width, and front and back might be of the same or different depth. All the stitches are cast off on the same row.

TAPERED NECK

Similar to a square neck, but the angles are not straight. Consequently, the central stitches are cast off on the same row, but additional decreases are worked at the sides at regular intervals.

V-NECK

The back is as for crew-neck, but the front plunges down to form an acute angle. The tip of the angle is generally sharp, but it could be made blunt. It can also be high or low, but high V-necks can easily look ill-balanced. When a border is to be added a classical start for the V is at 1–2cm ($\frac{1}{2}$–1in) below the beginning of the armholes. Work is divided at the centre, where a stitch might be cast off, and regular decreases are worked on either side.

FIVE-SIDED NECK

Generally higher than a V-neck. It has a short, wide V at the base, and two vertical sides thereafter.

STRAIGHT NECK

Just a straight line. Unless the opening is fairly wide, the front will stand up uncomfortably against the person's neck.

BOAT NECK

Like a wide straight neck, but it is cast off in three of four stages to make a gentle curve. If the curve is more pronounced, the two edges can be made to overlap at the sides.

KEYHOLE NECK

The general shape is that of a crew-neck, but it has a round or wedge-shaped opening at the front, which the border keeps in place. If the garment is very tight fitting, a couple of stitches cast off at the centre when dividing the work will be enough to shape the opening.

YOKES

Yokes highlight the bust and neckline. They are usually worked so that they contrast with the rest of the garment. Knit them, therefore, in a different colour, yarn, or stitch pattern, or in a Jacquard design. The garment can be gathered underneath the yoke.

Yokes are a good way of finishing sleeveless garments. When the yoke would require picking up stitches from non-existent sleeves, the appropriate number of stitches should be cast on instead of picked up.

LARGE ROUND YOKE

This is worked in rounds, picking up the stitches once the rest of the garment has been blocked and put together.

Front, back and sleeves are shaped as for set-in shoulders, but only for the first few rows—just enough to stop the yoke from 'hiding' under the arms. The number of stitches cast off in the first row is not critical, but it should approximate to 3cm ($2\frac{1}{4}$in) for an adult. If you want the yoke to fit exactly around the neck, front and back of the body will need a soft curve. This curve should be deepened at the front, and this is obtained by

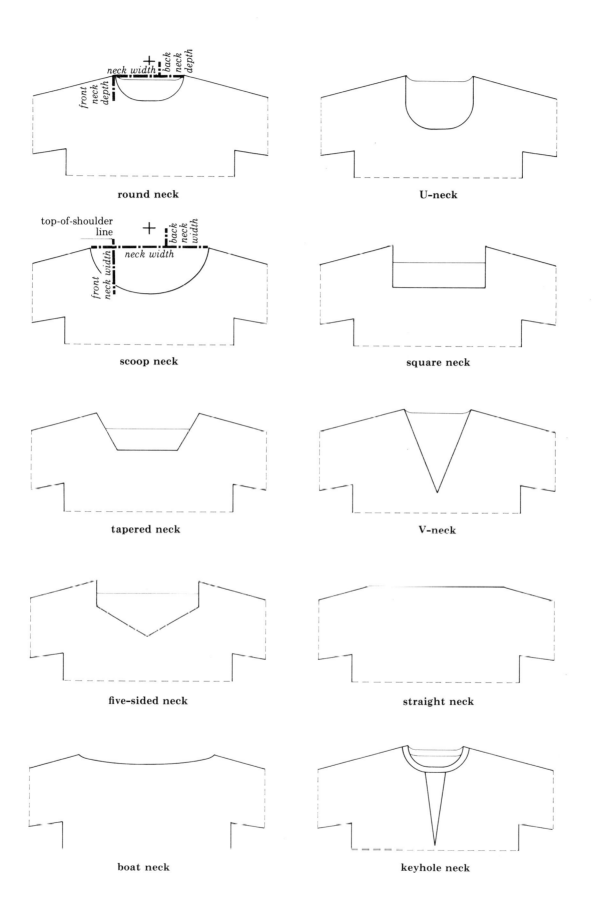

round neck

U-neck

scoop neck

square neck

tapered neck

V-neck

five-sided neck

straight neck

boat neck

keyhole neck

front neck depth

neck width

back neck depth

top-of-shoulder line

front neck width

neck width

back neck width

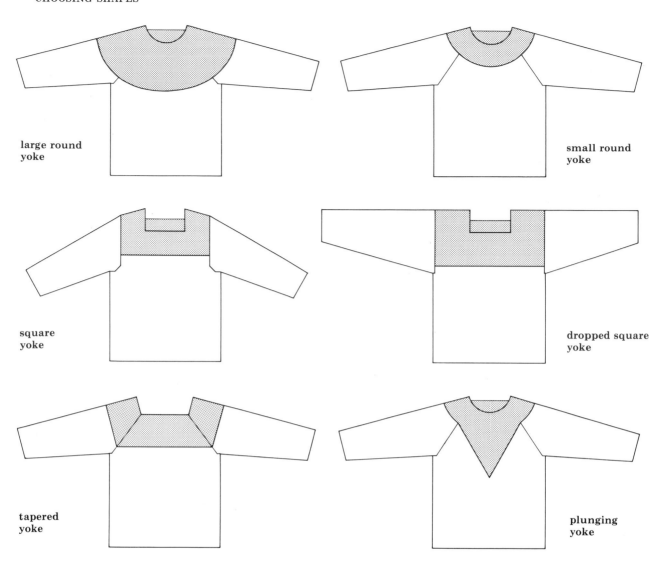

large round
yoke

small round
yoke

square
yoke

dropped square
yoke

tapered
yoke

plunging
yoke

progressively casting off the central stitches at the same time as you decrease for the armholes. Use a provisional cast off, or put the stitches on safety pins, ready to be picked up for the yoke.

To work the yoke, first pick up the stitches from the back, then one sleeve, then the front, and finally the other sleeve. Calculate the stitches that you will need at the neck, from the *round-the-neck* measurement, and subtract them from the number of stitches on needles. This will give you the total number of decreases to be worked. Next calculate the number of rows you will have to knit to reach the neck. How you distribute the decreases amongst the rows greatly depends on the stitch pattern or Jacquard design of the yoke, and it is best worked out on special graph paper. As far as possible, decrease the same amount of stitches per row, at equal intervals. Depending on your circumstances, this will best be done a few stitches every two or three rows, or a much larger proportion of stitches at longer intervals. The decreases can be single or double, and the number of stitches between them need not be constantly the same, but a certain pattern must exist eg:

single decrease, 7 sts, double decrease, 12 sts, single decrease, 7 sts, double decrease, 12 sts, etc. Jacquard yokes are usually decreased on the background stitches. The pattern has to be very carefully studied so that it forms a sort of star.

SMALL ROUND YOKE
This is similar to a large round yoke but the stitches are picked up nearer the neck. Between the beginning of the armhole and the beginning of the yoke, decrease as for raglan shoulders.

SQUARE YOKE
This is worked as a continuation of the front and back, although you may need to change the needles if it is in a different yarn or stitch pattern. The garment can have set-in shoulders, in which case the yoke is started at any point after finishing the decreases for the armholes, or false set-in shoulders: the yoke gathers the body to shoulder-to-shoulder width, somewhere above the armholes, and no decreases need to be worked. Front and back can start at different or similar heights.

DROPPED SQUARE YOKE

A variation of a square yoke, used when the garment has dropped shoulders. The yoke is started at any point after reaching the armhole openings.

TAPERED YOKE

Another variation on a square yoke, used when the garment has raglan shoulders. This time the yoke is worked partly on the sleeves, and can be started at any point after the beginning of the armholes, but it must be at the same point for front, back and sleeves, so that they meet at the seams.

PLUNGING YOKE

This may be considered as a small round yoke with a V at the front. Knit the V with the body, but otherwise work as for small round yoke.

COLLARS

Collars are good examples of the wisdom of using simple shapes—easy to obtain with knitting techniques—in preference to more complex shapes requiring a different type of fabric to be really successful. A shawl collar, for instance, can look very good with little effort because the knitted fabric naturally takes the right shape. Lapels, on the other hand, almost without exception lack crispness, because they should be stiff and knitting is soft.

To vary the collars illustrated, try them with necklines different from the ones shown. Try, for example, a ruff collar with a scoop neck, a tie with a square neck, or a wing collar with a V-neck. Or try leaving a gap between the ends of the collar, working circular collars flat and fastening them with buttons, or anything else suitable. In fact, collars can take so many shapes that it would be impossible to cover them all.

POLO-NECK COLLAR

Probably the best collar for people who feel the cold but it does not always suit those who have short necks. Pick up the necessary number of stitches from a round neckline with a medium or wide fit. Knit, at least, for a length that will allow the collar to be folded at the top of the person's neck, and come down to the base. If you prefer a softer, bulkier look, allow for a further fold at the base. Use any of the ribbed stitch patterns (see page 58), so that the collar will be elastic. Cast off loosely.

COWL-NECK COLLAR

This is attached to a scoop neck. It can be worked on the round from stitches picked up from the edge, like a large polo-neck, or transversely. In the latter case, a wide enough strip is worked separately, and then sewn to the neckline. Cowl-necks can be worked in ribbing or in a flat stitch pattern, and need at least two folds.

STANDING COLLAR

This is attached to a round neckline, and needs to be quite strong so that it stays upright. For a small collar, work a thin strip the length of the neckline, using a flat stitch pattern and perhaps two or three strands of yarn for added body. Sew the strip to the edge of the neckline, making sure it stays quite vertical. For a larger collar, pick up the necessary stitches from the edge, and work in a pattern with some degree of elasticity for twice the required length. Fold in two and, without casting off, sew each stitch to the back loop of the picked up stitches, as if sewing a hem at the end of work.

TIE COLLAR

This is worked separately, as a long strip, later to be joined to the neckline. The tie itself should be straight but the rest should follow the shape of the neckline, otherwise it will stand up. If the neckline is curved, use the curving technique explained for bias bands.

RUFF COLLAR

This can be worked on any neckline depending on the stitch pattern chosen, either pick up the necessary stitches from the neckline and work the ruff, or work the ruff separately and then join it to neckline. For a higher ruff, work as for polo-neck until the required height is reached (it will not be folded this time), and then knit the ruff. The finer the yarn, the more gathers the ruff can have.

SHAWL COLLAR

This is generally worked in ribbing. The two sides of the collar overlap at the front, and are fixed to a tapered or square neckline. The outer edges are kept straight. Either pick up the stitches and work the collar transversely, if the neckline is square, or work it separately and sew it later to the neckline. In the latter case, work a straight strip if the neckline is square, and a double-wedged strip if the neckline is tapered: start at one end, increasing on one of the sides to obtain a tapering that matches the one worked at the front of the garment, continue straight for a length that will go round the back of the neck, and decrease on the same side as you increased, following the same sequence, for a symmetrical tapering.

STRAIGHT COLLAR

Pick up the stitches from a round neckline, and work in ribbing or a flat stitch for the required length. When working in ribbing, the last row and the cast-off row might need to be in a flat stitch pattern, such as garter stitch, to open up the edge.

WING COLLAR

As for straight collar, but just before reaching the collar's folding line, work a few increases at either side of the neck. Alternatively, work regular increases at the edges.

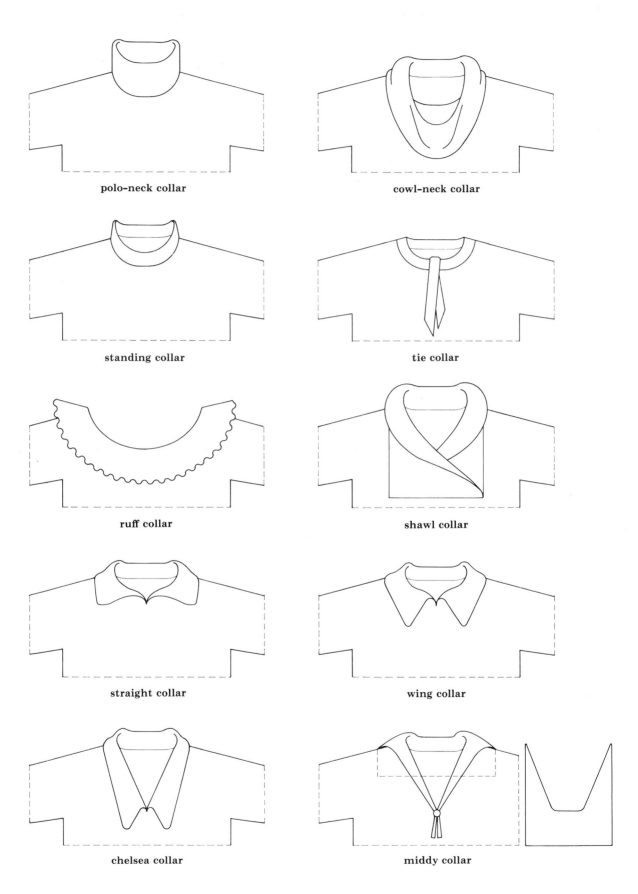

polo-neck collar

cowl-neck collar

standing collar

tie collar

ruff collar

shawl collar

straight collar

wing collar

chelsea collar

middy collar

102

CHELSEA COLLAR

This is worked in the same way as for a wing collar but in this case pick up the stitches around a V-neckline.

MIDDY COLLAR

This is worked separately and then joined to a V-neckline. Start work at the wider end, and shape as for diagram. When casting off the central stitches, follow the same shape as the back of the neckline. The two wedge-shaped sides can be just as long as the V-neck, or longer, in which case they will need a small band to tie them at the end of the V. Join the collar to the neckline with a backstitch seam, placing the collar right inside the finished garment, so that the right side of the collar is against the wrong side of the garment. The seam is then worked on the right-side of the garment, and the collar is turned and blocked so that it hides the seam.

POCKETS

Pockets can either be worked separately and then sewn to the finished garment, or they can be knitted-in. When the pockets are on the wrong side of the work, and only a slit shows, picking up the stitches for the base and the sides of the pocket lining gives the best results; pockets worked in this way are elastic, strong and very neat. If you do not feel confident enough to pick up the side stitches, try at least to pick up those for the base and later sew the sides with a slipstitch. If the garment has a horizontal change in stitch pattern (if, for instance, it has a border at the base of the body), it is best to pick up the stitches for the base of the lining from the line where the stitch pattern changes; it will then show less. The slit of this type of pocket may or may not be emphasized by a border. The border can only be knitted at the same time as the main section of the garment when the same size needles are to be used, and when the slit is horizontal or vertical. Otherwise, leave the stitches on a holder

and knit the border when the rest is finished. Sew the sides to the main section or, preferably, use knitted joins.

Applied pockets are easier: they are knitted separately, and can even be positioned when the garment is finished and can be tried on. The only difficulty is how to sew them so that they look neat and are strong. To turn the edges in is not a very good idea because it creates unwanted thicknesses. One possibility is to work a border with turned corners. The pocket is then sewn from the wrong side of work with a backstitch, making sure that no stitches show on the right side. This means that the stitch used for the border must be fairly thick: moss stitch, garter stitch or ribbing with an invisible casting on or off would be very suitable. Other possibilities are to work a crochet corded edging, or to trim the pocket with a bias band. Both these solutions would give a strong, thick edge, easy to sew from the wrong side of work.

Knitted flaps are best avoided. They tend to curl and look too bulky and fussy. They also lack crispness.

APPLIED PATCH POCKETS

These can have any shape and be of any size. Work them separately and fix them as explained above.

Assuming the pocket has only four sides, if it has been worked in a flat stitch pattern the border or edging need only be applied to the three sides to be sewn up. If the stitch pattern is not flat, all four sides will have to be edged.

PICKED-UP PATCH POCKETS

These can be square or tapered. After finishing the work, pick up the appropriate number of stitches for the base and sides, working on the right side of work, and proceed as explained on page 24. These pockets need a flat border at the top, unless they are all knitted in a flat stitch pattern.

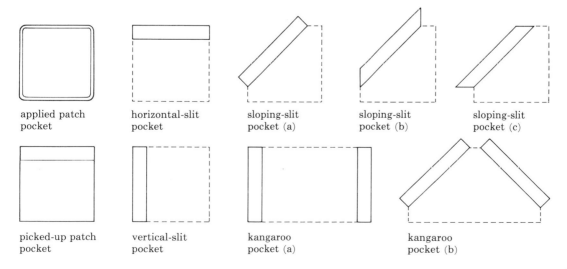

| applied patch pocket | horizontal-slit pocket | sloping-slit pocket (a) | sloping-slit pocket (b) | sloping-slit pocket (c) |

| picked-up patch pocket | vertical-slit pocket | kangaroo pocket (a) | kangaroo pocket (b) |

HORIZONTAL-SLIT POCKETS

Work normally until you reach the top end of the pocket, or the lower edge of the border if this is to be knitted in different size needles. Cast off pocket or leave its stitches on a holder. Leave all the other stitches on holders, too. Working on the wrong side, pick up the stitches for the base and sides of the lining, and knit the lining until the row on the holders is reached. Now work across the full width, knitting first the appropriate side of the main section, then the lining, then the rest of the main section.

For extra strength, pick up two stitches more than needed to give the correct width, one from each side. When joining the lining to the main section, knit together this stitch and the adjoining stitch from the main section.

SLOPING-SLIT POCKETS

Work the main section to the lower end of the slit. For pockets with a slant to the right, put all the stitches to the left of the pocket on a holder. For pockets with a slant to the left, put all the stitches to the right of the pocket on a holder. Continue working the remaining stitches, shaping the slit as if it were a dart, until the top of the slit is reached. Leave the stitches on holders, using a separate holder for the slit.

Start the lining as for horizontal-slit pockets, but join in the stitches left on the first holder when you reach the lower end of the slit. At the top of the slit, join in the rest of the main-section stitches. If the lining and the main section overlap, knit together one stitch from each of them, as you would do for a hem.

When the main section is finished, pick up the slit stitches and knit a border as explained for horizontal-slit pockets (a), or cast them off and work an edging. If you would prefer the ends of the border to be vertical (b), increase one stitch at every row at the top end and decrease one stitch at every row at the lower. For horizontal ends (c), decrease at the top and increase at the lower end.

VERTICAL-SLIT POCKETS

Divide the work at the beginning of the slit as for sloping-slit pockets, and continue knitting the side of the main section that includes the pocket. Either knit a border or work a chain selvedge on the pocket side. Once you reach the top of the slit, leave the stitches on a holder.

Pick up the stitches for the lining and work until you reach the lower end of the slit. Or, if the pocket is just as deep as the slit, pick up the stitches at that level. Join in the stitches left on the first holder, and knit across full width until you reach the top end of the slit. Join in the stitches on the second holder. Knit together one stitch from the lining and one stitch from the main section, as for hems, for the whole length of the overlap.

When the main section is finished, pick up the

stitches and knit the pocket border, or trim as necessary.

KANGAROO POCKETS

These are large pockets with a slit on each side, and are always placed at the front of a garment, in a fairly high, central position.

Knit them as vertical or sloping slit pockets with two symmetrical openings.

SKIRTS

Because knitted skirts are far less common than knitted tops, you might feel strongly inclined to think of shapes commonly used for skirts made out of cloth, when first thinking of knitting one. Again, the advice is: forget what can be done with cloth, and any dressmaking experience you might have. Now you are *knitting*.

Skirts can either be knitted in rounds, avoiding seams, or flat, in two or more pieces. Whichever way you choose, you do not need to restrict the shaping to a few darts at the top and a few decreases along the seams. A knitted skirt can be shaped all along its length, following twenty different lines, and still have only two seams, or no seams at all. This can be achieved by simply decreasing at regular intervals, if you are working upwards, or increasing at regular intervals, if you are working downwards. How often to increase or decrease will depend on whether your design requires wide or narrow panels but, whether you are knitting flat or in rounds, it is a good idea to pinpoint the lines where the shapings are taking place with markers. Skirts can also be knitted transversely, and still be wider at the lower edge than at the waist. This time, the shapings are achieved with darts which are as long as the skirt itself. Their frequency and depth will vary with the amount of flare desired.

Pleated skirts are not very satisfactory, because it is impossible to give them the crispness achieved with cloth unless one indulges in knitting acrobatics or endless sewing with matching cotton. An illusion of pleats, however, can easily be achieved by working narrow panels separated by two or three stitches in reverse stocking stitch.

The top of wide skirts can be kept elastic, so as to prevent the need for petersham bands, zips and other fasteners. The necessary adjusting to the wearer's waist can be achieved with a change in stitch pattern, so that the waist is tightly ribbed. See also 'Waistbands'.

To make a skirt fit more tightly just below the waist, increase the frequency of the shapings over the last 5–8cm (2–3in), or change to a more elastic stitch pattern. If neither of these solutions is desirable, change to needles one or two sizes smaller. This will give a tension that would normally be too tight but, if the stitch pattern is

Pompon skirt in hand-spun wool (see page 157)

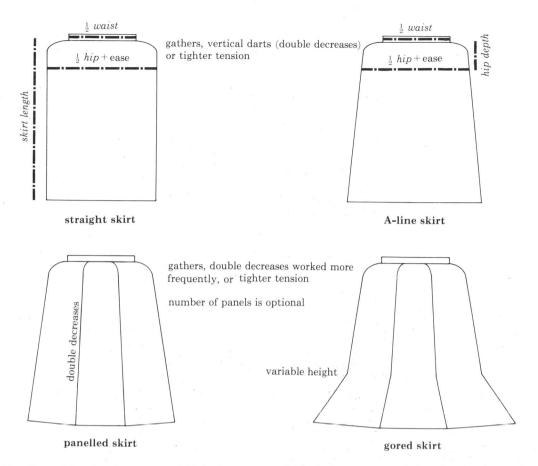

straight skirt

A-line skirt

panelled skirt

gored skirt

not badly affected by the change, it will be a lesser evil than a badly fitting garment.

For a good fit round the seat, make sure that the skirt gives a full *hip* measurement 5cm (2in) above the point where it is actually needed.

The lower edge of a skirt should be flat so that it will not curl. If the main stitch pattern is not flat, knit a border in a different pattern. Use hems only as a last resort. Do not use ribbing for the border —unless the whole skirt is ribbed—because it would gather the edge in.

Finally make sure the tension is right. Skirts are long projects, and it is very tempting to use needles thicker than required. Unfortunately, loosely knitted skirts lose their shape even faster than jumpers and jackets, and a loose skirt soon becomes useless.

STRAIGHT SKIRT
This is just a simple tube, gathered at the waist. It can be tight or loose fitting but, in either case, some decreases or a change to an elastic stitch pattern above the hips will reduce the amount of gathering.

A-LINE SKIRT
This is wider at the base than at the waist. It has only two lines of decreases, one at each side,

Little girl's red coat, boy's bomber jacket and girl's square-necked striped top (see pages 157 and 158)

which is not very satisfactory because the two lines are longer than the rest of the skirt and they tend to sag. To avoid this, either the lower edge has to be worked with a slight curve, which might not suit the design, or a ribbon has to be sewn in, on the wrong side of the seams, to shorten them. This has to be followed by careful blocking, in order to spread the shrinkage evenly over the sides.

PANELLED SKIRT
The panels are outlined by a series of double decreases and can be worked together or separately. The shapings can be made nearly invisible or form a prominent part of the design. It is easy to work in ribbed panels, either keeping the panels constant and decreasing the number of stitches between panels, or vice versa.

GORED SKIRT
This is similar to a panelled skirt but the panels have more pronounced shapings on the lower end, increasing the overall width of the skirt.

DRESSES
Simply combine any of the shapes given for the body and sleeves with one of the shapes given for skirts. Or, easier still, lengthen one of the bodies to dress length.

Dresses can either be left loose at the waist or tied with a belt, or they can be made to fit tightly.

107

This is best achieved with a change to an elastic stitch pattern.

COATS

Again, combine a body with a skirt but, obviously, work the front in two halves. In general, only straight and A-line skirts are used for coats.

TROUSERS

Most of the following shapes are only for babies, as they are designed to take the extra bulk of the nappy or diaper, but the last one can also be used for older children and adults.

Trousers can be worked flat or in rounds. In the latter case, work a couple of tubes for the legs and, depending on what shape you are knitting, knit one tube, cast on for the crotch, knit the other tube, cast on again and continue with a single, larger tube, or work a line of double increases or decreases at the top of the leg tubes, and knit one leg after the other to make the larger tube.

When working flat, two sections are needed. These can be either front and back, joined with side seams, or right and left legs, joined with central seams. Central seams show less, except with small babies that spend most of the day in a cot or pram.

The waist will need some sort of finish to keep it in place, which could just be a ribbed border or, for babies, a drawstring (see also 'Waistbands'). For dungarees, add a bib and straps over the shoulders. Whatever its finish, the front of the waist should be straight, but the back should have a curve to make it longer at the centre. This is to make sure that the trousers stay in place when bending down.

Long legs usually end straight, in which case the base needs to be knitted in a flat stitch. With babies, however, it is frequent practice to end the legs gathered in a cuff, to keep them in place.

BABY BRIEFS

These are worked in one piece, starting with the front waist and finishing with the back waist. The decreases at the front can be more or less sharp. The sharper they are, the more the baby's legs will show. The increases at the back are far more regular: one stitch at either side on every row, or two stitches at either side every two rows. A border is usually worked in rounds around the leg openings after sewing the side seams.

BABY SLIT-LEG BRIEFS

These are also worked in one piece, starting with the front waist and finishing with the back waist, but this time front and back have the same shape. The front has two slits for the baby's legs. A border can be worked in rounds around the slits.

STRAIGHT-CROTCH BABY TROUSERS

These are most often worked with short legs, and in this way they are an alternative to briefs. They do not fit as nicely as the other types of baby trousers, but they are the easiest for beginners to knit.

If worked as front and back (a), the two half-legs are worked first. Once the top of the legs is reached, they are joined by working first one half-leg, then increasing the appropriate number of stitches for the crotch, then working the second half-leg.

If worked as right and left (b), knit two identical pieces, starting with one leg, increasing at either side for half the crotch width, and finishing with a slant for the back waist, which has to be on the right side on one of the pieces, and on the left side on the other piece.

TAPERED-LEG TROUSERS

These trousers are common in all leg lengths. They are worked very similarly to straight-crotch trousers, the only difference being that the stitches needed for the crotch are increased at regular intervals along the leg (either along the whole leg, as illustrated, or only at the top of the leg, as shown by the dotted line), instead of all at once.

GUSSET-CROTCH TROUSERS

These trousers are worked without any increases or decreases, and the crotch is formed by means of a diamond-shaped gusset. The dimensions of this gusset are not critical; for a 6–12 month-old baby, it should measure 5–7cm (2–2½in) in width, and 7–8cm (around 3in) in depth. Knit it starting with 3–4 stitches, and increasing one stitch on either side, every two rows, until the full width and half the depth are obtained. Work two rows straight, and start decreasing, following the same sequence used for increasing, until only 3–4 stitches remain. Cast off.

When sewing up, start by tacking the gusset. Join the cast-off end to the meeting point of the legs at the front and the cast-on end to the meeting point of the legs at the back. Join the sides of the gusset to the corresponding leg sides. The two sides of each leg will meet at the widest points of the gusset. Now tack the leg seams, starting at the base to make sure that one of the sides is not longer than the other at that point. If one of them is longer at the top, that means that one of the leg sides was pulled more than the other when tacking the gusset. Adjust as necessary before sewing.

ORDINARY TROUSERS

The difference between these and the last three types of trousers is that the crotch is shaped with decreases rather than increases. This means that the garment legs fit much more loosely on babies but it makes them suitable for older children and adults, unburdened by nappies. The legs can be of any length. They can also be tapered or straight.

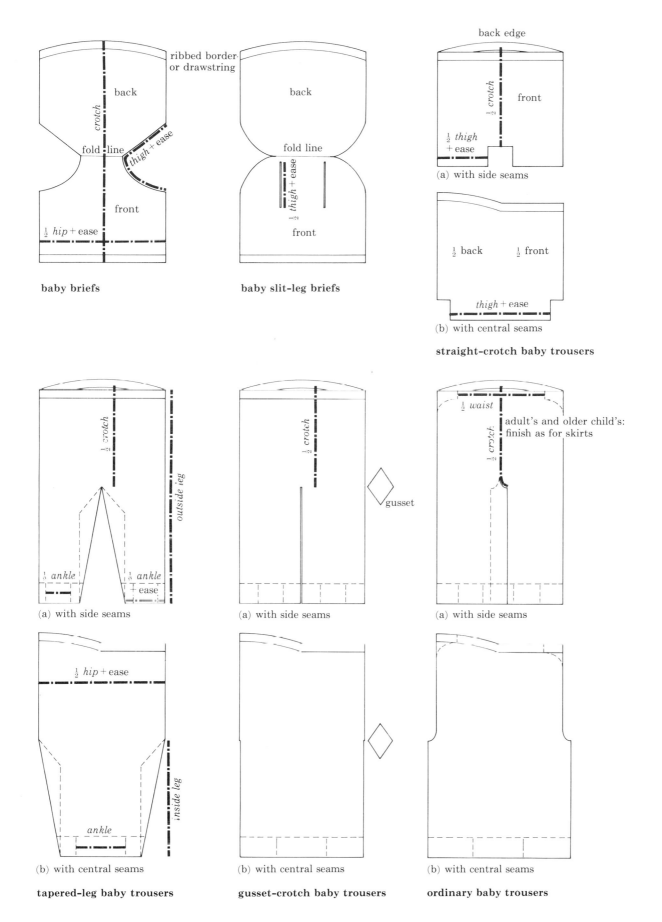

baby briefs

ribbed border or drawstring

back

crotch

fold line

thigh + ease

front

$\frac{1}{2}$ *hip* + ease

baby slit-leg briefs

back

fold line

$\frac{1}{2}$ *thigh* + ease

front

straight-crotch baby trousers

back edge

$\frac{1}{2}$ *crotch*

front

$\frac{1}{2}$ *thigh* + ease

(a) with side seams

$\frac{1}{2}$ back $\frac{1}{2}$ front

thigh + ease

(b) with central seams

tapered-leg baby trousers

$\frac{1}{2}$ *crotch*

outside leg

$\frac{1}{4}$ *ankle* $\frac{1}{4}$ *ankle* + ease

(a) with side seams

$\frac{1}{2}$ *hip* + ease

inside leg

ankle

(b) with central seams

gusset-crotch baby trousers

$\frac{1}{2}$ *crotch*

gusset

(a) with side seams

gusset

(b) with central seams

ordinary baby trousers

$\frac{1}{2}$ *waist*

adult's and older child's: finish as for skirts

$\frac{1}{2}$ *crotch*

(a) with side seams

(b) with central seams

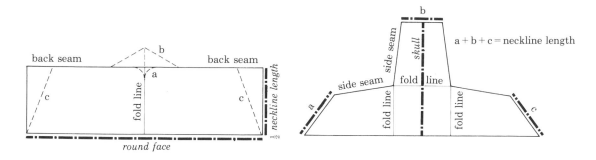

pointed hood   **rounded hood**

HOODS

Hoods are good additions to winter garments, but can also be used as decorative elements. They are usually worked separately and then attached to a round or high V-neck, but pointed hoods can also be picked up from one side of the neckline and grafted to the other side.

POINTED HOOD

The simplest of all hoods, it consists of a long rectangle folded along its centre line, with one of its sides becoming a back seam. Vary this basic hood by shortening (a) or lengthening (b) the fold line, to obtain hoods that are less or more pointed (see dotted lines). Another variation consists of tapering the sides (c), for a tighter fit around the neck.

ROUNDED HOOD

These are most often used for babies and small children because they fit tightly round the head. Start work at the front. Fold along the three lines indicated in the illustration, to obtain two back seams.

CHAPTER 7
Choosing Styles

Style refers to the way shapes are put together and, in particular, to how they are constructed. It is the variation in style that makes it possible for a limited number of shapes to offer what amounts to an unlimited number of knitting possibilities.

CONSTRUCTING SHAPES
The most obvious elements that will make two garments look different, even if they have used exactly the same shapes, are texture, colour and stitch pattern. Not so obvious, but equally important, are direction of work, stitch-pattern combinations and borders.

DIRECTION OF WORK
Generally, knitting is carried out from bottom to top (1), but it is also possible to work from top to bottom (2), transversely (3), diagonally (4) or forming chevrons (5 and 6).

To work diagonally, cast on three stitches to form corner A, and increase regularly to obtain two straight sides, until corners B and C are reached (one will probably be reached earlier than the other). To turn the corners, start decreasing for side B–D just as you increased for side A–C, and decrease for side C–D just as you increased for side A–B.

To calculate increases, decreases and shapings, follow the general instructions given in Chapter 8, with the following changes. Calculate how many stitches and rows the section would need if it was to be knitted from bottom to top. Now, draw the section on a sheet of tracing paper placed on top of the appropriate page of special

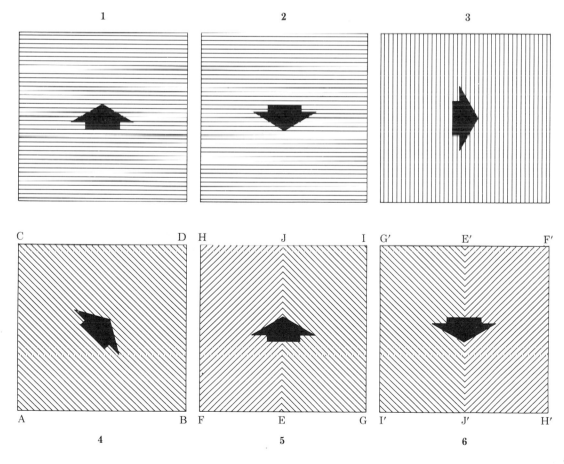

graph paper, and trace an oblique line from corner B to corner C, or to somewhere along the side A–C. This line will fix the direction of the rows, and its inclination should be the one that fits in best with the overall design. Turn the tracing paper so that the oblique line is made to lie on top of one of the thicker lines dividing rows on the graph paper, and corner A is on top of one of the thicker lines dividing stitches. Proceed, now, in the ordinary way.

To work chevrons pointing upwards (5), start with 3 stitches. These will now correspond to the spot marked E, at the base of the section. Work three sets of regular increases: one set of single increases at either end of the rows, and one set of double increases in the middle. The number of stitches cast on at the beginning could vary if the double increases were to have a wider central axis. F and G are reached at the same time and, from that moment, one stitch is decreased at either end of the rows, every time a double increase is worked at the centre. After reaching J, divide the work and finish both sides separately, decreasing for H–J and I–J as you increased for E–F and E–G, and continuing the regular decreases at the sides. To calculate increases, decreases and shapings, take half the section say E–G–I–J, and proceed as for diagonals. This will give you one side only, but the other one is identical, so the only adjustment will be to work double increases in the centre instead of the calculated single increases.

To work chevrons pointing downwards (6), the easiest method is to proceed as for chevrons pointing upwards, but from top to bottom instead of from bottom to top. These chevrons are very often combined with V-necklines. This means that the front of the body does not start at E', but lower down, at a row long enough to form the correct neckline shape.

Garments worked in diagonals or chevrons usually have straight borders, knitted on stitches picked up from base or sides.

STITCH-PATTERN COMBINATIONS
Combining two or more stitch patterns can have dramatic effects on shape itself. If you take any of the sections explained in Chapter 6 and you knit strategically placed panels in a stitch pattern that takes in, or pulls up, while working the rest flat, you will create arrangements of gathers that will effectively give a three-dimensional section. Obviously, you must not allow extra stitches or rows for the panels; otherwise, the section would be its usual flat self.

BORDERS
Borders, also called *welts*, are bands placed around the free edges of a garment to prevent it from curling or stretching, or to give it a neater finish. Sometimes, they also serve the additional purpose of gathering the main sections.

Borders are most often knitted on needles one or two sizes smaller than would normally be used for the yarn and stitch pattern involved, to make them firmer than the rest of the garment.

When the main section is knitted as a continuation of the border (or vice versa), changing needles is very straightforward. When the border is finished, knit the first row of the main section with the needle that has the border stitches in your left hand, and one of the main-section needles in your right hand. Any necessary increases or decreases should be worked on this row. Once the row is finished, continue work using both main-section needles.

When the border is at the right or left edge of work, you have three options: knit the border and main section together, using for the border a stitch pattern that gives a tighter tension with the same size needles: for instance, use Twisted Ribbing for the border and Stocking Stitch for the main section. (See 'Working Two Stitch Patterns Together' for more details.) You can also knit the border separately, in the same direction as the main section, and join them afterwards. Or you can pick up the stitches from the edge of the main section and knit the border transversely.

If the main section is already flat and strong, a proper border may not be necessary. In this case, crochet edgings or bias-band trimmings are often used, if the edge needs a better finish. Apply these edgings after the garment has been put together, so that they can run across the edge of the seams.

Suitable stitch patterns for borders are: most types of ribbing, garter stitch, moss stitch, welting and fur stitch. When a large border in one of these patterns would not blend in well with the design, try working only a couple of rows in ribbing or garter stitch. Ribbing will tend to pull in the edge, while garter stitch will tend to stretch it. The first effect will be best for, say, the bottom of a jumper, and the second for the bottom of a coat.

PUTTING SHAPES TOGETHER
Most common shapes can be put together without any problems, but it is useful to keep the following points in mind.

Sleeves and body are more easily matched if they have something in common: both flat or gathered at the base, both sharply tapered in the same direction; both fitting tightly or loosely at the underarm, etc. However, this should not be taken to extremes: there is no need to limit straight bodies to straight sleeves, for instance.

All necklines do not match equally well with all shoulders. Avoid those that are obviously going to give you problems; boat necks with raglan sleeves are a good example.

Similarly, not all necklines go well with all yokes. Round necks can normally be used with any yoke, but, in general, it is preferable to use necklines that are parallel to at least part of the yoke's outline. For instance, use a tapered neck with a tapered yoke, or a straight neck with a square yoke.

Joins betweens shapes should be as simple as possible. Avoid awkward corners, narrow strips that belong neither here nor there, crooked joins, etc. Mix only shapes you fully understand and feel confident in tackling. The number of these will soon grow with practice.

LAYING OUT AND MATCHING UP MOTIFS

When a garment is more than just a series of faintly textured shapes put together, it is important that stitch patterns, colours, textures, etc are laid out in an organized way. This, in turn, will affect the position of pockets, necklines, collars and seams. It might also affect the dimensions or the choice of individual shapes.

The colour illustrations, and the line drawings at the end of this chapter, give examples of motifs laid out in a variety of shape combinations. Each page of line drawings has a 'theme': sleeveless and short-sleeve garments, jumpers, cardigans, coats and jackets, skirts and dresses, baby and toddler garments.

The shaded areas in the line drawings represent one of many different possibilities: a change in stitch pattern, texture or colour; a band of Jacquard, stripes, bobbles, floral motifs or embroidery, rows of eyelets threaded with ribbon or contrasting yarn; or anything else you can think of. The dividing lines are shown straight, but they could also be scalloped or in zigzag. The unshaded areas may be plain, textured or coloured, but in general they are made to stand out less than the motifs. When borders are shown unshaded, they can be in the same or a different stitch pattern from the other unshaded areas, providing they are not over-emphasized.

It is impossible to give strict design recipes because so many variables are involved, which is fortunate because design recipes too often lead to stale results. The following notes, however, might prove of help as reference points.

Shape Let the general shape dictate where the motifs should go. Make use of outlines offered by seams, shoulders, necklines, pockets, etc.

Motifs Be bold. If a motif needs to be large or small, make it large or small. Do not make 'average' or 'medium' something that should be large or small.

Positioning of motifs When laying out motifs, better proportions are obtained if dimensions are interrelated as much as possible. For instance, start a motif at one-third, one-half or three-quarters of the total length; work a Jacquard band twice the width of the ribbing; make a scoop neck two-thirds the total shoulder width;

make the distance between stripes, alternately, one-quarter and three-quarters of the stripe width; start the neckline at four-fifths of the total length, etc.

Increases and decreases Use visible and decorative increases and decreases as motifs, for instance along raglan seams (19), when the garment has a very plain texture. Otherwise, increase or decrease at the edge, or use those techniques that will give you a no-fuss, sloping band of stocking stitch, two or three stitches wide, all along the edge.

Borders Preferably, use the same type of border throughout and, at the most, use only two types: one for elastic edges and one for non-elastic edges. Do not keep varying the border's depth. If narrow and wide borders are needed, make the wide border a multiple of the narrow one; say, two, three or six times as deep.

Blending in seams Blend seams with the rest of the garment in one of two ways. Either emphasize them, using them as the edge or the axis of a motif; for instance, work a band at the top of the sleeves in garments with dropped shoulders (33), or use the seam to outline colour areas (26), or work a line of bobbles at either side of raglan-shoulder seams, or trim the seams with bias bands (36). Or, if you prefer to hide the seams, adjust their position so that they are where they will show the least with the particular stitch pattern used. This may mean making the garment *slightly* larger or smaller than you first intended, so that each section can be made to accommodate the appropriate number of stitch pattern repeats. It might also mean making the front fractionally larger than the back.

Seam position Allowing for the adjustments just mentioned, seams usually coincide with the sides of the shapes described in Chapter 6. However, they do not really need to be in those places. A garment with side panels, for example, could have four seams: two between front and side panels and two between back and side panels (22), instead of just two seams between front and back. This is especially advisable if the panels need to be knitted on different size needles. To find out the shape of the new sections, make a scaled drawing of front and back, marking the side panels. Cut the drawing with a pair of scissors, join the 'seams' with tape, and cut along the side-panel lines.

Seams and motifs Make motifs and stitch patterns meet neatly at the seams. If the motifs are at a distance from the seam, try to make this distance the same at either side. Motifs and stitch patterns can be made to meet at a join in two ways. Either the two sides end at the same point

113

in the sequence, in which case both sides of the seam will look symmetrical; or one of the sides can continue the sequence where the other one has left it, as if the seam did not exist.

Seams and all-over patterns   If all-over patterns do not match perfectly at some important seam, eg at the shoulders, you can use the pattern only for one of the sections of the garment and leave the other section(s) plain (18); continue both sections in pattern, if you want, after the seam. Or, you can work in pattern only those parts of the garment that do not have problem seams (27). Or, you can work a band in a different colour, texture or stitch pattern along the seam, which is an example of a widely-used design trick: if you cannot join it, break it (7).

Shapings   Do not interrupt the flow of a motif with shapings and, if possible, relate motifs to shapings. For instance, make the top of a band across the chest and sleeves coincide with the beginning of the armhole shapings (52).

Stripes   Striped garments should be plotted carefully, so that seams and shapings do not break the rhythm of the stripes (25).

Bands   When matching horizontal bands run across body and sleeves, it is safer, from a design point of view, either to keep all the bands at precisely the same height (28), or to place the sleeve bands at a very different height from the body bands. For example, the body bands could be just above the bottom border, and the sleeve bands could be by the armholes (33).

Oblique lines   Make sure any oblique lines (38) can be easily worked: make them move, for instance, one stitch further every row, or every two rows, or every eight rows. If the whole garment is to be covered in oblique lines (32), try working it diagonally or forming chevrons.

Optical effects   Motifs can be used to emphasise or play down specific areas of garments. A wide band at the base of the body (15), for instance, can make the hips look larger if it has horizontal stripes, is of a lighter colour than the rest, or has a heavier texture than the rest. On the other hand, the same band can make the hips look smaller if it has vertical stripes, is darker, or has a finer texture than the rest. The same would apply to motifs elsewhere. The emphasis on specific areas can be taken a step further with double layers. If, for example, the extra emphasis should be on the shoulders, try a raglan with two shoulder caps, one knitted with the sleeve in the usual way, and the other, slightly wider, worked separately and joined at the seams (37).

1

6

11

2

7

12

3

8

13

4

9

14

5

10

15

16

21

17

22

18

23

19

24

20

25

116

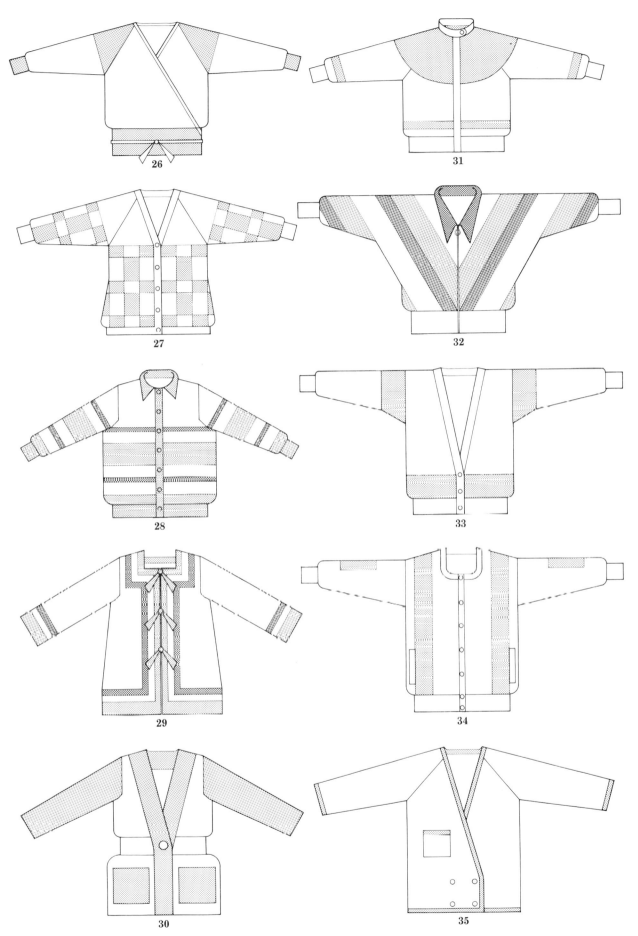

26

31

27

32

28

33

29

34

30

35

117

36

37

38

39

40

41

42

43

47

44

48

45

46

49

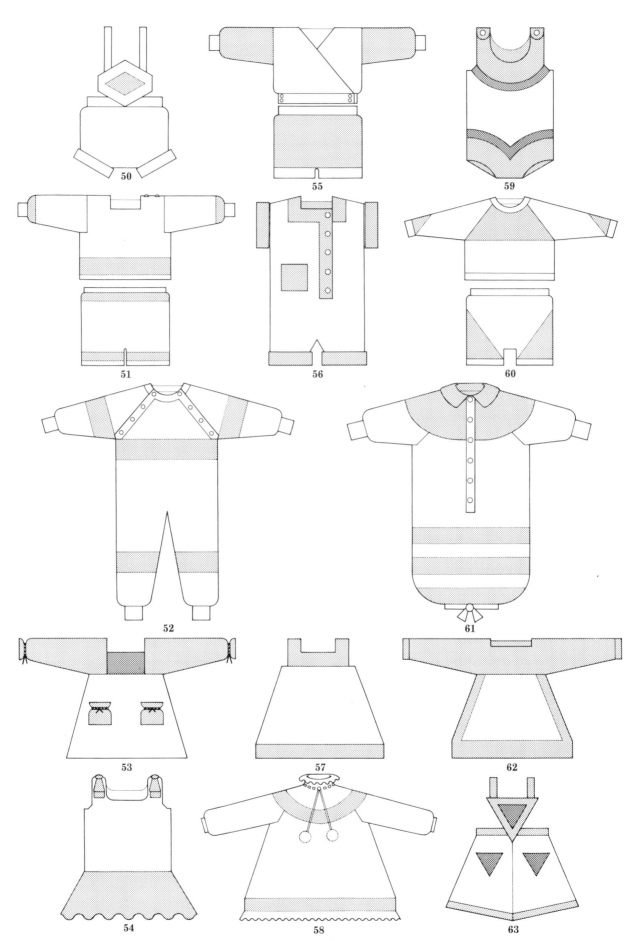

50

55

59

51

56

60

52

61

53

57

62

54

58

63

120

CHAPTER 8
Drawing Visual Patterns

Very often, people who possess no drawing skills are nervous about designing their own garments, fearing that it will be beyond their abilities. This book caters for two types of knitter: those who are eager to draw and those who are not. If you are in the second group, you will only be asked, at the most, to do two things. First, after choosing a style—which could be one of those illustrated to save you drawing it—you will have to draw a sketch for every section that needs knitting. These sketches can be as good or as bad as you can produce them, using only paper and pencil. They certainly do not need to be to scale, and the lines do not need to be perfectly straight. They are only for you to write down your own instructions, and to keep by your side while you are knitting.

Secondly, and this is only if the style requires any tapered or curved shapings, you will need to draw straight lines and curves on special graph paper. These will be to calculate the necessary increases and decreases. The alternative would be to do some arithmetical calculations, which most people find more confusing and difficult to master than elementary drawings.

If, however, you are interested in exploring the much wider range of possibilities offered to those who can draw, you will find details in this chapter on how to draw your chosen style to scale, and on how to draw details of sections and motifs. Some people go as far as enlarging each section to full size, and then cutting them out, so that they can have a direct check for their work. It is not really necessary but, if it helps you, go ahead.

A final word for anyone who might still not be fully convinced that knitting drawings are within everyone's reach. Knitting is a very ancient craft that has been practised for many centuries in many parts of the world. Not until comparatively recently have knitters in general been able to read and write. Traditionally, knitting was understood and handed down from generation to generation—and still is in many places—by word-of-mouth and through more or less crude *drawings*. If illiterate people have used a method of communication with success, over centuries, it is to be assumed that those who can read will be able to use it just as well.

RELATIONSHIPS BETWEEN GARMENT AND BODY MEASUREMENTS
To obtain a perfect fit, a garment's measurements have to be based on the body measurements of the person who is going to wear it. These should be taken with a dressmaker's tape. When taking your own measurements you will need somebody else to help you, because it is impossible to measure oneself accurately.

All measurements should be taken wearing the same amount of clothes that are to be worn underneath the finished garment.

Some body measurements can be used directly on the garment, while others need a certain proportion added or subtracted to allow for *ease*, a vague term indicating how tightly or loosely a garment will fit. How much to allow for ease depends on the measurement itself, the thickness of the yarn, and the type of fit desired. The Ease Allowance table in the Appendix gives all the necessary details. Do not allow for shrinkage at this stage; this can be done, if necessary, when calculating the tension.

Measuring children has the added problem of having to allow for growth. Obviously, it is impossible to give a true prediction of how much a child will grow in one year, but the two tables on Growth Allowance, also in the Appendix, will help you make a more informed guess. Another table, Babies' Measurements from Birth to Three Months, will help you overcome the impossibility of measuring a baby before it is born—the only case that justifies the use of average measurements.

When taking measurements, the body should be kept in an upright, natural position, and the tape should be held so that it is neither loose nor tight.

A number of the following measurements refer to the 'bone at the top of the spine'. This is a slightly protruding, easy to locate bone, above which the neck rotates.

Round the neck (1) Might be necessary for some round necks or yokes. Also for some high collars. Measure round the lowest part of the neck.

Front neck depth (2) This can only be an approximate figure, but it is necessary for most necklines. Measure from the top of the shoulder to the desired deepest point in neckline. For tight round necks, the depth will be that of the lowest point in the round-the-neck measurement.

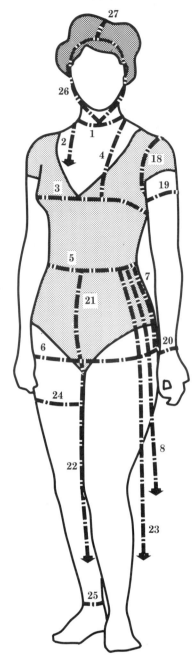

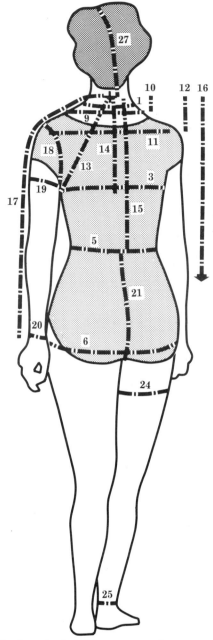

Bust or **chest** (**3**)   The tape should go all the way round the body. Women should be measured around the fullest part of the bust, keeping the tape high at the back. Men and children should be measured with the chest expanded. Add an allowance for ease as shown in the Appendix on page 151.

Bust depth (**4**)   Necessary for women's garments, but only when the bustline is critical; for instance, to make sure that a stripe, a change in pattern, or the beginning of a yoke does not coincide with it, or to place darts. It is taken from the shoulder down.

Waist (**5**)   In general, this will only be needed for skirts and trousers, or for garments with a

tight band of ribbing round the waist. The tape should go round the natural waistline.

Hip (**6**)   For skirts, trousers, dresses and long jackets or tops. It should be measured round the fullest part. Add an allowance for ease as shown in the Appendix.

Hip depth (**7**)   This applies to the same garments as for *hip* measurements. From waistline to hipline, measured along the side of the body.

Skirt length (**8**)   Hold one end of the tape at the waist, and let the rest of the tape hang loose

Heavy winter coat in Unst pure wool (see page 158)

122

over the body's side; measure desired length. It is a good idea to measure the length while wearing a favourite skirt and shoes of the appropriate type and height for the garment. Allow for heavy skirts that might tend to get longer under their own weight.

Neck width (9) Place tape across back, and measure the distance between the two points at which you want the neckline to rest on the shoulders.

Back neck depth (10) This can only be taken approximately. Measure from the bone at the top of the spine to the *neck-width* line. Write down zero if the *neck-width* line goes across the bone.

Shoulder to shoulder (11) Essential for set-in shoulders, and useful for checking other types of shoulder. Place tape high and straight across back, from one shoulder to the other, but not quite reaching the edge of the shoulders. If you try on a good-fitting garment with set-in shoulders, you will understand what 'not quite reaching the edge' means.

Shoulder depth (12) Essential for set-in shoulders, and useful for other garments. It can only be taken approximately. Measure from the bone at the top of the spine to the *shoulder-to-shoulder* line.

Neck to underarm (13) Essential for raglans, but useful for other garments. Measure from the bone at the top of the spine to the point on your side at which you want the sleeve to meet the body of the garment. It can be anywhere along the side, between the underarm and the waist. Add one fifth of total *chest* or *bust* ease allowance, calculated as indicated in the Appendix.

Underarm depth (14) Essential for raglans when a style diagram will not be drawn. It can only be taken approximately. Measure from bone at top of spine to the point on the spine which is at the same height as the meeting point of body and sleeve in (13).

Waist length (15) Measure between bone at top of spine and waistline. If you want the garment to be full at the waist, allow for extra length.

Total length (16) Essential for all garments. From bone at top of spine to lower edge of garment. It is useful to try on a similar garment to decide whether the new one should be shorter or longer. Allow for heavy coats and dresses that might tend to get longer under their own weight.

Thick jumper in three shades of blue and sleeveless blue V-neck top (see page 158)

Neck to wrist (17) Essential for all garments with long sleeves. For those with shorter sleeves, adapt to *neck to sleeve edge*. Measure from bone at top of spine to wrist, keeping the arm hanging loose alongside the body, and taking the tape over the shoulder. Check both arms, as one could be longer than the other. Add as much as desired for full sleeve bases ending in tight cuffs.

Sleeve seam This measurement is extremely confusing and should therefore be avoided. Its use as the only way of indicating the length of the sleeve in many British knitting patterns has caused headaches to large numbers of knitters.

Round shoulder (18) Essential for set-in shoulders and useful for checking other shoulders. Place tape over shoulder, down under the underarm and up again over shoulder. The tape should not restrict the movement of the arm. Add an allowance for ease as shown in the Appendix.

Upper arm (19) Essential for all garments with sleeves. It is taken placing the tape around the fullest part of the arm, above the elbow. Add an allowance for ease as shown in the Appendix. It is closely related to *round shoulder*, since if less ease is given to the *round shoulder* than to the *upper arm* measurement, the sleeve will look tighter at the top than it should.

Wrist (20) Essential for garments with long sleeves. Add an allowance for ease as shown in the Appendix, but note that it is common to give more ease to the *wrist* than to the *upper arm*. When calculating tight cuffs, check that the cuff will stretch enough for the closed fist to go through without difficulty.

Crotch (21) Only necessary for trousers. Take tape from centre of waist at the front to centre of waist at the back, passing tape between legs. Flex your legs and bend over in order to make sure that you have freedom of movement; the tape measure should never be allowed to hide between the buttocks.

Inside leg (22) Only necessary for trousers. Measure from the point where the tape passed between the legs for *crotch*, to the desired lower edge of trousers. Check both legs, as one could be longer than the other.

Outside leg (23) Only necessary for trousers. Place tape at side of body, holding one end at waist. Let the rest of the tape hang loose. Measure down to the desired lower edge of trousers.

Thigh (24) Only necessary for trousers. Measure round the fullest part of the thigh. Add an ease allowance as shown in the Appendix.

125

Ankle (25) For baby trousers ending in cuffs. Ensure that the cuff will stretch enough for the foot to go through without difficulty. Add an ease allowance as shown in the Appendix.

Round face (26) Essential for hoods. Place end of tape on desired deepest point in neckline, which will generally be a round neck or a high V-neck, take tape round face and back to starting point. Hold tape as tightly or as loosely as you want the hood to be.

Skull (27) Essential for rounded hoods. Measure from highest point in (26) to *neck-width* line at back of neck.

DRAWING STYLE DIAGRAMS

These diagrams should give you a clear picture of what the garment will look like when finished. They are essential when you want to experiment with styles or motifs with any degree of complexity, or when you want to make doubly sure that motifs and shapes, complex or simple, will have the correct proportions.

If you are planning a simple everyday garment, ignore these diagrams. Instead, copy or adapt one of the styles illustrated in Chapter 7.

Style diagrams show the garment flat. This is the best way of showing shapes and motifs, but it makes the garments look much wider than they do when worn. You might find it odd at first, but you will soon adapt to it.

Generally, only a diagram of the front is needed, with perhaps a rough sketch of the back, not to scale. Sometimes, however, the back might be more important than the front, and rarer cases might require scaled diagrams of both front and back.

The illustration shows how to construct the body, and then how to construct the three most common types of shoulder: dropped, raglan and set-in. The general style is that of a long, mixed-body cardigan with medium-tapered sleeves and a wide-fitting neck. Once this garment is understood, it should not be difficult to follow similar processes for any of the shapes explained in Chapter 6.

Drawing style diagrams is not especially difficult, but it requires patience and critical thought; otherwise, there is no point in drawing them. Their function is to show whether the garment will look right or not, and therefore one has constantly to assess whether borders are too wide or too narrow, whether a neckline is too high or too low, etc.

When the outline is finished, it is time to lay out any motifs. This is done following the notes at the end of Chapter 7, and it often requires stitch counts and tension diagrams that are bound to have an effect on the general outline. For instance, a Jacquard band that needs to be a third of the total height might prove, after counting the number of rows involved, that it is over or under the required dimension; this will mean using a different band, or making the garment longer or shorter, as the case may be.

Although the illustrations have been drawn on a white background for clarity, the easiest way to draw style diagrams is on ordinary graph paper (see Equipment in Chapter 1). Each square is made to correspond to one centimetre (half an inch, or one inch if the squares are large enough). This avoids the need for rulers and set squares, and at the same time provides a guide for straight lines.

Before starting, cut off a narrow strip of graph paper for measuring lines that do not follow the graph lines.

Use a medium to soft pencil; they are best for drawing and erasing. Make your lines fine to start with, and thicken up the relevant ones once you are sure of them.

All necessary allowances for ease are understood to have been added when taking the body measurements.

CONSTRUCTING THE BODY

1. Draw a cross, to mark the position of the bone at the top of the spine, on the intersection of two of the lines at the centre top of your graph paper.
2. Extend the cross down, with a broken line, to indicate the centre line of the garment. Extend the cross sideways, also with a broken line, to indicate the neck.
3. Mark *waist length* on centre line, measuring from top cross, and draw a horizontal line through this mark. Mark one quarter of *bust* or *chest* measurement at either side of centre line, on horizontal line just drawn.
4. Mark *total length* on centre line, measuring from top cross, and draw a second horizontal line through this mark.
5. Mark *hip depth* on centre line, measuring from waistline, and draw a third horizontal line through it. Mark one quarter of *hip* measurement at either side of centre line, on horizontal line just drawn.
6. If the body is to have a border at the lower edge, mark tentative border depth on centre line, measuring from *total-length* line, and draw a fourth horizontal line through this mark.
7. At either side of centre line, join the mark for *bust* or *chest* measurement on waistline to the *hip* measurement on hipline. Extend this oblique line with a vertical line above the waist, and another vertical line below the hip.
8. Using the strip of graph paper as a measuring tape, mark *neck-to-underarm* measurement from top cross to upper vertical line.
9. If the border is to be in ribbing, draw the border narrower than the hips, and turn the side lines into small curves just above the border; this gives a more realistic effect, but does not imply

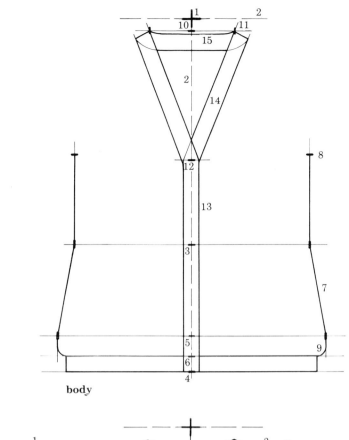

body

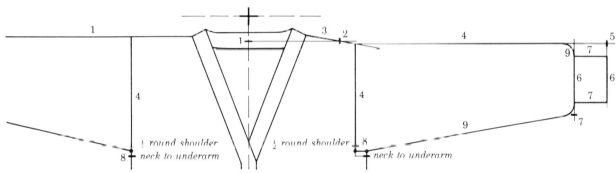

dropped shoulder (a)　　　　　　　　dropped shoulder (b)

½ round shoulder
neck to underarm

½ round shoulder
neck to underarm

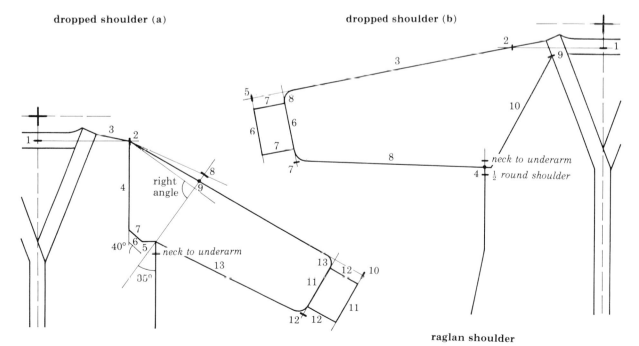

set-in shoulder

right angle

40°

35°

neck to underarm

raglan shoulder

neck to underarm
½ round shoulder

127

that the sides will have to be knitted with a curve.

10. Mark *back neck depth* on centre line, measuring from top cross, and draw a short horizontal line through this mark.

11. Mark half the *neck width* at either side of centre line, on horizontal line just drawn.

12. Mark *front neck depth* on centre line, measuring from top cross, and draw a very short horizontal line across this mark.

13. Mark half the tentative front-border width at either side of centre line, and draw the corresponding vertical lines for the border, between *front-neck-depth* and *total-length* lines.

14. Join the left front-border line to the right *neck-width* mark, and the right front-border line to the left *neck-width* mark. Mark border width at right angles from both these lines, and draw parallels to them to complete the borders.

15. To finish the neckline, join the two *neck-width* marks with a shallow curve, representing the back of the neckline. Draw a second curve, under and parallel to the first, at a distance equal to the border width. Join the points at which both curves cross the front borders, to show the border's folding line.

CONSTRUCTING DROPPED SHOULDERS

1. If the top of the body is to be cast off as a straight line (a), draw a horizontal line, starting at the outer edge of the neckline border, to indicate the sleeve's folding line. Omit steps 2 and 3 below.

If the top of the body is to be cast off following the natural shoulder slope (b), mark *shoulder depth* on centre line, and draw a horizontal line through this mark.

2. Mark half *shoulder-to-shoulder* measurement at either side of centre line, over horizontal line just drawn.

3. Join the outer edge of neckline border and the *shoulder-to-shoulder* mark. Extend line past this last mark.

4. Extend vertical lines defining the sides of the body upwards, until they reach the shoulder's folding line (a). For a smaller drop, make the vertical lines move nearer the centre line before extending them up (b). If working as for (b), draw a horizontal line starting at the point where the last two lines met, to mark the sleeve's folding line.

5. Mark the *neck-to-wrist* measurement on horizontal line, measuring from top cross, and following the shoulder slant if there is one.

6. Draw a vertical line from last mark down, and one parallel to this one at tentative border, or cuff, depth.

7. Mark half the *wrist* measurement on second vertical line, starting from the horizontal line. If the sleeve has a cuff requiring a smaller ease allowance than the base of the sleeve, mark half this measurement on both vertical lines, so that the cuff occupies a central position. Join the marks with horizontal lines.

8. Mark half the *upper-arm* measurement down the vertical line at the top of the sleeve. Ideally, it should coincide with the *neck-to-underarm* mark (a), or fall on the same horizontal line (b). If theory and reality are close, compromise on a spot between the two. If they are wide apart, check with the *round-shoulder* measurement (same ease as for *upper arm*!), to make sure that the sleeve will not be too tight at the top. From *shoulder-to-shoulder* mark (which in (a) should be determined, not along the real line, but along the sleeve's folding line instead) to *neck-to-underarm* mark, the distance should be half the *round-shoulder* measurement. If it is not, check whether you took the measurements correctly before proceeding any further. If the half *round-shoulder* mark falls near the *upper-arm* mark, compromise between these two. If it falls near the *neck-to-underarm* mark, you will have to widen the top of the sleeve. Draw a horizontal line through the *upper-arm* mark, and determine the point on the line that is at a distance of half *round shoulder* from the *shoulder-to-shoulder* mark. This will be the starting point of your increases (see also page 91).

9. Join point just determined to half-*wrist* mark. If the sleeve is gathered in a cuff, draw small curves near the cuff, for a more realistic effect.

CONSTRUCTING RAGLAN SHOULDERS

1. Mark *shoulder depth* on centre line, and draw a horizontal line through this mark.

2. Mark half the *shoulder-to-shoulder* measurement at either side of centre line, on horizontal line just drawn.

3. Join the outer edge of neckline border with the *shoulder-to-shoulder* mark. Extend line well past this last mark; it will indicate the sleeve's folding line.

4. Check whether the distance between *shoulder-to-shoulder* mark and previously made *neck-to-underarm* mark is half the *round-shoulder* measurement. If it is not, check that you took the measurements and ease allowances correctly. If necessary, find a compromise point between the two, along the side-of-body line.

5. Mark the *neck-to-wrist* measurement on the sleeve line, starting at top cross. Place the strip of graph paper from cross to outer edge of neckline border, and then along the sleeve's folding line.

6. Draw a line at right angles from the last mark, and another line parallel to this one at the tentative border, or cuff, depth. Use a book to obtain the right angle if you do not possess a protractor or set square.

7. Mark half the *wrist* measurement on the second of the two lines just drawn, starting from the sleeve's folding line. If the sleeve has a cuff requiring a smaller ease allowance than the base of the sleeve, mark half this measurement on both parallel lines, so that it occupies a central

position. Join the marks with lines parallel to the sleeve's folding line to indicate the cuff.

8. Join the half-*wrist* mark to the checked *neck-to-underarm* mark. If the sleeve is gathered in a cuff, draw small curves near the cuff for a more realistic effect.

9. Determine width at the top of the shoulder cap (see page 92); mark half this width, vertically, along the neckline border.

10. Join point just marked with checked *neck-to-underarm* mark, making the joining line end in a very short horizontal stretch at the underarm.

CONSTRUCTING SET-IN SHOULDERS

1. Mark *shoulder depth* on centre line, and draw a horizontal line through this mark.

2. Mark half the *shoulder-to-shoulder* measurement at either side of centre line, on horizontal line just drawn.

3. Join the outer edge of neckline border with the *shoulder-to-shoulder* mark.

4. Draw a vertical line from *shoulder-to-shoulder* mark downwards.

5. Draw a horizontal line from the previously made *neck-to-underarm* mark inwards. It should cover half the distance between the side-of-body line and the vertical line just drawn.

6. Join the end of the horizontal line just drawn to the vertical line, at an angle of approximately 40 degrees. Because at this scale there is no need to be exceptionally accurate, if you do not possess a protractor take a sheet of paper and fold it at one corner, so that two of the sides that normally form a right angle now lie on top of each other. The corner has become a 45-degree angle. A 40-degree angle will be eight ninths of what you now have, so just make it slightly smaller.

7. Take your measuring strip of graph paper and place it from *shoulder-to-shoulder* mark to *neck-to-underarm* mark, following the broken line. It should give half the *round-shoulder* measurement. If it does not, move the *neck-to-underarm* mark up or down the side, for as much as the measurement is over or under what it should be. Repeat steps 5 and 6.

8. Draw a line through *neck-to-underarm* mark, at an angle of about 35 degrees with the side-of-body line; it will be seven ninths of the folded-paper angle. On this line, and from *neck-to-underarm* mark up, mark half the *upper-arm* measurement.

9. Join *shoulder-to-shoulder* mark with mark just made, extending line well past the mark. This will be the sleeve's folding line. This line should cross the 35-degree line previously drawn at approximately right angles. If it does not, the *upper-arm* measurement is probably too wide or too narrow for the *round-shoulder* measurement. Check and, if necessary, adjust one or the other, or find a compromise between the two.

10. Mark the *neck-to-wrist* measurement on the sleeve line, starting at top cross, and following all

the time the outer line of the garment with the strip of graph paper used for measuring.

11. Draw a line at right angles from last mark, and one parallel to this one at the border, or cuff, depth. Use a book to obtain a right angle if you do not possess a protractor or set square.

12. Mark half the *wrist* measurement on the second of the two lines just drawn, starting from the sleeve's folding line. If the sleeve has a cuff requiring a smaller ease allowance than the base of the sleeve, mark half this measurement on both parallel lines, so that it occupies a central position. Join the marks with lines parallel to the sleeve's folding line to indicate the cuff.

13. Join half-*wrist* mark to the checked *neck-to-underarm* mark. If the sleeve is gathered in a cuff, draw small curves near the cuff, for a more realistic effect.

The diagram is now ready for laying out any motifs. Tension diagrams might need to be drawn as well, to study the motifs in more detail. This, in turn, might make changes in the style diagram necessary. The depths of the borders will also have to be checked, so that they are in proportion with the rest. Sketches of the individual sections, not to scale but fully dimensioned, will also have to be drawn.

DRAWING INDIVIDUAL SECTIONS

Whether you have drawn your own style diagram or not, you will need to draw a sketch for every major section to be knitted excluding any borders to be picked up or joined later. Collars, belts, pockets, etc, rarely need such sketches, but if you ever feel they do, do not hesitate to draw them as well. As explained at the beginning of the chapter, only rough sketches are necessary.

Let us imagine that the style chosen is that of garment 27 in Chapter 7, which also fits the raglan-shoulder version of the example used for the style diagrams. A raglan garment is a good example because it is probably the most difficult to dimension correctly. Let us also imagine that the garment will be knitted in a medium-thick yarn such as 'double knitting', that a medium-fit is desired, and that it has to fit the following body measurements:

	cm	in
Front neck depth	25	10
Bust (5% added)	92	$36\frac{1}{2}$
Waist length	42	$16\frac{1}{2}$
Hip (5% added)	102	40
Hip depth	18	7
Neck width	16	$6\frac{1}{4}$
Back neck depth	1	$\frac{1}{2}$
Underarm depth	25	10
Neck to wrist	72	$28\frac{1}{2}$
Upper arm (20% added)	36	14
Wrist (40% added)	24	$9\frac{1}{2}$
Wrist for cuffs	17	$6\frac{3}{4}$

In addition to these, it has also been decided:

Cuff depth	6	$2\frac{1}{2}$
Borders	3	$1\frac{1}{4}$
Top of sleeve cap	6	$2\frac{1}{2}$
Total length	to allow the body to match the sleeves from lower edge to underarm	

(The above measurements are not exact equivalents; always follow the same system.)

SKETCHING THE SECTIONS

The sections are drawn so that they show units to be knitted. These units, more often than not, are made up of two or more of the shapes explained in Chapter 6. For instance, the sleeves will show, in the example, the sleeve proper, the cuff and the shoulder cap. All sections have to be drawn, unless two of them are symmetrical, in which case only one needs sketching.

The sections must include those borders that will be knitted as part of the sections, but not those knitted separately or picked up from the edge at a later stage. Changes in texture, colour or stitch pattern are also shown. And the by now familiar point of reference, the bone at the top of the spine, is shown in position as a cross.

In the example, three sections need drawing: back, half-front and sleeve. They should all be drawn with the cast-on edge at the bottom, so that you will always work up when knitting.

Use a medium to soft pencil. Do not worry if your sketches are not very good, but make them large enough for you to be able to annotate them afterwards.

DIMENSIONING THE SECTIONS

If you have drawn a style diagram, the dimensions will be those that the scaled diagram shows. Otherwise, follow the notes on the shape diagrams in Chapter 6, but make allowances for any borders. For instance, the *neck width* of 16cm ($6\frac{1}{4}$in), will become 22cm ($8\frac{3}{4}$in) when the neckline border is removed from the back; the half-front will be 21·5cm ($8\frac{1}{2}$in) instead of half the back, which would be 23cm ($9\frac{1}{8}$in), because of the missing half border; the half-*neck width* at the front will be 9·5cm ($3\frac{3}{4}$in) instead of 11cm ($4\frac{3}{8}$in) for the same reason; and the *back neck depth* of 1cm ($\frac{1}{2}$in), added to the border and to an approximate distance of 1cm ($\frac{1}{2}$in) between the *neck-depth* line and the top of the border, will give a distance of 5cm (2in) between the centre top of the back and the bone at the top of the spine.

Having written down all the known measurements (a), we have to find out those that are missing (b).

We know that the *neck width* is 22cm ($8\frac{3}{4}$in). This means that the distance between the centre top of the sleeve and the bone at the top of the spine will be 11cm ($4\frac{3}{8}$in), or half the *neck width*. If the *neck-to-wrist* measurement is 72cm ($28\frac{1}{2}$in),

the sleeve will have to be $72-11=61$cm ($28\frac{1}{2}-4\frac{3}{8}=24\frac{1}{8}$in) along its centre line. We can assume that the top of the sleeve will rest on the shoulder at 2cm ($\frac{3}{4}$in) from the bone at the top of the spine, which is the *neck depth* plus allowance for the border at the side of the neck. This means that there will be 5cm (2in) between the bone at the top of the spine and the top of the back. This is the same dimension calculated for the *back neck depth*, which means that the top of the back will be on a straight line.

There are now only 20cm ($7\frac{3}{4}$in) left between the top of the back and the underarm line. This will also be the distance between the sleeve's underarm line and the highest point of the sleeve, which is the top end of the back shoulder seam. We can guess that the top end of the front shoulder seam will be some 2cm ($\frac{3}{4}$in) lower, giving a height of 18cm (7in) between this point and the underarm line. And this will also be the height of the top end of the front, measured from the front's underarm line.

We can now say that the sleeve has to be 42cm ($16\frac{3}{4}$in) long, from cast-on edge to underarm. This is calculated by subtracting the 11cm ($4\frac{3}{4}$in) between the bone at the top of the spine and the top centre of the shoulder cap, plus the average 19cm ($7\frac{3}{4}$in) between the shoulder-cap top and the underarm line, from the *neck-to-wrist* measurement of 72cm ($28\frac{1}{2}$in).

Since the body has the same length as the sleeves between cast-on edge and underarm, we can also say that the back will have a total length of 62cm ($24\frac{1}{2}$in), and the front a total length of 60cm ($23\frac{3}{4}$in). Do not worry about the 2cm ($\frac{3}{4}$in) difference in height; it will fall into place when the garment is put on.

Finally, we can say that the shapings for the hips will start at 7cm (3in) from the cast-on edge, having subtracted the 37cm ($14\frac{1}{2}$in) between the top of the back and the waist, plus the 18cm (7in) between the waist and the hipline, from the 62cm ($24\frac{1}{2}$in) of the total back length.

It looks very complicated when it is explained in so many words, but do try to spend some time over it, following every step, and you will soon realise that it all makes good sense. What is more important, effort spent on this exercise will ensure far less effort at a later stage, and well-fitting garments.

ARRANGING DIMENSIONS

Measurements need to be arranged in an orderly way, so that they make sense when knitting. This has been done in (c).

To start with, omit all dimensions that are not needed for knitting; that is, those dimensions used merely to calculate the rest. All measurements taken from bone at top of spine, for instance, will fall in this category. Now, write down all width dimensions, using fine lines to show those parts of the garment to which they

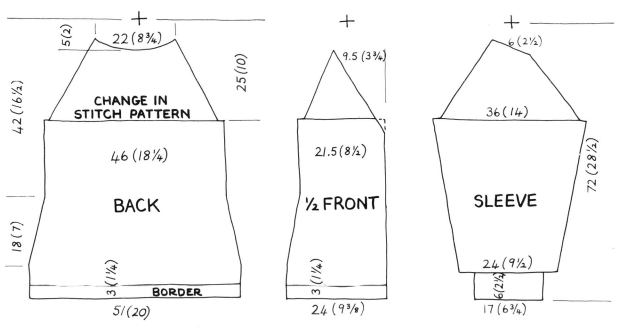

(a) known measurements (the first figure indicates centimetres; the figure in brackets indicates inches)

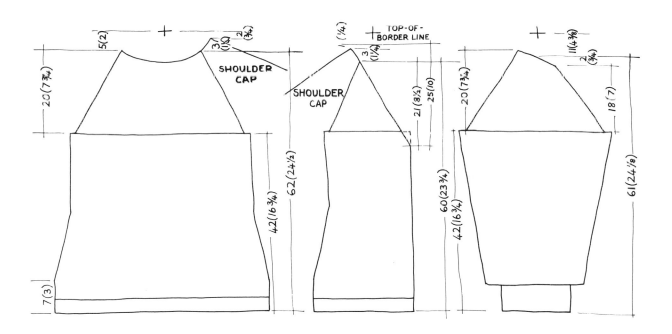

(b) measurements that require calculation

131

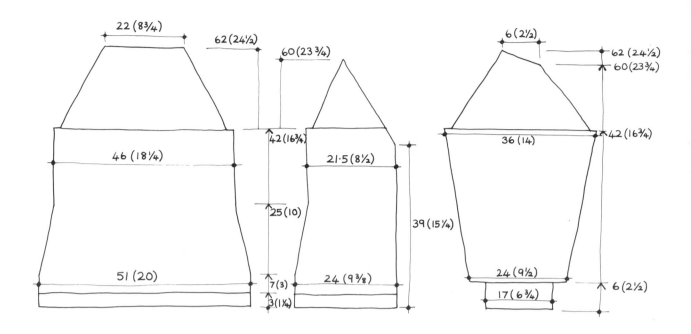

(c) measurements relevant to knitting

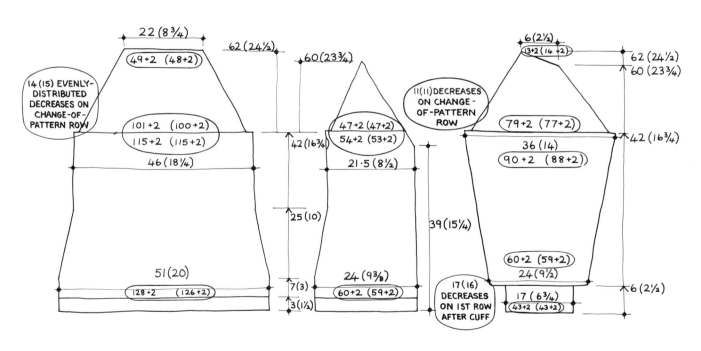

(d) number of stitches

132

apply. Mark the intersection of these lines with the outline of the garment with thick dots.

Finally, write down the vertical measurements on a fine line placed to the side of the sketch. Front and back can share the same line so long as they follow the same dimensions. The best way to write the vertical measurements is to refer all of them to the cast-on edge, because later this will make easy work of checking the overall progress. Every time you reach a critical point on the section (start or finish of shapings, change in pattern, etc), cross the vertical line with short horizontal lines. Draw an upwards pointing arrow at each intersection, except at the ones at the cast-on and cast-off edges which should have thick dots like those of the horizontal dimensions. In this way, dots will always indicate beginning or end of dimensions, and arrows will indicate intermediate, running dimensions. Now, re-calculate the vertical dimensions so that they are all measured from the cast-on edge. If, however, a specific dimension makes more sense by itself, keep it so, but write it down on an individual vertical line, away from the line with arrows.

The drawings are now ready for the stitch count.

CALCULATING NUMBER OF STITCHES AND ROWS

To transform the dimensions on the sketched sections into number of stitches and rows, it is essential to knit a swatch in the appropriate yarn, and with the correct tension. The details on how to knit such a swatch and how to judge whether the tension is correct have been explained in Chapter 5. Table 2, in the Appendix, also gives an idea of how many stitches might be necessary to obtain a large enough swatch.

When the swatch is finished, block or press it and, with the help of a measuring tape, mark with pins a width and a height of 10cm (4in). Make sure that the swatch is on a flat, hard surface when measuring it, and take care not to stretch it.

Now count the number of stitches and rows between pins. Do not disregard any half stitches or rows.

If you suspect that the yarn might shrink when washed, wash the swatch before counting the stitches. If your swatch is a small one, knitted in fine yarn, count stitches and rows per 5cm (2in), and double these numbers.

You will now know the number of stitches and rows per 10cm (4in). To convert this into the rows and stitches needed for each part of the garment, turn to tables 7 and 8 in the Appendix. These show exactly how many stitches and rows a particular dimension will require with a particular tension. If necessary, add two columns together. If your tension is so-many-stitches-*and-a-half*, approximate between the tensions immediately above and below.

Convert all your horizontal dimensions into stitches, and write these down on your sketch, next to the appropriate dimension, using a contrasting pen or drawing a circle around them. Whenever selvedge stitches are necessary, add those to the total number of stitches. It is best to mark them as +1 or +2, in order to remember what they are.

If you are intending to work a stitch pattern or Jacquard motif requiring multiples of a certain number of stitches, you may have to alter the total number of stitches just calculated to accommodate the pattern. This, in turn, will mean a wider or narrower garment, and you can use the tables in reverse to find out the new width. When an exact number of repeats cannot be accommodated, follow the advice given for *Seams and Motifs* in Chapter 7.

When the garment uses more than one type of yarn or more than one stitch pattern, it will be necessary to knit a swatch for each of the yarns or stitch patterns involved, because the tension will probably be different for every one of them. When changing texture, all necessary increases or decreases must be *evenly* distributed along the first new-texture row.

You will only need to convert vertical dimensions into the number of rows for some types of shapings, and when the number of vertical repeats of a stitch pattern need to be known.

If, in the cardigan previously used as an example, we consider the tension to be 22sts per 10cm (4in) for the upper stitch pattern, and 25sts per 10cm (4in) for the lower stitch pattern and the border, the resulting number of stitches will be those shown in (d). Differences between stitches in the metric and imperial versions are due to the fact that only approximate, not exact, equivalents have been used throughout.

The drawings are now ready for the final stage.

DRAWING TENSION DIAGRAMS

Tension diagrams are only needed for shapings involving curves or oblique lines, and for stitch patterns and motifs requiring special attention. This means that, often, only part(s) of a section will require a tension diagram. If the sections do not possess any oblique or curved shapings, and the stitch pattern presents no special problems, no diagrams at all will be needed.

Tension diagrams have traditionally been drawn on ordinary graph paper, each square representing one stitch in width and one row in height. This, however, has a significant drawback in that it is extremely rare to find a knitted stitch that is square. Given time, one gets used to the unavoidable distortion, and allows for the fact that a knitted motif will always look squatter on the finished garment than it does on paper. But it is very confusing for beginners, and even experienced knitters find it difficult at times.

This book solves the problem with the introduction of a series of especially designed graph papers, which are collected at the end of the book. These graph papers are not square, but rectangular. They should be looked at from the side of the book, so that the rectangle lays flat on its longer side. There are a total of ten pages, each one showing a different stitch proportion, from almost square to a rectangle twice as wide as it is high.

To use the graph papers, start by counting the number of stitches and rows in your swatch. You can either count them per 10cm (4in) or per 5cm (2in); providing you are counting a square the proportion will always be the same. Now, divide the number of stitches into the number of rows. The result will tell you what graph-paper to use; if necessary, approximate to best fit.

In the example, if we consider the already mentioned horizontal tension of 22sts, with a vertical tension of 30 rows, we will have:

$$\frac{30 \ (\text{number of rows})}{22 \ (\text{number of stitches})} = 1.36$$

The result falls between pages 1.3 and 1.4, but 1.4 is the nearest and, therefore, this is the one to use.

To use the graph papers without damaging the book, either take photocopies or fix a piece of tracing paper over the appropriate page with paper clips. If you need a larger piece of graph paper, take several photocopies and tape or paste them together.

CALCULATING OBLIQUE SHAPINGS
For reasons of clarity, only the stitches and rows of the metric count have been used in the example; the procedure is exactly the same whatever the measuring system used.

To calculate shapings, the first thing is to calculate the number of stitches and rows involved. Lines of the appropriate shape are then drawn on the graph paper, spanning the calculated number of stitches and rows. Finally, the lines are adapted to the graph, so that only whole stitches are used.

134

The cardigan in the example provides a very good illustration, because of its raglan sleeves. Raglans are very easy to knit and fit, but can be trickier to calculate than other types of shoulder. This is because the widths of body and sleeve are highly interrelated. It is therefore important to explain them in greater detail.

Start by repeating the top of your sketches on a separate piece of paper, indicating the number of stitches required for each part of the sections. Calculate the number of stitches involved in each of the shapings, and write them down as well (e). This is done as follows:
—to calculate the stitches for the back raglan shapings, deduct stitches needed for the neck from the total number of stitches at the underarm. Halve the result.
—to calculate the stitches for the front raglan shapings, deduct two stitches from the back raglan shapings. If the top of the shoulder cap was narrower, the difference would only be one stitch. If the top of the shoulder was wider, the difference would be three or four stitches.
—to calculate the stitches for the front neckline shapings, subtract the stitches needed for the front raglan shapings from the stitches needed for the half-front at the underarm.
—the sleeve shapings will require the same number of stitches as the corresponding back and front shapings.

The next step is to check whether the resulting figures make sense.

Adding up all the stitches for the cap of the sleeve $(26 + 13 + 24)$, we obtain a total of 63 stitches. This is 16 stitches less than we had first assumed.

Fortunately, *slight* adjustments will not substantially affect the final result, and it is possible to introduce *small* changes in the first figures, so that they become consistent. In this case, the sleeve is made 2 stitches narrower, the back 4 stitches wider, and the half-front 2 stitches wider. At the top of the sketches, the sleeve is made 6 stitches wider, and the back of the neckline 4 stitches narrower. The stitches required for the shapings will now be 30 for the back and 28 for the front. These changes will obviously affect the measurements, and the section sketches will need correcting accordingly (f).

The decreases for the sleeve cap can now be calculated. With a tension of 30 rows per 10cm, the back will need 60 rows, while the front will only need 54 rows.

Draw the sleeve cap on graph paper 1.4, making sure that you have the right number of rows and stitches. Use a ruler to give you straight lines, but first do not forget to mark the two or three stitches that are cast off at the beginning of raglans. This leaves 27 stitches to be decreased at the back in 60 rows, and 25 stitches to be decreased at the front in 54 rows. It is obvious that if we decrease every other row—one of the

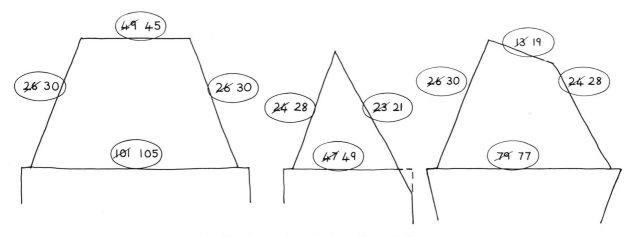

(e) adjusting raglan shapings (figure indicates number of stitches)

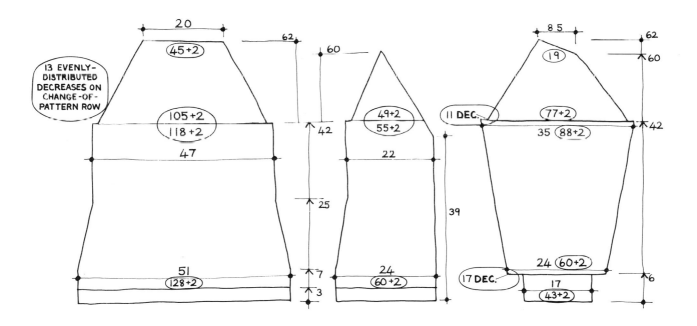

(f) corrected measurements and number of stitches

most usual ways of decreasing—we will run out of stitches before the sleeve is finished. Therefore, some decreases will have to be worked every four rows instead of every two rows. This is best done near the underarm, because it will show less. Mark a few decreases every four rows from the underarm up, and then start marking decreases every two rows from the top of the sleeve down, until both series of decreases meet.

Front and back will have similar decreases to those calculated for the sleeves.

If there had been the same amount of decreases and more rows, it might have been best to introduce every-four-row decreases at regular intervals, amongst the every-two-row decreases. If there had been less rows, then we would have needed occasional double decreases instead of more widely spaced decreases.

To cast off the cap, there are 19 stitches and, in theory, 6 rows left. This means casting off at rows 1, 3 and 5, with no row 6 because there will be no stitches left. Therefore, the top will be cast off in groups of 6, 6 and 7 stitches.

The shapings for front of neckline, hip and lower part of sleeve are calculated in a similar fashion, although the sleeve will have increases instead of decreases, and the adjustments might need to be different:

—hip shapings must be regular; if necessary, adjust total height over which they are worked, but do not change the intervals.

—V-neck shapings also need to be regular; depending on circumstances, you might need to work them alternating, for example, decreases every-four-row with decreases every-six-row, or you might need to finish them before the top of the front is reached, thus creating a short, vertical stretch near the neck.

—normal tapered sleeves also need regular increases. However, if these are difficult to fit within a given length, which is quite common, the increases are finished early, thus creating a short stretch without shapings before the armholes are reached.

CALCULATING CURVED SHAPINGS

The shapings are drawn on graph paper as they are intended to look, making sure that they span the right number of stitches and rows. Coins, cups and plates are all good aids for drawing curves, but you might need different objects to help you with different parts of one single curve. A set of French curves would, of course, be far better.

When a curve has two symmetrical sides, only half of it needs calculating.

Because the cardigan in the example does not possess any curved shapings, let us introduce a new example: a round neck, which is a very common design. This time we will imagine that the garment is to be knitted with a thicker yarn, giving a tension of 17 stitches and 24 rows per 10cm square (4in square). Dividing the number

of stitches into the number of rows we now obtain a result of 1.41. This means that we will need to use the same graph-paper size of 1.4. Also imagine that the neck width requires 31 stitches, the front neck depth requires 22 rows, and the back neck depth requires 6 rows.

We know, from Chapter 6, that the front of a round neck is 'like a flattened semicircle', while the back is 'basically a straight line curving gently upwards at the ends'. Therefore, we will have to draw two curves, following these shapes and spanning the appropriate number of stitches and rows. However, when drawing the front curve we realise that the flattened semicircle is shallower than the depth required by the example, and this means that the semicircle will have to be extended up with straight lines.

Having drawn the curves, it is just a question of marking a series of steps on the graph paper, making sure that the curves always remain on the inside of the edge. The steps represent cast-off stitches. These stitches will usually be cast off every other row, and this is the reason why most of the steps are two rows high. After casting off the first large group of stitches from the centre, the decreases to the left will be worked on right-side rows, while those to the right will be worked on wrong-side rows, starting with the row immediately after the central casting off. A new ball of yarn will have to be introduced for working to the right of the centre.

The diagrams show the following results. For the front, cast off 11 stitches at the centre; cast off at either side, every two rows, 4, 2, 1, 1 and 1 stitches; then another stitch after 4 rows. For the back, cast off 19 stitches at the centre; then cast off at either side, every two rows, 3, 2 and 1 stitches.

CALCULATING MOTIFS

When working with motifs, graph papers can be used in a variety of ways. They can be used, for instance, to see how a stitch pattern will be affected by shapings, or to calculate mock patchwork pictures (as explained in Chapter 5).

Sometimes, a whole section needs to be drawn for the effect to show, but most often drawing part of the section will be enough. The technique is simply to draw as much of the outline of the section as is necessary, and then experiment until the motif fits inside the section in the best possible way. These sketches will help you see whether you are approaching the motif in the right way, and whether it would be best to add or subtract a couple of stitches or rows to the section. For these reasons, it is best not to wait until all the shapings have been calculated before starting work on the motifs; otherwise, you might have to calculate rows and stitches twice.

Referring to the cardigan again, imagine that the highlight of the design is not the checked pattern of the illustration in Chapter 7, but a

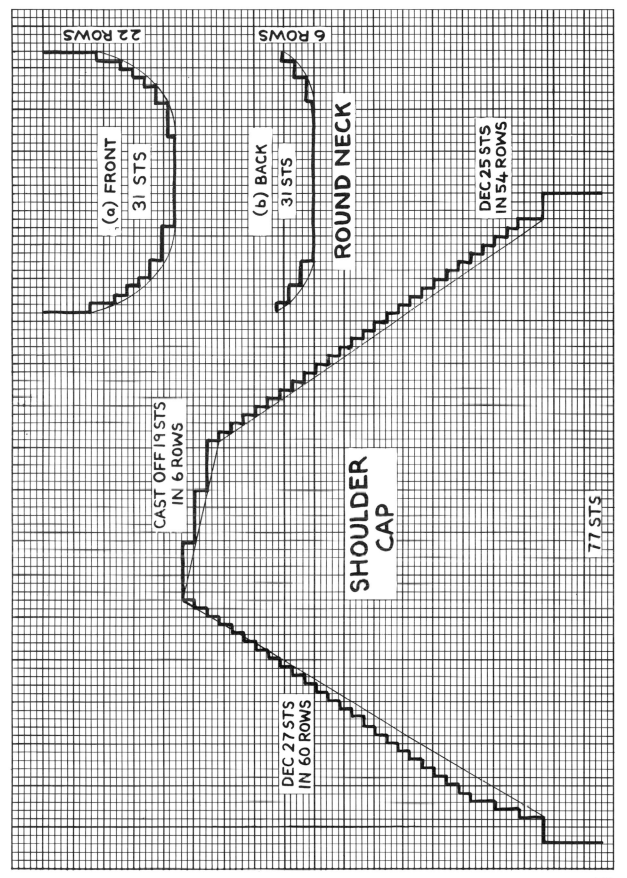

22 ROWS

6 ROWS

(a) FRONT
31 STS

(b) BACK
31 STS

ROUND NECK

DEC 25 STS
IN 54 ROWS

CAST OFF 19 STS
IN 6 ROWS

SHOULDER
CAP

77 STS

DEC 27 STS
IN 60 ROWS

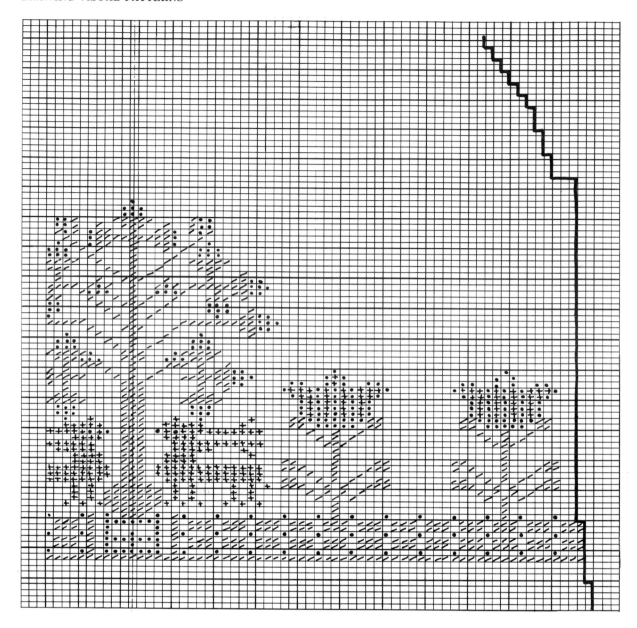

three-colour Jacquard motif placed in the centre of the back. It is especially important to see the effect, because the motif was originally designed for cross stitch.

Being a symmetrical design, there is no need to draw both sides in detail. Therefore, only part of the back will have to be drawn: from top of hip shapings to beginning of armholes, and from one side seam to just after the centre line.

Once the drawing is finished, it is clear that, although it fits very well on the back, if the 'tulips' are to be continued at the front it might be better to add one or two extra stitches at each side, so that the sequence in which they appear is maintained at the seams. On the other hand, a drawing of the front might prove that an easier way of maintaining the sequence is to place the first front tulip further away from the seam than the last back tulip. Which solution is best will depend on how near the front border the last tulip

should be. If you do not wish to draw the front as well as the back, cut a strip of graph paper, mark on it the front width, and slide it over the tulips already drawn until you find the right position for the front edge.

SHORTCUTS AND OTHER PRACTICAL HINTS

With many garments, it is not necessary to follow every one of the steps explained, in the order in which they have been explained. The following hints should all be preceded by 'Should the design allow it':

—make a swatch of the correct width but of only half the height, and count only the number of stitches. Start work. If you need to know the number of rows per 10cm (4in), count them once the work has reached a long enough length.

—do not make a special swatch for ribbed borders. Instead, knit them with the same

138

amount of stitches as the main section for a slight gathering, and with 10 to 20 per cent less stitches for a heavier gathering.

—to calculate the number of stitches needed for a cuff, secure a portion of the back's border with safety pins, so that it forms a short tube, and pass your closed fist through it. Move pins until you find a comfortable fit.

—avoid lengthy calculations for shapings at top of back when working round necks or necklines with similar back shapes. For raglans, cast off top of back in a straight line. For all other shoulders, start shapings at 1·5–2cm (about ⅔in) from highest back point, for an adult, casting off between one half and two thirds of the total number of stitches in the centre. Cast off the rest of the stitches in progressively smaller numbers, every two rows, half to the right and half to the left of the central cast-off group.

—knit the back up to armhole level before calculating the rest, to make sure that you are maintaining the correct tension.

—start knitting the back to see how a stitch pattern or motif develops, before deciding how deep to make a band near the lower edge, and/or how long to make the garment.

—instead of drawing different positions for a seam, place a small mirror upright on top of the swatch, or on top of any design, and move the mirror sideways, until the right position for the seam is found.

—use the mirror again, this time at a 45-degree angle, to find out the best way of making a band turn a corner.

—wait until part of the back has been knitted, to decide how best to make stripes fit in with shapings.

CALCULATING AMOUNT OF YARN

There is only one reliable way of finding out how much yarn a garment will need, and that involves knitting part of the garment. This is because the amount of yarn depends on many variables: style, size, stitch pattern, thickness of yarn, weight of fibre, etc. Manufacturers can help by stating the amount of metres (yards) in a given weight, something that they do not very often do in Great Britain. Unfortunately, the length of a ball only allows an accurate comparison between yarns that give the same tension when knitted but, of course, it is better than nothing and at least it can be used as an initial guide. Indeed, manufacturers would help knitters greatly if they included this information in their labels.

A first assessment of what is needed has to come from experience, either your own or the shop assistant's. Your own will grow gradually and it is important to keep a record of how much yarn you have used for each garment, together with one of the labels. If you are going to use a yarn that you know nothing about, then it is best to ask the assistant for advice.

The first assessment should always be made well in excess to ensure that enough of a particular dye lot is reserved.

For a final assessment, you need to knit at least one, but preferably two or three balls, especially if part of the first one was used to knit a border in a different stitch pattern. Calculate the area of the rectangle you have knitted; simply multiply the height by the width. If it is not a rectangle, roughly convert it into one. The result does not need to be one hundred per cent accurate. For instance, if you are working a tapered sleeve, consider the width halfway along; if you have worked the back with set-in shoulders, disregard all the shapings, both the slant at the top for the shoulder seams, and the narrowing at the sides to take in the sleeves; if the back had raglan shoulders, divide it into two rectangles, one under and the other above the underarm, and calculate the area of the one at the top by multiplying its height by the width halfway along.

Once you know the area of the knitted rectangle, divide it by the number of balls used, so that you know how much you can do with one ball. Now calculate the total area of the garment, always considering simple rectangles. You can easily do that from the section diagrams, but do not forget to add any borders, collars, pockets, etc, that are not shown in the diagrams. Dividing the total area by the area that can be knitted with one ball will give you a fairly accurate estimate of how many balls you will need in total.

Always approximate in excess. If the last result is very close to an exact number of balls, add one extra ball. For instance, if your calculations tell you that you need 18·8 balls, buy 20.

KNITTING FROM DIAGRAMS

The diagrams you will be using for knitting are the rough section diagrams, plus the tension diagrams if any. It is therefore important that you write down on them as many notes as you feel necessary, regarding type of increases and decreases, selvedges, changes in stitch pattern, etc. Some of these you will annotate from the start, and others while you are already knitting. The more notes you write, the better you will remember, later, what you have done.

Start following the diagrams from the bottom up, because the bottom is where the cast-on row is. Shapings and changes in stitch pattern should be introduced when the height indicated in the diagram is reached. This means that, with rare exceptions, you will be checking the work's progress with a measuring tape.

To measure the work, stop knitting in the middle of a row, and move the stitches along both needles so that the work is as flat as possible. Place the work on a hard, flat surface, and measure it. The end of the tape should be against the side of the needle, and the measurement should be read at the cast-on edge. *Do not pull or*

139

compress the work. If it does not stay flat easily, pin it down.

The width needs also to be checked, as otherwise the length measurement might not be a true one, but if you have started with a ribbed border, you will not be able to check it until well past the border. Then, you will have to stretch the ribbing and pin it down to measure the rest. In any case, do not attempt to measure the width after the first few rows, because it is then easily distorted.

Do not deceive yourself into thinking that you have reached the required length if you know that, in fact, you still need a couple of rows. One always regrets these things afterwards, because if the diagrams are not accurately followed the garment will not fit.

Do not try to assess the final effect by putting individual sections against you. If they are not all there, properly pinned together, the effect will be misleading and unnecessarily worrying.

Occasionally, it will be necessary to count the number of rows to assess progress. This will happen when working in stripes or stitch patterns that need to be fitted in with special accuracy. Counting rows will also be necessary to make sure that front and back are exactly the same; if the number of rows is different, then one side of the seam will be longer than the other and puckers will form.

Unless special circumstances suggest otherwise, work the back first, then the front(s), and finally the sleeves.

The back is knitted first because it is the section that will show less if, at first, the work is not very even. Another reason is that mistakes can be more easily made good at the back than at any other part of the garment. If the back turns out to be too narrow, make up for it with a wider front. If it is too wide, and front and back look alike, transform it into the front before shaping the armholes, and knit a narrower new back.

If the work is not the required measurement, always check whether the mistake has been in calculating one particular figure, or whether the mistake was to use the wrong tension throughout; in the latter case, you will have to re-check all calculations.

Whenever possible, work together those sections that are symmetrical, such as fronts and sleeves. Remember that they should be *symmetrical, not identical*. You will need two balls of yarn, which you should keep separate, one to your right and one to your left, so that they do not get tangled. Working these sections together has two advantages: one is that you only have to worry once about measurements, shapings, changes in stitch pattern, etc, and the other is that the finished sections will have exactly the same length, whether or not your tension is very even. Some people take this as far as working together the front and back lower borders; the rest of the sections are then worked individually. In this way they avoid having to count the number of rows in the border.

Off-white summer suit in silk noil and linen top (see page 161)

CHAPTER 9
Amending and Altering

Knitted garments may need alterations for a number of reasons: mistakes may occur when working the stitch pattern, the design may have a major flaw, dimensions or number of stitches may be wrongly calculated, a child may grow too fast, fashion may change while the garment is still in good condition, an accident may cause obvious damage, wrong cleaning may cause felting or stretching, or the garment may just wear out in places after long use. Whatever the reason, it is very often possible to do something about it

The illustration shows one of those 'fateful' garments, where almost everything that could go wrong actually did go wrong. I designed it for my husband, a thin, long-bodied man who likes bright colours and casual clothes. The colour, a leafy green, looked slightly light in the shop but it was a perfect match for some of his shirts and trousers. The first snag was that the stitch pattern (Ladder and Rope) pulled in and took up, a fact I had not allowed for when buying the yarn or calculating the stitches. I had foolishly assumed that the tension would be as for stocking stitch. The shop had some extra yarn reserved for me, but this proved not to be enough, and it was impossible to obtain any more of that particular dye lot. Hoping it would stretch when pressing it (this was before I had tried cold blocking), I carried on working, shortening somewhat the length and making a low front opening to use less yarn. Eventually, I cast off the last stitch, and had to face the full extent of my miscalculations. No amount of pulling was enough to make the stitch pattern stretch more than a mere centimetre in width, but after two hours of pressing and pulling the pattern was noticeably flatter. I sewed the pieces together only to make matters worse. When buttoned up, the waistcoat fitted so tightly that the two fronts were pulled apart and looked terrible. The armholes, on the other hand, were too small and, being made to go round the shoulders, looked rather feminine. So did the stitch pattern, too elaborate for the occasion, and in any case not appropriate, because the vertical motifs emphasised the long, thin body. As for the colour, it was now a bright green that could be seen from miles away.

Navy-blue cardigan and V-neck jumper with Jacquard bands (see page 161)

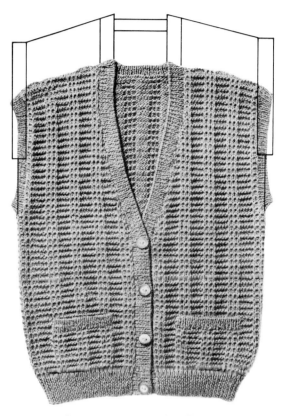

If the colour had been right, I would probably have unravelled the waistcoat and started again. But, the colour being wrong, I decided that the best course of action would be to alter it so that it could be worn by somebody else: me! I removed all the borders, and unravelled the shoulders until the total length was right and the V-opening was also right. I then reshaped the armholes, unstitching the top of the side seams, and cutting away some of the knitting, after securing what was to be left with three runs of the sewing machine. I finally re-knitted the borders, placing the buttonholes on the other side. Even the colour looks right now.

MISTAKES IN THE STITCH PATTERN
These happen to everybody at some time or other, and it is best to watch for them, because the sooner they are spotted the easier they are to correct. Do not be tempted to leave mistakes as they are; you would always be aware of their existence. If something is worth doing, it is worth doing correctly.

143

MISSING ROWS OR EXTRA ROWS IN PATTERN

The only solution is to unravel the work, so that the extra rows can be omitted or the missing rows can be added.

If only the last row needs unravelling, do it stitch by stitch. Insert the point of the needle into the stitch below the stitch being unravelled, and drop the stitch above from its needle. Pull yarn at the same time. Work from right to left or from left to right, as you prefer.

If more rows need unravelling, pull needles out, unravel all the rows that need unravelling except one, and unravel this last row stitch by stitch (it will not be on a needle, but otherwise work as previously explained). Alternatively, thread a length of contrasting yarn through last correct row with a tapestry needle, pull knitting needles off, unravel, and pick up stitches from contrasting yarn.

Unravelled stitches are easier to pick up with a knitting needle one or two sizes smaller than those used for knitting.

When unravelling, it is easy to twist the stitches. Watch out for this when you start knitting again.

Check the number of stitches on the needle before continuing work.

ONE-STITCH ERRORS

If they have been committed in the same row, unravel as explained. Unravel two or three stitches extra, if you think the error might have affected their tension.

If the error occurred a few rows further down, try the crochet-hook method. Work to a stitch just above the mistake, drop this stitch and let it

ladder all the way down to the row below the error. Work your way up again with the help of a crochet hook.

This method is very easy with stocking stitch, but with practice, care and courage it can be applied to more complicated patterns, including cables and some types of lace. It is well worth trying because, even if you cannot make it work, it will help you tremendously to understand the nature of knitted fabrics. In the worst of cases,

you will have to unravel down to the error. But, since you would have done this anyway had you not tried with a crochet hook, nothing will be lost.

When picking up reverse stocking stitch, turn the work round, so that it becomes stocking stitch. In knit and purl combinations, keep turning the work so that you always pick up knit stitches.

Whenever the pattern has overs or twist-stitches, leave all the rungs of the ladder on a cable needle or stitch holder, so that you will know in which order and in what way to pick them up. In these cases, it is sometimes necessary to ladder as well the stitches next to the error.

When the error is a missing increase or decrease, it is best not to use this method, because the amount of yarn used in the mistake is different from the amount of yarn the correction would need.

LARGER ERRORS

If more than one, or perhaps two, stitches are wrong, proceed as for missing rows in pattern. If you think the tension might have been affected, unravel two or three stitches past the error.

CORRECTING SIZE OR STYLE

Chapter 8 dealt with minor problems arising from miscalculations. However, there are cases when these are not spotted until the garment is actually being fitted. It might be too short, or too tight, or the sleeves might not fit. Some cases will need partial or total unravelling but, before you do that, make sure you understand what went wrong and recalculate it.

Luckily, many garments can be saved without completely unravelling them. The following suggestions can be used to trigger off your own thoughts, when faced with a particular problem. They not only apply to ill-fitting new garments, but also to cases of children outgrowing their knitwear, garments changing owners, and new fashion trends.

If, at the time of finishing a garment, you foresee there will be a need to re-shape it or re-style it in the future, make sure you have matching yarn when the times comes by knitting loosely whatever yarn you have to spare and cleaning this extra piece of knitting every time you clean the garment.

Alterations will sometimes create new problems. For instance, shortening the body from the shoulders may make the armholes too small. Keep this in mind when deciding what alterations to undertake.

When the design is affected by the alterations, proceed with care. If necessary, introduce extra alterations, even if they are not needed from a fitting point of view, so that the unity of the design is maintained. It is often a good idea to transform alterations into design features, instead of trying to half-conceal them.

TOO LONG

One way of shortening a garment is to unravel part of it, starting at the cast-off edge, and to cast off again when the right length is obtained. If the cast-off edge is at the shoulders, this might affect the armholes and the neckline.

A second way is to pick a strand from the edge, and pull it as far as it will go, to draw out a row. Cut the yarn at the other end of the row, half a dozen stitches before the edge as a safety measure, and pull it further. The knitting will then open in two. Unravel the last few stitches one at a time with a tapestry needle. Pick up the stitches

at the top with a knitting needle. Unravel the other side as required, and pick up the stitches with another knitting needle, making sure it points in the same direction as the first needle. Graft the two sections.

It is best to graft next to a change in pattern; for instance, just above or below a border. A stocking-stitch grafting might not matter at that point, if it is not possible to graft in pattern.

Any differences in width between the two sections will have to be evened up at the seams, trimming off any unnecessary knitting.

TOO SHORT

One way to lengthen a garment is to introduce a border, or widen an existing border. New borders can be picked up and worked in the opposite direction to the main section. Existing borders can rarely be widened in that way. If the edge of the border is a cast-off row, unravel that row and add directly to the border. If the edge is a cast-on row, pull a thread as explained to divide the knitting, pick up the border stitches, knit as necessary, and graft to the main section.

Another way of lengthening a garment is to make the main section longer. Again, it will be a question of pulling a thread, knitting and grafting. This is best done on straight sections, or where there is a change in pattern. If you have run out of yarn, a change in colour might be necessary. Either knit stripes in one or more new colours, or work a Jacquard band. You could also unravel the borders and use the yarn to lengthen the garment; then re-knit the borders with contrasting yarn or yarns.

A last possibility is to lengthen the garment from the cast-off edge. Unravel the last row, pick up the stitches, and knit to the required length. If the shoulders had been cast off with a slant, a few more rows will have to be unravelled, so that the addition starts on a straight line. This method cannot be applied when there are any shapings which would be affected, such as armholes, unless the work is unravelled further and the additional knitting is introduced before those shapings start.

TOO WIDE

The most common solution is to take in the extra width at the seams. Unless special circumstances do not recommend it, take in half the extra width from each side.

If little is taken in, the seams need not be trimmed. Large seams, however, could be bulky and they are best trimmed off (see page 148).

TOO NARROW

If the garment is open from top to bottom, it might be possible to add a make-up piece, or wide border, along the opening. Otherwise, make-up pieces will have to be introduced at the seams, or as front or back centre panels.

Only a few stitch patterns allow the introduction of invisible, or almost invisible, additional sections. These are patterns with vertical panels or ribs, and stocking stitch. Ribbed sections should be added with backstitch seams in that part of the rib where the join is less likely to show. Stocking stitch sections should be joined with invisible seams.

If the new sections are going to be visible, it is usually best to make them stand out from the rest. Knit them as contrasting bands, either in a different colour or yarn, or in a different stitch pattern. You can even work them picking up stitches along one of the edges, knitting transversely, and grafting to the other edge.

If the extra width is only necessary for part of the length, for instance, below but not above the waist, try knitting one or more panels of the required length, and fixing them as if they were short box pleats. Obviously the pleats will remain open at the lower end.

OPENINGS TOO LARGE

Add a band or border all the way round. Either pick up the stitches and knit in rounds, or knit the band separately and sew it in position.

Alternatively, add a make-up piece of appropriate shape to one section of the opening, when that might solve the problem. For instance, add a triangle to the corner of a V-neck that has turned out to be too low; it will change the neckline, but if the result looks right it may not matter.

OPENINGS TOO SMALL

Sew seams or place borders correctly and trim away excess (see page 148).

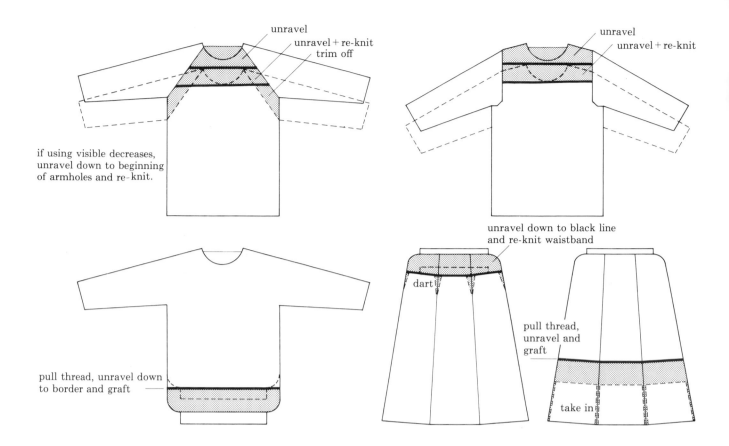

unravel

unravel + re-knit
trim off

if using visible decreases,
unravel down to beginning
of armholes and re-knit.

unravel

unravel + re-knit

unravel down to black line
and re-knit waistband

dart

pull thread,
unravel and
graft

pull thread, unravel down
to border and graft

take in

TOO LONG

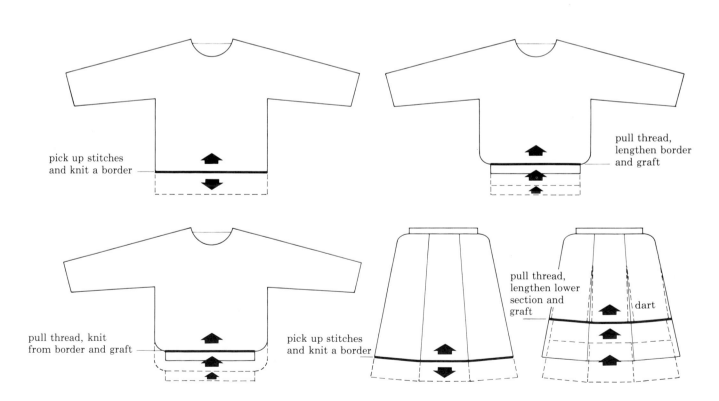

pick up stitches
and knit a border

pull thread,
lengthen border
and graft

pull thread, knit
from border and graft

pick up stitches
and knit a border

pull thread,
lengthen lower
section and
graft

dart

TOO SHORT

146

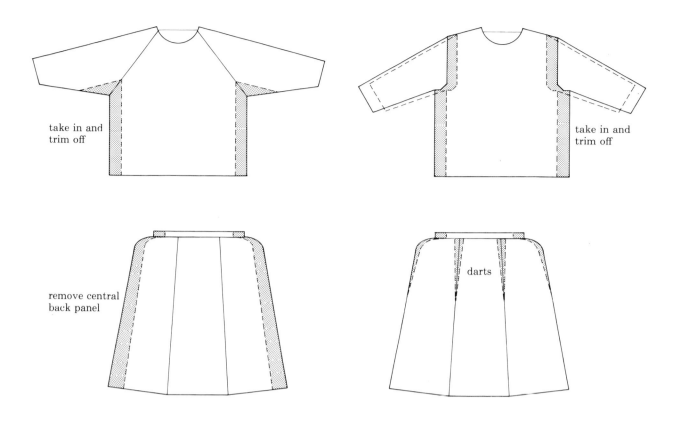

take in and
trim off

take in and
trim off

remove central
back panel

darts

TOO WIDE

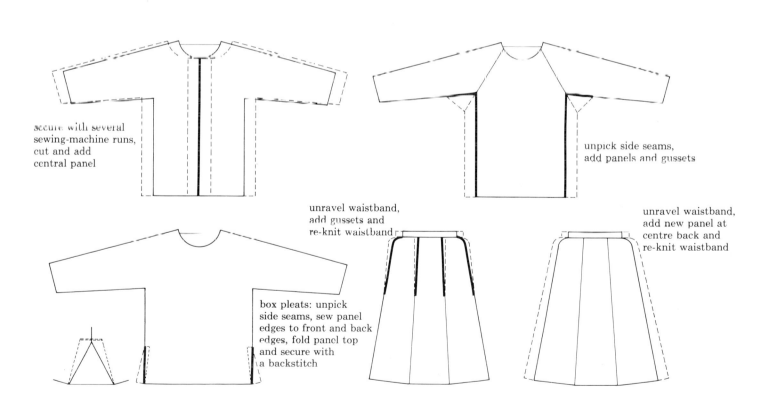

secure with several
sewing-machine runs,
cut and add
central panel

unpick side seams,
add panels and gussets

unravel waistband,
add gussets and
re-knit waistband

unravel waistband,
add new panel at
centre back and
re-knit waistband

box pleats: unpick
side seams, sew panel
edges to front and back
edges, fold panel top
and secure with
a backstitch

TOO NARROW

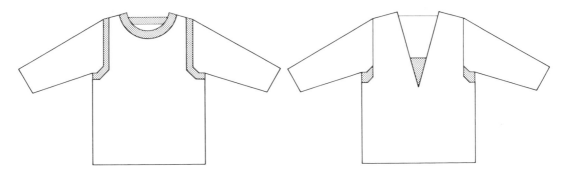

OPENINGS TOO LARGE

Alternatively, trim first and fix a bias band round the edge, if no other section is to be attached to the opening.

TRIMMING OFF EXCESS FABRIC

If you possess a sewing machine, stitch the knitting two or three times with very tight, ordinary stitching, using matching cotton. Work at a distance of about one centimetre (half an inch) outwards from the correct seam position. Cut excess fabric near the last machine run; the stitching will stop the fabric from unravelling.

Without a sewing machine, stitch by hand once, with a short, taut backstitch and two strands of matching cotton. Cut excess fabric near but not too close to the backstitch, and thoroughly overcast the raw edge. It is a good idea to cut a little at a time, overcasting one section before cutting the next one.

DARNING BUTTONHOLES

If horizontal buttonholes are not overstretched, it may be possible to eliminate them. Carefully unpick any stitching they might have, and see whether it would be possible to unravel the edges if one or two key stitches were to be cut. If the answer is yes, unravel the buttonhole stitches, and graft them together with a length of matching yarn to close the opening.

SPOT ACCIDENTS

These are best dealt with before they spread and cause more damage. Holes of any type, acid burns, permanent stains, can be overcome in two ways, depending on their size and their place.

FIRST METHOD: COVERING

Just cover the spot or hole with something else. This works well for accidents in prominent places, where the addition of a pocket, patch or embroidered motif will not be unwelcome. Add anything you want, knitted or not, that might look decorative and blend in well with the rest of the garment.

If colour cannot be perfectly matched, aim for contrast. If necessary, add similar motifs in other parts of the garment to maintain the unity of the design.

SECOND METHOD: REPLACING

Replacing the knitted fabric is the method to use when the accident occurred in a place awkward to cover with a patch or motif, or when the design or the stitch pattern make any additions impossible. Unfortunately, replacing can only be totally successful when the new yarn matches to perfection the old yarn. When stitches in only one row have been affected, cut the stitch in the centre of the damage, and, working in both directions, unravel the damage plus two or three stitches extra on each side. Pick up the free stitches with a pair of knitting needles, and graft them. Weave in the four ends of yarn.

When more than one row has been affected, start work on a row below the damage. Cut the stitch in the centre of this row and, working in both directions, unravel the stitches of the row until the section unravelled is wider than the damage. Pick up the lower stitches with a

knitting needle and, with matching yarn, work in pattern until the whole area is well covered. Unravel a second row, this time above the damage but again starting from the central stitch, and graft the new knitting to it. Make sure you unravel the correct row for the patch to be flat after grafting. Join the sides of the patch to the garment, if possible with an invisible seam. Using two strands of matching cotton, work a line of taut backstitch on the damaged area, parallel and fairly close to each of the seams. Trim away damage near the backstitch lines and thoroughly overcast raw edges. Weave in yarn ends left from unravelling top and bottom rows.

RENOVATING BORDERS

Most renovations can be approached by methods already explained for ill-fitting garments. The only difference will be that the yarn will now be fully set and its crinkles will have to be removed before re-knitting it. Borders, however, have not yet been covered.

Borders, especially those worked in ribbing, often lose their shape and get torn while the rest of the garment is still in good condition. This should not really happen, and the best policy is prevention. Knit borders with needles one, two, or even three sizes smaller than the rest of the garment. Cast on, or cast off, borders with two strands of yarn when knitting for a child or adult who tends to tear the edges. For especially bad problems, use two strands of yarn to knit the whole border. Use natural yarns in preference to man-made, because these have a greater tendency to stretch. And make sure you have a sufficient number of stitches.

To repair stretched ribbing, try threading shirring elastic through the ridges, every row or every other row, working on the wrong side.

When the borders are badly misshapen or torn, unpick them if they have been sewn to the garment, or pull a thread to cut them free if they have been worked in one piece. Unravel them, remove the crinkles and re-knit them.

It is best to change the position of the yarn when re-knitting it, so that the areas that normally receive the worst wear-and-tear are worked with the yarn that has received the least.

If the yarn is too damaged to be used again, re-knit the borders in contrasting yarn.

UNRAVELLING TO START AFRESH

This is a good way of recycling yarn that still has some life left, when a garment will not be worn any more in its present shape. Proceed with great care and patience, and follow in reverse the sewing up sequence you used when putting the garment together.

Use a blunt tapestry needle to unpick the stitching. Only use scissors to trim yarn ends from the seam. Be careful not to cut any small loops; they could easily be part of the garment.

Unravel starting at the cast-off edge; it is impossible to unravel from the cast-on edge. Pull firmly but carefully. If you find any resistance, stop pulling. Examine the problem, and gently ease any entangled loops. Brushed yarns and some fancy-textured yarns can be very difficult to unravel. Take your time with them.

Trim any damaged lengths, and make skeins with the help of a swift or two chairs placed back to back, but with a space in between. When the skein is finished, tilt back one of the chairs to retrieve the skein. Tie skeins *loosely* at three or four places with strong strips of fabric, and use some sort of identification to know what part of the garment the skein is from. Do not make skeins too large.

Wash skeins gently, rinse well and hang to dry, securing them by one of the ties. They should be thoroughly wet, so that the weight of the water can straighten the crinkles. Let them dry naturally, away from direct sun and direct heat. When dry, wind into loose balls.

Because some yarn is always lost while unravelling, the new garment will have to be smaller than the original one, or yarn in contrasing colour or colours will have to be added.

When knitting the new garment, do not use the same yarn for the same sections. Follow the advice given for renovating borders.

If a solid-colour garment has faded, and you would like to restore it to its original colour, dye it before unravelling. In this way, you will not be wasting your time should anything go wrong with the dye.

Appendix

TABLE 1: Comparative sizes of knitting needles and crochet hooks

International Standard Range (ISR), or metric (diameter in mm)	UK Old Nos	USA Nos	USA Letters (only for crochet hooks)
10	000	15	
9	00	13	
8	0	12	
$7\frac{1}{2}$	1	11	
7	2	$10\frac{1}{2}$	K
$6\frac{1}{2}$	3	10	J
6	4	9	I
$5\frac{1}{2}$	5	8	H
5	6	7	
$4\frac{1}{2}$	7	6	G
4	8	5	F
$(3\frac{3}{4})$	9	4	E
$3\frac{1}{2}$			
$(3\frac{1}{4})$	10	3	D
3	11	2	C
$(2\frac{3}{4})$	12	1	B
$2\frac{1}{2}$			
$(2\frac{1}{4})$	13	0	
2	14	00	

(The metric sizes in brackets are only available in the United Kingdom.)

TABLE 2: Tentative needle size and tentative number of stitches for tension swatches

This table should only be used as a rough guide when knitting test tension samples. The real needle size and the real number of stitches required will depend on the actual stitch pattern, the brand of the yarn and how tightly or loosely you knit.

The needle sizes should be considered 'average' in stocking-stitch. The number of stitches gives an idea of how many to cast on for a stocking-stitch swatch that is large enough to measure the tension per 10cm square (4in square).

Yarn	Tentative needle size (mm)	USA	Tentative number of stitches
Two-ply	2	00	46
Three-ply	$2\frac{3}{4}$	1	38
Four-ply	3	2	32
Quick knit	$3\frac{3}{4}$	4	30
Double knitting	4	5	28
Triple knitting	$4\frac{1}{2}$	6	22
Double-double knitting	6	9	18
Extra chunky	9	13	14

TABLE 3: Babies' measurements from birth to 3 months

Body measurement	cm	in
Chest	44–46	17–18
Hip (including nappies/ diapers)	46–48	18–19
Shoulder to shoulder	19–20	$7\frac{1}{2}$–$7\frac{3}{4}$
Total height	56–64	22–25
Waist length	16·5–18	$6\frac{1}{2}$–7
Outside leg (including nappies/ diapers)	34–36	13–14
Inside leg	17–18	$6\frac{3}{4}$–7
Neck to wrist	27–29	10–$11\frac{1}{2}$
Upper arm	17–18	$6\frac{3}{4}$–7
Wrist	14·5–15	$5\frac{7}{8}$–6

TABLE 4: Growth allowance in children's and teenagers' measurements (metric)

| Body measurement | Growth allowance (cm) | | | | | | | | | | | | | | |
| | months | | years | | | | | | | | | | | (Boys only) | |
	3–6	6–12	1–2	2–3	3–4	4–5	5–6	6–7	7–8	8–10	10–12	12–14	14–16	16–18
Chest	2·5	2·5	2·5	2·5	2·5	2·5	2·5	2·5	2·5	2·5	5	5	4	4
Waist	1·5	1·5	1·5	1·5	1·5	1·5	1·5	2	2	2·5	2·5	2·5	2·5	2·5
Hip	2·5	2·5	2·5	2·5	2·5	2·5	2·5	2·5	2·5	G 5 / B 2·5	G 5 / B 2·5	G 5 / B 2·5	2·5	2·5
Shoulder to shoulder	1	1	1	1	1	1	1	1·5	1·5	1·5	2	2	2	2
Total height	8	8	8	8	8	8	8	6	5	6	G 15 / B 10	G 8 / B 15	15	5
Waist length	1·5	1·5	1·5	1·5	1·5	1·5	1·5	G 2·5 / B 3·5	G 1·5 / B 1	G 2 / B 1·5	G 8 / B 6	G 5 / B 8	1·5	1·5
Neck to wrist	1·5	1·5	2	2	2	2	2	2·5	1·5	2	4·5	4·5	4·5	2·5
Upper arm	1	1	1	1	1	1	1	1	1	1	1	1	1	1
Wrist	0·5	0·5	0·5	0·5	0·5	0·5	0·5	0·5	0·5	0·5	0·5	0·5	0·5	0·5

G = girls
B = boys

TABLE 5: Growth allowance in children's and teenagers' measurements (imperial)

| Body measurement | Growth allowance (inches) | | | | | | | | | | | | | | |
| | months | | years | | | | | | | | | | | (Boys only) | |
	3–6	6–12	1–2	2–3	3–4	4–5	5–6	6–7	7–8	8–10	10–12	12–14	14–16	16–18
Chest	1	1	1	1	1	1	1	1	1	1	2	2	1½	1½
Waist	½	½	½	½	½	½	½	¾	¾	1	1	1	1	1
Hip	1	1	1	1	1	1	1	1	1	G 2 / B 1	G 2 / B 1	G 2 / B 1	1	1
Shoulder to shoulder	¼	¼	¼	¼	¼	¼	¼	½	½	½	¾	¾	¾	¾
Total height	3	3	3	3	3	3	3	2½	2	2½	G 6 / B 4	G 3¼ / B 6	3	2
Waist length	½	½	½	½	½	½	½	G 1 / B 1¼	G ½ / B ¼	G ¾ / B ½	G 3¼ / B 2½	G 2 / B 3¼	½	½
Neck to wrist	½	½	¾	¾	¾	¾	¾	1	½	¾	1¾	1¾	1¾	1
Upper arm	¼	¼	¼	¼	¼	¼	¼	¼	¼	¼	¼	¼	¼	¼
Wrist	⅛	⅛	⅛	⅛	⅛	⅛	⅛	⅛	⅛	⅛	⅛	⅛	⅛	⅛

G = girls
B = boys

TABLE 6: Ease Allowance

Note that some allowances are negative. This means that the garment should be smaller than the body measurement. See page 121 for general comments on ease allowance.

| Body measurement | Type of yarn | | |
	fine	medium	thick
Bust or Chest, and Hip			
tight garments	−6% to −2%	−4% to 0%	−2% to +2%
medium-fit garments	0% to 4%	2% to 6%	4% to 9%
loose garments	6% or more	8% or more	12% or more
Wrist, Upper Arm, Round Shoulder, Thigh and Ankle			
tight garments	−6% to −1%	−2% to +3%	0% to 5%
medium-fit garments	0% to 10%	10% to 20%	20% to 30%
loose garments	20% or more	30% or more	40% or more

TABLE 7: Number of stitches or rows in a given measurement, depending on tension of work (metric)

Tension (total number of stitches *or* rows in 10cm)	1 cm	2 cm	3 cm	4 cm	5 cm	6 cm	7 cm	8 cm	9 cm	10 cm	20 cm	30 cm	40 cm	50 cm	60 cm	70 cm	80 cm	90 cm
									Total number of stitches or rows									
10	1	2	3	4	5	6	7	8	9	10	20	30	40	50	60	70	80	90
11	1	3	4	5	6	7	8	9	10	11	22	33	44	55	66	77	88	99
12	2	3	4	5	6	8	9	10	11	12	24	36	48	60	72	84	96	108
13	2	3	4	6	7	8	9	11	12	13	26	39	52	65	78	91	104	117
14	2	3	5	6	7	9	10	12	13	14	28	42	56	70	84	98	112	126
15	2	3	5	6	8	9	11	12	14	15	30	45	60	75	90	105	120	135
16	2	3	5	7	8	10	11	13	15	16	32	48	64	80	96	112	128	144
17	2	4	5	7	9	10	12	14	16	17	34	51	68	85	102	119	136	153
18	2	4	6	7	9	11	13	15	16	18	36	54	72	90	108	126	144	162
19	2	4	6	8	10	12	14	15	17	19	38	57	76	95	114	133	152	171
20	2	4	6	8	10	12	14	16	18	20	40	60	80	100	120	140	160	180
21	2	4	6	9	11	13	15	17	19	21	42	63	84	105	126	147	168	189
22	2	5	7	9	11	13	16	18	20	22	44	66	88	110	132	154	176	198
23	2	5	7	9	12	14	16	19	21	23	46	69	92	115	138	161	184	207
24	3	5	7	10	12	15	17	19	22	24	48	72	96	120	144	168	192	216
25	3	5	8	10	13	15	18	20	23	25	50	75	100	125	150	175	200	225
26	3	5	8	10	13	16	18	21	23	26	52	78	104	130	156	182	208	234
27	3	5	8	11	14	16	19	22	24	27	54	81	108	135	162	189	216	243
28	3	6	8	11	14	17	20	22	25	28	56	84	112	140	168	196	224	252
29	3	6	9	12	15	17	20	23	26	29	58	87	116	145	174	203	232	261
30	3	6	9	12	15	18	21	24	27	30	60	90	120	150	180	210	240	270
31	3	6	9	12	16	19	22	25	28	31	62	93	124	155	186	217	248	279
32	3	6	10	13	16	19	22	26	29	32	64	96	128	160	192	224	256	288
33	3	7	10	13	17	20	23	26	30	33	66	99	132	165	198	231	264	297
34	3	7	10	14	17	20	24	27	30	34	68	102	136	170	204	238	272	306
35	4	7	11	14	18	21	25	28	32	35	70	105	140	175	210	245	280	315
36	4	7	11	14	18	22	25	29	32	36	72	108	144	180	216	252	288	324
37	4	7	11	15	19	22	26	30	33	37	74	111	148	185	222	259	296	333
38	4	8	11	15	19	23	27	30	34	38	76	114	152	190	228	266	304	342
39	4	8	12	16	20	23	27	31	35	39	78	117	156	195	234	273	312	351
40	4	8	12	16	20	24	28	32	36	40	80	120	160	200	240	280	320	360
41	4	8	12	16	21	25	29	33	37	41	82	123	164	205	246	287	328	369
42	4	8	13	17	21	25	29	34	38	42	84	126	168	210	252	294	336	378
43	4	9	13	17	22	26	30	34	39	43	86	129	172	215	258	301	344	387
44	4	9	13	18	22	26	31	35	40	44	88	132	176	220	264	308	352	396
45	5	9	14	18	23	27	32	36	41	45	90	135	180	225	270	315	360	405
46	5	9	14	18	23	28	32	37	41	46	92	138	184	230	276	322	368	414
47	5	9	14	19	24	28	33	38	42	47	94	141	188	235	282	329	376	423
48	5	10	14	19	24	29	34	38	43	48	96	144	192	240	288	336	384	432
49	5	10	15	20	25	29	34	39	44	49	98	147	196	245	294	343	392	441
50	5	10	15	20	25	30	35	40	45	50	100	150	200	250	300	350	400	450
Tension	1 cm	2 cm	3 cm	4 cm	5 cm	6 cm	7 cm	8 cm	9 cm	10 cm	20 cm	30 cm	40 cm	50 cm	60 cm	70 cm	80 cm	90 cm

TABLE 8: Number of stitches or rows in a given measurement, depending on tension of work (imperial)

Tension (total number of stitches or rows in 4in)	$\frac{1}{4}$ in	$\frac{1}{2}$ in	$\frac{3}{4}$ in	1 in	2 in	3 in	4 in	5 in	6 in	7 in	8 in	9 in	10 in	11 in	12 in	24 in	36 in
								Total number of stitches or rows									
10	1	2	2	3	5	8	10	13	15	18	20	23	25	28	30	60	90
11	1	2	2	3	6	9	11	14	17	20	22	25	28	31	33	66	99
12	1	2	3	3	6	9	12	15	18	21	24	27	30	33	36	72	108
13	1	2	3	4	7	10	13	17	20	23	26	30	33	36	39	78	117
14	1	2	3	4	7	11	14	18	21	25	28	32	35	39	42	84	126
15	1	2	3	4	8	11	15	19	23	26	30	34	38	41	45	90	135
16	1	2	3	4	8	12	16	20	24	28	32	36	40	44	48	96	144
17	1	2	3	4	9	13	17	21	26	30	34	38	43	47	51	102	153
18	1	2	4	5	9	14	18	23	27	32	36	41	45	50	54	108	162
19	1	3	4	5	10	15	19	24	29	33	38	43	48	52	57	114	171
20	1	3	4	5	10	15	20	25	30	35	40	45	50	55	60	120	180
21	1	3	4	5	11	16	21	26	32	37	42	47	53	58	63	126	189
22	1	3	4	6	11	17	22	28	33	39	44	50	55	61	66	132	198
23	2	3	4	6	12	17	23	29	35	40	46	52	58	63	69	138	207
24	2	3	5	6	12	18	24	30	36	42	48	54	60	66	72	144	216
25	2	3	5	6	13	19	25	31	38	44	50	56	63	69	75	150	225
26	2	3	5	7	13	20	26	33	39	46	52	59	65	72	78	156	234
27	2	3	5	7	14	20	27	34	41	47	54	61	68	74	81	162	243
28	2	4	5	7	14	21	28	35	42	49	56	63	70	77	84	168	252
29	2	4	5	7	15	22	29	36	44	51	58	65	73	80	87	174	261
30	2	4	6	8	15	23	30	38	45	53	60	68	75	83	90	180	270
31	2	4	6	8	16	23	31	39	47	54	62	70	78	85	93	186	279
32	2	4	6	8	16	24	32	40	48	56	64	72	80	88	96	192	288
33	2	4	6	8	17	25	33	41	50	58	66	74	83	91	99	198	297
34	2	4	6	9	17	26	34	43	51	60	68	77	85	94	102	204	306
35	2	4	7	9	18	26	35	44	53	61	70	79	88	96	105	210	315
36	2	5	7	9	18	27	36	45	54	63	72	81	90	99	108	216	324
37	2	5	7	9	19	28	37	46	56	65	74	83	93	102	111	222	333
38	2	5	7	10	19	29	38	48	57	67	76	86	95	105	114	228	342
39	2	5	7	10	20	29	39	49	59	68	78	88	98	107	117	234	351
40	3	5	8	10	20	30	40	50	60	70	80	90	100	110	120	240	360
41	3	5	8	10	21	31	41	51	62	72	82	92	103	113	123	246	369
42	3	5	8	11	21	32	42	53	63	74	84	95	105	116	126	252	378
43	3	5	8	11	22	32	43	54	65	75	86	97	108	118	129	258	387
44	3	6	8	11	22	33	44	55	66	77	88	99	110	121	132	264	396
45	3	6	8	11	23	34	45	56	68	79	90	101	113	124	135	270	405
46	3	6	9	12	23	35	46	58	69	81	92	104	115	127	138	276	414
47	3	6	9	12	24	35	47	59	71	82	94	106	118	129	141	282	423
48	3	6	9	12	24	36	48	60	72	84	96	108	120	132	144	288	432
49	3	6	9	12	25	37	49	61	74	86	98	110	123	135	147	294	441
50	3	6	9	13	25	38	50	63	75	88	100	113	125	138	150	300	450
Tension	$\frac{1}{4}$ in	$\frac{1}{2}$ in	$\frac{3}{4}$ in	1 in	2 in	3 in	4 in	5 in	6 in	7 in	8 in	9 in	10 in	11 in	12 in	24 in	36 in

Guidelines for Knitting Illustrated Garments

POLO-NECK JUMPER WITH CHEVRON DESIGN
(see colour photograph on page 33)

Yarn Shetland-type pure wool. Thickness between 'quick knit' and 'double knitting'.

Finished weight 450g (16oz).

Shapes Straight body, fairly wide tapered sleeves, ordinary cuffs, raglan shoulders, small round yoke ending in polo-neck collar.

Stitch patterns Stocking stitch. Fish scales for the chevrons. Ribbing for cuffs, borders, yoke and collar.

Techniques Shapings worked one stitch after the selvedge for shoulders. Real double decreases (no 3) for yoke shapings. Chain selvedges. Backstitch seams.

Remarks Front and back have similar chevrons. The yoke decreases were worked in three regularly spaced rows.

ALPACA WAISTCOAT
(see colour photograph on page 33)

Yarn Pure alpaca. Thickness similar to '4-ply'.

Finished weight 250g (8¾oz).

Shapes Straight body, set-in armholes, U-neck, edge-to-edge opening fastened with ties and rounded at the lower edge.

Stitch patterns Stocking stitch and Quilted lattice edged with small tufts. Bias bands and ties in stocking stitch.

Techniques Double slipped garter-stitch selvedges, except for side seams that have chain selvedges. Backstitch seams. Bias bands fixed with slipstitch on front and back. Ties left to curl naturally then edges joined with a running stitch.

Remarks Repeated blocking was needed to keep edges from curling inwards.

MAROON POLO-NECK WITH CHEVRONS ON SLEEVES
(see colour photograph on page 34)

Yarn Machine-washable 'double-knitting' pure wool.

Finished weight 550g (19½oz).

Shapes Straight body, narrow tapered sleeves, set-in epaulette shoulders, polo-neck collar.

Stitch patterns Stocking stitch with Jacquard motifs. Crossed double ribbing for collar, cuffs and border.

Techniques Shapings at two stitches from the selvedge. Stocking-stitch selvedges. Invisible seams.

Remarks To compensate for the slant that the crossed ribbing was giving to the collar, a few rows before reaching the fold line the garment was turned inside out. The rest of the collar was knitted in the opposite direction. Only the knit stitches were worked through the back of the loop, both before and after changing direction. In this way, the front and back of the ribbing are different, but time is saved because then stitches only need to be twisted every other row.

BLUE/GREY TWEED COLLARED JUMPER
(see colour photograph on page 34)

Yarn Pure wool tweed.

Finished weight 1050g (37oz).

Shapes Straight body, medium tapered sleeves, raglan shoulders, high V-neck, variation of middy collar, ordinary cuffs.

Stitch patterns Brioche rib. Single ribbing for borders, cuffs and collar.

Techniques Shapings worked after selvedge stitch. Chain selvedges for seams and garter-stitch selvedges for collar. Backstitch side seams. Invisible seams for raglan. Collar worked separately, then fixed with an invisible join.

Remarks The collar is basically a very short middy collar that can be fastened round the neck with a button and loop. It was knitted starting with the widest edge, and a few double decreases were worked 2.5cm (1in) before starting to shape the neck.

154

BABY BRIEFS AND MATINEE JACKET
(see colour photograph on page 51)

Yarn Machine-washable 'three-ply' pure wool.

Finished weight 110g (4oz).

Shapes Straight body, medium tapered sleeves, round yoke, overlapping opening fastened with buttons at back for jacket. Slit-leg briefs.

Stitch patterns Stocking stitch for background. Reverse garter stitch for stripes. (To work reverse garter stitch, start stripe on a wrong-side row.) Colour is changed every two rows. Simple eyelets for threading faggot cords.

Techniques Chain selvedges. Shapings were worked at the edge when it was not possible to do them after the selvedge. Invisible seams.

Remarks Borders around legs worked in rounds from stitches picked up from the edge of the slits. (To work garter stitch in rounds, knit one row and purl one row.) The body was worked in one piece, without side seams, and was only divided to shape the beginning of the armholes before starting the yoke.

TODDLER'S CHENILLE TOP
(see colour photograph on page 51)

Yarn Fine cotton and rayon chenille. Mercerised cotton for cords.

Finished weight 200g (7oz).

Shapes Straight body, medium straight sleeves, right-angle shoulders, straight neck, shoulder openings.

Stitch patterns Stocking stitch with garter-stitch borders. Simple eyelets for threading the plaited cords.

Techniques Worked transversally in two sections, back and front. Borders knitted with the main sections. Stocking-stitch selvedges. Invisible seams sewn with mercerised cotton.

Remarks The border along the sleeve openings and along the neckline needed extra rows to keep the sections flat. However, no extra rows were added to the lower border, because it was very convenient to have gathers at that point.

CAMISOLE
(see colour photograph on page 52)

Yarn Acrylic and mohair blend. Shetland-type wool for Jacquard motif.

Finished weight 90g (3oz).

Shapes Straight body.

Stitch patterns Purse stitch for background. Single ribbing for bottom border. Moss stitch and two rows of stocking stitch in contrasting yarn for top border. Stocking stitch and Jacquard for front motif. Crochet chain with crochet corded edging on both sides for straps (the chain worked in contrasting yarn).

Techniques Worked from top to bottom, to avoid a cast-off chain at the top edge. The side seams have one stitch in stocking stitch after the chain selvedge, to emphasize the join, and were sewn with a backstitch.

Remarks The ribbed border is only to keep the camisole gathered at the waist, and should be worn inside a skirt or trousers. It is narrower than the rest, so that it does not look bulky.

MOHAIR CARDIGAN
(see colour photograph on page 52)

Yarn Pure mohair.

Finished weight 380g (13½oz).

Shapes Mixed body, medium tapered sleeves, set-in shoulders, sloping-slit pockets, ordinary cuffs, V-neck, overlapping opening fastened with buttons.

Stitch patterns Single ribbing for cuffs and borders. Shetland shell stitch:
Multiple of 18 sts plus 1
Row 1 (right side) *k1, (k2tog)3 times, (yf, yon, k1)5 times, yf, yon, (k2tog-b)3 times*, k1
Rows 2 and 4 purl
Row 3 knit
Repeat rows 1 to 4

Techniques Chain selvedges for seams and garter-stitch selvedges for front border. Backstitch seams. Shapings worked after selvedge. Front border knitted separately, then sewn with an invisible join. Pocket borders knitted from stitches left on holders.

CAMEL-COLOURED V-NECK WITH STRIPED BORDERS
(see colour photograph on page 69)

Yarn 'Double-knitting' pure wool.

Finished weight 620g (22¾oz).

Shapes Straight body, wide tapered sleeves, yoke shoulders, V-neckline, ordinary cuffs.

Stitch patterns Fancy rib (10 stitches knit, 2 stitches purl). Double ribbing for borders.

Techniques Shapings one stitch after selvedge in sleeves, and just at the edge for lower part of V-neck. Chain selvedges. Backstitch seams at the sides. Top of body grafted to yoke.

Remarks The front is four stitches wider than the back, to ensure that the seams do not break the patterns. The seams are placed between a knit stitch and a purl stitch.

155

GREEN COTTON TWIN-SET
(see colour photograph on page 69)

Yarn 'Double-knitting' pure cotton.

Finished weight Top 470g (16½oz). Cardigan 750g (26½oz).

Shapes Top: straight body, tapered armholes (becoming wider), wide scoop neck. Cardigan: straight body, dropped shoulders, medium tapered sleeves, ordinary cuffs, V-neckline, overlapping opening fastened with buttons.

Stitch patterns Stocking stitch. Zebra chevron. Ordinary ribbing for cuffs and borders.

Techniques Shapings for top worked at the edge. Stocking-stitch selvedge. Invisible seams. Front border for cardigan worked separately and fixed with a flat join.

Remarks Some stitches needed to be increased before starting the patterned band round the sleeves.

PEACH MOHAIR JACKET
(see colour photograph on page 70)

Yarn Pure mohair.

Finished weight 380g (13½oz).

Shapes Mixed body, wide tapered sleeves, flat-stitch cuffs, raglan shoulders, U-neckline, edge-to-edge opening slightly rounded at the bottom, tapered yoke.

Stitch patterns Reverse stocking stitch. Raspberries for the yoke and borders. Bias garter stitch for tie-up band round neck. Two rows of garter stitch at cast-on edges.

Techniques Shapings after selvedge stitch. Chain selvedge and backstitch seams at joins. Double garter-stitch selvedge at front. The borders are worked with the main sections.

Remarks The yoke and the bottom band have more stitches than the rest of the body.

BOUCLÉ CARDIGAN WITH EYELETS
(see colour photograph on page 70)

Yarn Acrylic and wool bouclé. Thickness similar to 'double knitting'.

Finished weight 360g (12¾oz).

Shapes Straight body, narrow tapered sleeves, set-in shoulders, ordinary cuffs, plunging V-neckline, overlapping opening fastened with buttons.

Stitch patterns Stocking stitch with eyelet motifs. Single ribbing for cuffs and borders.

Techniques Shapings worked at the edge. Chain selvedges. Backstitch seams. Front borders fixed with a flat join. Eyelets embroidered with tapestry wool of a slightly darker shade.

Remarks Body and sleeves have exactly the same length, so that the eyelet pattern reaches the armholes at the same time. The continuity of the pattern is maintained across the side seams. Cold blocking was needed to open up the eyelets after embroidering them. Several pins were placed on the inside of every eyelet, pushing the sides apart to obtain a round hole, before spraying.

GIRL'S CARDIGAN IN BLUE AND WHITE
(see colour photograph on page 87)

Yarn Acrylic and wool 'four-ply'.

Finished weight 180g (6½oz).

Shapes Straight body, medium tapered sleeves, ordinary turned-up cuffs, raglan shoulders, round neck, overlapping front opening fastened with buttons.

Stitch patterns Stocking stitch. Waves for the colour changes. Swiss darning for the fish and bird motifs. Single ribbing for borders and cuffs.

Techniques Decorative shapings for raglan seams. Chain selvedges. Backstitch seams. Front border worked separately and fixed with flat join.

BOY'S JUMPER WITH DIAGONAL STRIPES ON FRONT
(see colour photograph on page 87)

Yarn Shetland-type pure wool. Thickness between 'quick knit' and 'double knitting'.

Finished weight 280g (10oz).

Shapes Straight body, fairly wide tapered sleeves, ordinary turned-up cuffs, dropped shoulders, straight neck.

Stitch patterns Stocking stitch. Single ribbing for cuffs and borders.

Techniques The front was knitted diagonally, with all increases and decreases being worked at the very edge. The lower front border was knitted separately and grafted. The back half of the neck border was worked as a continuation of the back, but some stitches were increased in order to keep the back flat. The front half of the neck border was picked up from the front (same number of stitches as the back), and grafted to the back border at the sides. Sleeve shapings worked one stitch after the selvedge. Invisible seams.

Remarks The front needed careful blocking to make sure that the angles were kept right, and that the overall dimensions were the same as the back's.

PURPLE TUNIC WITH JACQUARD DESIGN
(see colour photograph on page 88)

Yarn Acrylic and wool bouclé. Thickness similar to 'double knitting'.

Finished weight 450g (16oz).

Shapes Straight body supplemented below the waist with a false pleat, medium tapered sleeves, set-in shoulders, flat-stitch cuffs, five-sided neckline, very wide plunging yoke matching the neckline and extending over the shoulder caps, shoulder opening fastened with buttons.

Stitch patterns Stocking stitch with Jacquard motifs. Moss stitch for cuffs, borders, false pleats and yoke. Simple eyelets for threading the drawstring belt. Crochet corded edging round yoke.

Techniques Shapings worked at the edge. Chain selvedges. Backstitch seams. Twisted cords and tassels for the belt.

Remarks The yoke and the neckline move one stitch further every row. The Jacquard was worked with a series of little bobbins; with another type of yarn the design could have been embroidered, although with bouclé it is difficult to see the stitches. However, bouclé was chosen to soften the lines of the design.

GREY WAISTCOAT
(see colour photograph on page 88)

Yarn Acrylic and wool 'double knitting'.

Finished weight 280g (10oz).

Shapes Straight body, set in armholes, V-neckline, horizontal-slit pockets, overlapping opening fastened with buttons.

Stitch patterns Hurdles and woven check for the body bands. Single ribbing for borders.

Techniques Shapings worked after the selvedge stitch. Chain selvedges. Backstitch seams at sides and horizontal knitted seams at shoulders. Front borders worked separately and fixed with flat joins. Armhole borders picked up from the edge.

Remarks The pockets end between the last two rows of hurdles.

POMPON SKIRT
(see colour photograph on page 105)

Yarn Hand-spun pure wool, coloured with natural dyes.

Finished weight 880g (31oz).

Shapes A-line skirt with six panels, slit opening fastened with drawstring at side.

Stitch patterns Stocking stitch for background. Irish moss stitch for diamonds and lower border. Scattered oats for stripes (change colour) on first slip-stitch row). Purl stitches to outline the diamonds around pompons. Single ribbing for waistband. Tufts (three and six loops), pompons and faggot cord.

Techniques Shapings worked as unobtrusive, paired single decreases, which double their frequency above the hipline. Stocking-stitch selvedges for side seams and slipped garter-stitch selvedges for slit opening. Reinforced eyelet buttonholes to thread drawstring at both sides of opening. Invisible seams. Faggot cord worked with two strands of yarn, except at the ends where the strands are worked separately. Gathers before starting to work waistband. Waistband reinforced with elastic. Loose lining.

Remarks The bands worked in scattered oats required more stitches than the rest. The yarn was very difficult to work with and had to be broken repeatedly, often in the middle of rows, because of sudden changes in colour and weak stretches. One of the skeins was also very badly spun and had large blobs that needed 'shaving'. Because of the different thickness of the skeins, the front was knitted with needles one size larger than the back and six stitches less; it also needed six rows less, and the diamonds were adapted accordingly.

LITTLE GIRL'S RED COAT
(see colour photograph on page 106)

Yarn 'Double-double' Shetland-type pure wool.

Finished weight 820g (29oz).

Shapes Tapered body, medium straight sleeves, turned-up cuffs, dropped shoulders, round neck, double-breasted opening, variation of tie collar.

Stitch pattern Staggered rib. Wave cable. Corded edging.

Techniques Neck shapings worked at the edge. Chain selvedges, backstitch seams. Invisible join between cuff and sleeve. Last row of cuff was grafted to the cast-on row. Tie collar joined with invisible join after crocheting edging. Sleeves first fixed to body with an invisible seam; then the edge of the body was folded in to emphasize the shoulders, securing it with a slipstitch.

Remarks The tapering of the body is achieved by the progressive introduction of cables, which have a gathering effect on the fabric.

BOY'S BOMBER JACKET
(see colour photograph on page 106)

Yarn 'Double-double' pure lambswool.

Finished weight 600g (21oz).

Shapes Straight body, wide tapered sleeves, ordinary turned-up cuffs, raglan shoulders, round neck, edge-to-edge opening.

Stitch patterns Stocking stitch. Single ribbing for cuffs, borders and side panels.

Techniques The body was worked in five parts: two fronts, two side panels and one back, although the lower part of the panels was worked at the same time as the ribbing for the front. The sleeve panels were also worked separately, except for the cuff. The sleeve increases were placed at either side of the panels, which makes for wedge-shaped panels and straight sleeves. The decorative increases for the shoulder seams were worked after the selvedge stitch. Stocking-stitch selvedges and invisible seams for joins. Garter-stitch selvedge at front openings.

GIRL'S SQUARE-NECKED STRIPED TOP
(see colour photograph on page 106)

Yarn Acrylic and wool 'four-ply'.

Finished weight 180g (6½oz).

Shapes Straight body, fairly wide tapered sleeves, ordinary turned-up cuffs, dropped shoulders, square neckline.

Stitch patterns Stocking stitch. Sawtooth for the colour changes. Single ribbing for cuffs and borders. Swiss embroidery.

Techniques Shapings worked after the selvedge stitch. Chain selvedges. Backstitch seams. Neck border picked up from the edge.

HEAVY WINTER COAT
(see colour photograph on page 123)

Yarn 'Extra-chunky' Unst pure wool. Three complementing shades of pure mohair for edging.

Finished weight 2100g (74oz).

Shapes Mixed body, skirt becoming A-line with a straight section at the lower edge, magyar shoulders, straight sleeves, round neck, variation of wing collar, applied patch pockets.

Stitch patterns Wasp's nest. Corded edging.

Techniques Shapings worked after selvedge on right-side rows. Garter-stitch selvedges. Invisible seams. Picked-up collar shaped by increasing on every right-side row.

Remarks Worked in one piece, starting with the back, using 55cm (21½in) long needles. The cast-on rows needed needles two sizes larger than

158

the rest. The large wing collar can be closed tightly round the neck, by means of a small button sewn to the underside of the right 'wing'. The edging was crocheted using one strand of the main yarn and three strands of mohair. Only one crochet stitch every two ridges or every two knitted stitches was necessary.

THICK JUMPER IN THREE SHADES OF BLUE
(see colour photograph on page 124)

Yarn 'Double-double' pure lambswool.

Finished weight 1050g (36oz).

Shapes Straight body, wide tapered sleeves, flat-stitch cuffs, dropped shoulders, straight neckline.

Stitch patterns Stocking stitch. Three-colour tweed for borders and band around armholes. Two rows of garter stitch at cast-on and cast-off edges.

Techniques The tapering for the shoulders was worked before the neckline border. A few decreases were necessary before changing to stocking stitch after the bottom border. Conversely, a few increases were necessary when returning to coloured pattern at the neck. The motif around armholes was worked with the body, with frequent extra rows to keep the work flat. Horizontal knitted seams at shoulders. Sleeves joined to body with grafting. Stocking-stitch selvedge and invisible seams at sides.

Remarks A running stitch needed to be worked on the wrong side along the armhole motif, to neaten up the change in pattern to stocking stitch.

SLEEVELESS BLUE V-NECK TOP
(see colour photograph on page 124)

Yarn 'Double-knitting' pure wool crêpe.

Finished weight 400g (14¼oz).

Shapes Straight body, straight armhole opening, V-neckline.

Stitch patterns Shadow rib. Crossed double ribbing for the borders.

Techniques Shapings worked at the edge. Neck and sleeve borders worked from stitches picked up from the edge. Two stitches were cast off at the sides to mark the armholes. Chain selvedges. Backstitch seams.

Remarks The front is two stitches wider than the back to ensure that the seams do not break the pattern. The seams are placed next to the rib.

Green chenille bomber jacket and tweed and chenille bomber jacket (see page 162)

OFF-WHITE SUMMER SUIT
(see colour photograph on page 141)

Yarn Silk noil. Thickness similar to 'double knitting'.

Finished weight Jacket 650g (23oz). Skirt 440g (15½oz).

Shapes Straight body, wide straight short sleeves, right-angle shoulders with slight tapering at the underarm, plunging V-neckline, overlapping opening fastened with buttons, horizontal-slit pockets stretching across the whole front for jacket. Straight skirt with darts at the top and short, overlapping opening fastened with buttons on one of the back vertical bands.

Stitch patterns Stocking stitch. Moss stitch for borders, bands and waistband.

Techniques Jacket shapings worked at the edge of the armholes, and just after the border at the neckline. Skirt shapings worked at either side of the vertical bands. Borders and bands knitted in with the rest, except around the sleeves, where the borders have been picked up from the edge. Stocking-stitch selvedges. Invisible seams except for horizontal knitted seams at shoulders.

Remarks Extra rows had to be worked on the vertical bands and borders to keep the garment flat. In addition to the darts, a few decreases had to be worked at the top of the skirt before knitting the waistband. The skirt also required lining and petersham at the waist, and was knitted in two sections: front plus side panels and back, so that the seams run along the edge of the vertical bands at the back.

LINEN TOP
(see colour photograph on page 141)

Yarn Fine linen tow.

Finished weight 250g (8¾oz).

Shapes Straight body, square yoke, side openings fastened with buttons.

Stitch patterns Stocking stitch with rows of diagonal eyelets. Stocking-stitch welts for yoke and lower band. Narrow edge in garter stitch around yoke, and garter-stitch bands at the sides. To work the welts:

Row 1 (right side) with red, knit
Row 2 with red, purl
Rows 3, 4 and 6 with contrast, knit
Rows 5, 7 and 8 with contrast, purl
Repeat rows 1 to 8

Baby's travelling bag and young child's dungarees (see page 162)

Techniques Stocking-stitch edge at back, and garter-stitch edge at front. Invisible seams. Crochet cast off for neckline. Straps worked as part of the front and grafted at the back on a red row. More stitches are increased after the lower band than are decreased at the start of the yoke.

Remarks The garter-stitch side bands have two buttonholes and are knitted as part of the front, with additional rows to keep them flat. On the lower side, another set of bands is knitted with the back, to which buttons were sewn. Before the start of the yoke, the armholes were shaped as for set-in shoulders. The garter-stitch edge around the yoke needed less rows than the yoke, to avoid stretching the welts.

NAVY-BLUE CARDIGAN
(see colour photograph on page 142)

Yarn 'Double knitting' pure wool crêpe.

Finished weight 600g (21¼oz).

Shapes Straight body, medium tapered sleeves, ribbed cuffs, mock set-in shoulders, plunging V-neckline, overlapping opening fastened with buttons, square yoke.

Stitch patterns Stocking stitch. False cable rib for borders, yoke and cuffs.

Techniques Shapings after selvedge stitch on sleeves. Chain selvedges. Backstitch seams. Front shapings worked after border. Front border worked with main section.

Remarks The shoulder caps were worked as for set-in, but the body has no armhole shapings. Instead, more stitches were decreased for the yoke than had previously been increased to keep the work flat at the top of the border. The extra decreases gather the body under the yoke, and obviously make the work narrower, so that it fits between shoulders.

V-NECK JUMPER WITH JACQUARD BANDS
(see colour photograph on page 142)

Yarn Acrylic and wool 'double knitting'.

Finished weight 410g (14½oz).

Shapes Straight body, medium tapered sleeves, dropped shoulders, V-neck, ordinary cuffs.

Stitch patterns Stocking stitch with Jacquard motifs. Single, twisted ribbing for cuffs and borders.

Techniques Shapings worked one stitch after selvedge. Backstitch seams. Neck border worked in the round from stitches picked up from the edge.

GREEN CHENILLE BOMBER JACKET
(see colour photograph on page 159)

Yarn Acrylic and wool chenille. Matching 'double knitting' pure wool for borders and collar.

Finished weight 690g (24½oz).

Shapes Straight body, wide tapered sleeves, ordinary ribbed cuffs, dropped shoulders, round neckline with straight collar, vertical-slit pockets, zip-and-flap opening.

Stitch patterns Garter stitch welting. Single ribbing for borders, flap, collar and bands at shoulders and armholes. Two rows of garter stitch at cast-off edge of collar.

Techniques Front and back were worked without interruption, changing from chenille to wool after shaping the front for the shoulders, and back from wool to chenille after working the shoulder band. The rest of the shapings were worked after the selvedge stitch. Chain selvedges and backstitch seams for the sides. Sleeves grafted to the body. Flap and collar picked up from edge.

Remarks The bottom border has more stitches than the body. The bands at the shoulders and armholes have twice as many stitches as the body or sleeves.

TWEED AND CHENILLE BOMBER JACKET
(see colour photograph on page 159)

Yarn 'Double-double' pure wool tweed. Acrylic and wool chenille, in one of the tweed's colours.

Finished weight 1250g (44oz).

Shapes Straight body, wide mixed sleeves, dropped shoulders, wing collar, patch pockets, buttoned-up cuffs, round neck.

Stitch patterns Vertical herringbone for tweed. Single ribbing for chenille.

Techniques Shapings worked after selvedge stitch. Chain selvedges. Backstitch seams. Picked-up collar. Garter-stitch selvedges and invisible joins for borders, cuffs and pockets.

Remarks Lower border, pockets, elbow patches and cuffs were knitted transversally. Special care had to be taken to maintain the verticality of the pattern when shapings were being worked on the right edge.

BABY'S TRAVELLING BAG
(see colour photograph on page 160)

Yarn Two strands of machine-washable 'double-knitting' pure wool.

Finished weight 720g (25½oz).

Shapes Wide, straight body, made long enough to take the whole child and rounded at the lower edge. Straight sleeves, right-angle shoulders, ordinary ribbed cuffs, high V-neck, rounded hood. Overlapping opening at lower edge.

Stitch patterns Welted brickwork. Double ribbing for borders and cuffs.

Techniques Stocking-stitch selvedges. Invisible seams. Front and back are joined along the top of the sleeves. Hood worked separately, then joined with invisible seam. Cuffs and lower borders worked from stitches picked up from the edge. Shapings worked at the edge.

Remarks No blocking was needed. Care had to be taken not to flatten the pattern when sewing the seams. When the top of the lower curve was reached, two stitches were increased at either side at both front and back. The gap thus created was later filled by the two overlapping borders that fasten the bottom of the bag.

CHILD'S DUNGAREES
(see colour photograph on page 160)

Yarn Real Shetland wool. Thickness similar to 'four-ply'.

Finished weight 220g (7¾oz).

Shapes Ordinary, straight-leg trousers, tapered bib.

Stitch patterns Stocking stitch for brown background. Garter stitch for stripes and straps. Single ribbing at waist. (To knit the stripes, work two rows of each colour in garter stitch, starting with a right-side row.)

Techniques Shapings worked after selvedge. Chain selvedges. Backstitch seams, except for lower bands of stripes, which have invisible seams.

Remarks The waistband has two buttonholes at the back to fasten the straps. Extra rows were needed at the sides of the bib to keep it flat.

GRAPH PAPERS FOR DRAWING TENSION DIAGRAMS
(pages 163–172)

The correct graph to use is the one that is nearest the result of the division:

$$\frac{\text{number of rows in 10cm (4in)}}{\text{number of stitches in 10cm (4in)}}$$

2.0

Index